The Iron Age in Northern East Anglia: New Work in the Land of the Iceni

Edited by

John A. Davies

BAR British Series 549
2011

Published in 2016 by
BAR Publishing, Oxford

BAR British Series 549

The Iron Age in Northern East Anglia: New Work in the Land of the Iceni

ISBN 978 1 4073 0885 2

© The editors and contributors severally and the Publisher 2011

COVER IMAGE *Enamelled and decorated lipped terret from Snettisham.*
Photograph by Neil Jinkerson. © *Norfolk Museums & Archaeology Service*

The authors' moral rights under the 1988 UK Copyright,
Designs and Patents Act are hereby expressly asserted.

All rights reserved. No part of this work may be copied, reproduced, stored,
sold, distributed, scanned, saved in any form of digital format or transmitted
in any form digitally, without the written permission of the Publisher.

BAR Publishing is the trading name of British Archaeological Reports (Oxford) Ltd.
British Archaeological Reports was first incorporated in 1974 to publish the BAR
Series, International and British. In 1992 Hadrian Books Ltd became part of the BAR
group. This volume was originally published by Archaeopress in conjunction with
British Archaeological Reports (Oxford) Ltd / Hadrian Books Ltd, the Series principal
publisher, in 2011. This present volume is published by BAR Publishing, 2016.

Printed in England

PUBLISHING

BAR titles are available from:

         BAR Publishing
         122 Banbury Rd, Oxford, OX2 7BP, UK
EMAIL   info@barpublishing.com
PHONE +44 (0)1865 310431
  FAX   +44 (0)1865 316916
         www.barpublishing.com

Contents

List of contributors ii

Acknowledgements iii
John Davies

Introduction. Ten years after: the Land of the Iceni in 2010 1
John Davies

The role of museums in the study of Iron Age Norfolk 3
John Davies

Late Bronze Age and early Iron Age pottery in Norfolk – a review 11
Matt Brudenell

Iron Age landscapes from the air: results from the Norfolk national mapping programme 25
Sophie Tremlett, with James Albone and Sarah Horlock

Excavations at Snettisham, Norfolk, 2004: re-investigating the past 41
Natasha Hutcheson

Iron Age coins from Snettisham 49
Adrian Marsden

Boars, bulls and Norfolk's Celtic menagerie 59
John Davies

Icenian coin production 69
John Talbot

The language of inscriptions on Icenian coinage 83
Daphne Nash Briggs

Closing thoughts 103
John Davies

List of Contributors

James Albone
Historic Environment Service
Union House
Gressenhall
Dereham, Norfolk
NR20 4DR
james.albone@norfolk.gov.uk

Matt Brudenell
Department of Archaeology
University of York
The King's Manor
Yo1 7EP
MatthewBrudenell@gmail.com

John Davies
Norfolk Museums & Archaeology Service
Shirehall
Market Avenue
Norwich
NR1 3JQ
john.davies@norfolk.gov.uk

Sarah Horlock
Historic Environment Service
Union House
Gressenhall
Dereham
Norfolk
NR20 4DR
sarah.horlock@norfolk.gov.uk

Natasha Hutcheson
Norfolk Museums & Archaeology Service
Shirehall
Market Avenue
Norwich
NR1 3JQ
natasha.hutcheson@norfolk.gov.uk

Adrian Marsden
Historic Environment Service
Shirehall
Market Avenue
Norwich
NR1 3JQ
adrian.marsden@norfolk.gov.uk

Daphne Nash Briggs
34 Thorncliffe Road
Oxford
OX2 7BB
daphne.briggs@waitrose.com

John Talbot
Cambridge
john.talbot@talbot7.com

Sophie Tremlett
Historic Environment Service
Union House
Gressenhall
Dereham
Norfolk
NR20 4DR
sophie.tremlett@norfolk.gov.uk

Acknowledgements

This publication represents the proceedings of a conference held in Norwich in May 2008 entitled 'Land of the Iceni, the Iron Age of Northern East Anglia'. The idea for the conference was developed through discussions with Amanda Chadburn, Megan Dennis and J.D. Hill, all of whom provided contributions to the proceedings in 2008. I am grateful for their enthusiasm, encouragement and involvement in the wider study of Iron Age East Anglia over many years. Special thanks must also go to my colleagues Tim Pestell, of Norfolk Museums & Archaeology Service, and Adrian Marsden, of Norfolk's Historic Environment Service, who assisted with the organisation of the conference and who have been actively supportive to the current local Iron Age project in many ways. John Jarman kindly assisted with the process of assembling information for this publication. I would also like to thank the Council for British Archaeology East Anglia for their enthusiastic support for the conference and for sponsoring the event.

John Davies
Norwich
May 2011

Introduction

Ten Years After: The Land of the Iceni in 2010

John Davies

The Iceni were a people who lived in the east of England during the Iron Age and into the Roman period. They are one of several tribal groups who were mentioned by classical writers, such as Julius Caesar, Tacitus, Cassius Dio and Strabo. Their territory occupied a substantial part of northern East Anglia, which includes land now covered by the counties of Norfolk, the northern part of Suffolk, and north east Cambridgeshire (Davies and Williamson 1999). The precise tribal boundaries are unclear and these almost certainly shifted over time. There is a degree of geographical cohesion to this region. Norfolk is bounded in the north and east by a lengthy coastline. In the west, the fenland formed a formidable barrier to easy movement, although a growing corpus of Iron Age finds suggest that there was another significant focus of Icenian settlement within the fens, centred around Stonea, Cambridgeshire (Jackson and Potter 1996). The southern boundary, in Suffolk, remains less clear (Martin 1999), and the River Waveney, which now separates Norfolk and Suffolk, may have formed a boundary for part of the time.

This volume is a compilation of essays which, together, represent a regional study of the Iron Age within the part of East Anglia that was occupied by the Iceni. It was born out of a conference held in Norwich in May 2008. Most of the participants on that day have contributed papers. The specific submissions received for publication mean that the emphasis here is on the Iron Age of Norfolk, although there were contributions from Suffolk at the conference. Matt Brudenell has provided an additional chapter, which considers Late Bronze Age and Early Iron Age pottery in Norfolk. I have also contributed additional papers, based on the developing Iron Age collection held at Norwich Castle Museum. The period covered in this volume spans the Iron Age, through to the time of the Boudican revolt of AD 60-61. The purpose underlying the conference was to review the progress made in our understanding of the Iron Age in northern East Anglia over the previous decade.

An earlier conference had been held at the University of East Anglia, Norwich, in 1995, which was subsequently published as a *Centre of East Anglian Studies monograph*, entitled *Land of the Iceni: the Iron Age in Northern East Anglia* (Davies and Williamson 1999). That conference helped to focus interest in Iron Age studies in the region and served to stimulate further research into the subject. Then, ten years on, in 2005, Norwich Castle Museum held a British Museum partnership exhibition called *'Buried Treasure: Finding Our Past'*. It was during the assembling of Iron Age objects for that exhibition and related conversations with J.D. Hill, Curator of the British Museum's Iron Age collections at that time, which stimulated the idea of holding a follow-up conference in which we could assess how far Iron Age studies in the region have indeed progressed. The idea and content was subsequently developed in discussion with Amanda Chadburn and Megan Dennis, during 2006-7.

In the 1995 conference, there was an emphasis on the question of regionality and a resulting awareness that areas like East Anglia should be studied in their own right and not in terms of generalisations made from Wessex or, in the case of the later Iron Age, from Hertfordshire and Essex. There was also a developing emphasis on the importance of *ritual* and *ideological* themes, as well as the *economic* aspects of everyday life. A number of new models were presented to explain the growing bodies of data. The Iceni were characterised as a people distinctive and different, while the nature and extent of those differences was targeted for further research.

During the intervening years, important new discoveries of Iron Age objects have continued to be made, largely through the agency of metal-detection, and reported through the county identification and recording services. In addition, fieldwork and landscape projects have provided important new information. Research has continued through the enthusiasm of scholars and new students, while records are being regularly supplemented and updated within the county museums and archaeology services.

The 2008 conference brought together some of the original contributors, with some more recent researchers of the region's Iron Age. The results of new in-depth studies into the region's material culture and landscape have been drawn together and new models and approaches have started to be developed, which go further towards providing an understanding of just how the Iceni were culturally different, and defining the nature of those differences. The subject matter of this volume includes both object-based and landscape-based studies.

The Iron Age collections held by Norfolk Museums and Archaeology Service, particularly at Norwich Castle Museum, have provided the subject matter for the object-based contributions from Matt Brudenell (Late Bronze

Age and Iron Age pottery) and myself (non-ceramics). A landscape context is provided by two contributions. Sophie Tremlett, James Albone and Sarah Horlock review their results from the National Mapping Programme and discuss the impact for what we know of Iron Age sites and settlement in Norfolk, while Natasha Hutcheson provides a review of her fieldwork at the site of Snettisham in 2004. The coinage has continued to be a rich source for study and has provided the core content of the papers by Daphne Nash Briggs, John Talbot and Adrian Marsden.

It has been stated that there is no single ready-made model through which we can understand the Iron Age in Britain as a whole (Gosden and Hill 2008). Elsewhere, commentators have sought to doubt the usefulness of regional archaeological studies within Britain. It is hoped that the contributions presented here may collectively help to justify this genre of publication and to present an enlightening way forward for increasing our understanding of Britain's Iron Age.

I would like to offer thanks to all of the contributors, both those who spoke at the conference and those who have provided papers for this volume. I am grateful to everybody who supported, organised, attended and helped on the day. In particular, I would like to give grateful thanks to the CBA East Anglia who sponsored the conference and enabled it to happen.

John Davies
Chief Curator and Keeper of Archaeology
Norfolk Museums & Archaeology Service
December 2010

Bibliography

Davies, J. and T. Williamson, T. (eds) 1999. *Land of the Iceni: the Iron Age in Northern East Anglia*. Norwich, Centre of East Anglian Studies.

Gosden, C. and Hill, J. D. 2008. Introduction: re-integrating 'Celtic' art. In D. Garrow, C. Gosden and J. D. Hill (eds.), *Rethinking Celtic Art,* 1-14. Oxford, Oxbow.

Hutcheson, N. C. G. 2004. *Later Iron Age Norfolk*. Oxford, British Archaeological Report 361.

Jackson, R. P. J. and Potter, T. W. 1996. *Excavations at Stonea Cambridgeshire 1980-85*. London, British Museum Press.

Martin, E. 1999. Suffolk in the Iron Age. In J. Davies and T. Williamson (eds), *Land of the Iceni: the Iron Age in Northern East Anglia*, 44-99. Norwich, Centre of East Anglian Studies.

Oppenheimer, S. 2006. *The Origins of the British: A Genetic Detective Story*. London, Constable.

The role of museums in the study of Iron Age Norfolk

John Davies

Introduction

One of the outcomes of my initial study of Iron Age Norfolk (Davies 1996) and the ensuing 'Land of the Iceni' conference held at the University of East Anglia in 1995 (Davies and Williamson 1999) was the development of a new gallery within Norwich Castle Museum & Art Gallery, designed specifically to showcase the county's late prehistoric collections within an appropriate context. The newest discoveries from the county were presented in ways intended to reflect the latest thoughts and ideas, and in order to provide an impact and meaning for all age groups. The *Boudica Gallery* opened in 2000 and, with ongoing developments, continues to be a major venue for visitors to the region (Collingridge 2005, 254). In this paper I shall look at the different ways in which museums have contributed towards the study of the Iron Age in Norfolk and consider the importance and wider relevance of a major regional collection for the understanding of the period in northern East Anglia.

The role of the Norfolk museums

Norwich Castle contains large and significant collections covering all archaeological periods. These collections received national recognition in 1998 when they were awarded Designation status from the Museums and Galleries Commission (to become the MLA in 2000). Norwich's Iron Age holdings currently number 1,200 items. This material reflects different aspects of everyday life, through objects in a variety of metals, bone and flint. King's Lynn Museum, in west Norfolk, has a much smaller but important collection for the period, which numbers approximately 230 items. To both of these can be added sizeable pottery collections, which have not been considered for the purposes of this paper (see Matt Brudenell's paper, this volume).

Such material provides an important resource with the potential to complement other forms of archaeological investigation within an area. Today, the Norfolk collections continue to be supplemented by an active programme of acquisition. Collecting policy governs that this material is restricted to finds from the modern county of Norfolk alone (as opposed to what may have been areas of significance to the people living across the region in the past). These collections have been steadily assembled since the mid-19th century.

The *Victoria County History*, published at the end of the 19th century, at around the time when Norwich Castle Museum was established, reflects how far our understanding of local Iron Age archaeology has progressed today. It states that *'the remains of this interesting period which immediately preceded the advent of the Romans are, as far as Norfolk is concerned, but few in number and only locally important'* (Victoria County History Norfolk, 273). Fortunately, the many discoveries since then have completely disproved this observation in every respect.

The earliest acquisitions were largely in the form of major donations, representing large personal collections. A significant change occurred during the career of R. R. Clarke, who became Deputy Curator of the Norwich Museums in 1946, and subsequently Curator at Norwich Castle until his death in 1961. Clarke undertook archaeological fieldwork and his policy was to develop the museum collections and displays with material from excavations. Clarke's favourite archaeological period was the Iron Age and his paper 'The Iron Age in Norfolk and Suffolk', was to become a standard work on the subject (Clarke 1940). Following the initial chance discovery of treasure at Ken Hill, Snettisham, it was Clarke who undertook the first excavations at this internationally important site in 1948 (Clarke 1954). Most of this material subsequently entered the Norwich collection.

It was during this period that Norwich Castle Museum's 'open door policy' was established, which encouraged members of the public to show their finds to staff for identification. In the 1970s this policy developed into the special relationship between metal-detectorists and museum professionals which was to become known as 'the Norfolk system' (Davies 2009, 5-8). It was through this liaison that very large quantities of information about sites, artefacts and coins came to be recorded. This data formed the starting point for later studies of the Iron Age in the area (Green 1993; Davies 1996).

The name of the late Tony Gregory is synonymous with early metal-detector liaison. Gregory, Assistant Keeper of Archaeology at Norwich Castle from 1974 to 1978, undertook major excavations at the important enclosure and sanctuary site at Fison Way Thetford. His popular book, co-written with Bruce Robinson, entitled 'Celtic Fire and Roman Rule', has endured as a starting point for those interested in Iron Age and Roman Norfolk (Robinson and Gregory 2003).

The growth of the collection at Norwich Castle

The 1970s saw a massive growth in the discovery of artefacts, through the agency of metal-detection. Increasingly large numbers of artefacts of all periods have been studied by museum staff and recorded in the county Sites and Monuments Record (SMR), which became the Historic Environmental Record (HER). Despite the significant amount of time invested in this recording process, very little of that material was ever acquired, displayed or made accessible to a wider audience, prior to the 2000s. The museum collections and displays did not reflect the important new discoveries being made. Despite the proliferation of metal-detector finds over the years, it was recognised that this is a finite and diminishing resource. It became increasingly important that this anomaly should be addressed and that a proportion of the material should be acquired for future generations to study, enjoy, and forge a connection with the past.

So, during the last decade, the policy of recording finds has been developed into one of active acquisition. Each year in excess of 20,000 objects continue to be studied by Norfolk's Identification and Recording Service. Alongside this, record numbers of Treasure cases continue to be achieved every year, with 107 cases in 2008, of which just two involved Iron Age artefacts. This material is part of a finite resource and this will be exhausted one day, whether it will be in the next five, ten or fifty years. It will not continue to be available indefinitely. It is surely our duty to collect and secure at least a representative sample of this material for future appreciation and study while we can. The low proportion of Iron Age finds among the high number of discoveries overall is a relatively constant situation. Figures compiled over the last three years show Iron Age finds to represent below 5% of Treasure cases in Norfolk, on each occasion.

Iron Age material is now being actively targeted for acquisition within Norfolk Museums. As a result, the Norfolk collection, supported by the generosity of grant giving bodies, as well as individual donors, is growing significantly. The Iron Age holdings at Norwich Castle currently number over 1,200 objects, of which 290 come from Snettisham. There are 760 Iron Age coins and items associated with coin production. The important collection of pottery can be added to these figures. Over 20% of individual accessions of Iron Age material have been added since 2000. This paper will initially consider the material acquired by Norwich Castle Museum. The much smaller collection at King's Lynn will then be reviewed.

The Norwich Castle collection

It was during the planning of Norwich Castle's *Boudica Gallery* that the peculiar composition of the county Iron Age collection became apparent. It became clear that there are distinctive features which set this collection apart from archaeological assemblages relating to other periods and which may reflect a distinctive character that we can associate with the Iron Age people of this region. For example, in complete contrast to those of earlier prehistoric and historical periods, the Iron Age collection does not contain material from burials. This is in marked contrast to those of Anglo-Saxon and Roman times, which contain significant examples of funerary material. Neither does it contain the sort of settlement occupation debris that one might associate, for example, with a Romano-British site. What it does have is fine bronze metalwork, much of which is beautifully decorated, frequently using enamel. In terms of function, it was clear that much of this is horse-related metalwork. There are also a number of items and groups of material which appear to have been intentionally buried in the ground, or in water, as formal deposits. Where records exist, we can detect that a number of these were deposited in an intentional and carefully structured way.

I shall now look in more detail at the composition of this currently modestly-sized but steadily growing collection. It should be noted that this paper is intended to be an initial overview, while a comprehensive and detailed study of the collection and catalogue is in progress (Davies, forthcoming).

Snettisham

The first discovery of gold torcs at Ken Hill, Snettisham was made in 1948 and small-scale excavations were subsequently carried out under the direction of R.R. Clarke (Clarke 1954). The three hoards discovered at this time, consisting of complete and fragmentary gold and bronze torcs, ingot rings, gold and potin coins and other scrap metal were acquired by Norwich Castle. Three more gold torcs, a gold bracelet and a coin were discovered in 1950 and went to the British Museum. Subsequent finds in 1964, 1968 and 1989 came to Norwich. In 1990 six more hoards of metalwork, mainly gold, silver and bronze torcs were excavated and went to the British Museum.

The Snettisham collection is the largest component of the Norwich Castle Iron Age collection. In summary, this comprises 146 complete or fragmentary torcs, 21 complete or fragmentary bracelets four rings and ten fragmentary torc terminals. There are also 119 pieces of scrap metal. These items are made from gold, silver, electrum and bronze. In addition, there are 16 gold coins and a hoard of 145 potin coins. This is an important and magnificent collection which, together with the British Museum finds, comprises a collection of Iron Age metalwork unique in western Europe.

Of particular importance within the Norwich component are three complete (and one partial) tubular gold torcs, which were the first part of the Snettisham Treasure to be discovered, in 1948, through ploughing. They are known as Hoard A. They are unlike other torcs because they are hollow and very light in weight. They also appear to have been made to easily come apart. It is possible that they were intended to be worn during tribal ceremonies only and stored in a safe place at other times.

The range of material

The rest of the Norwich collection will be summarised without the inclusion of the Snettisham component. It contains a wide range of material. In terms of classification, it can be broken down into:

objects of personal adornment or dress	41.5%
objects associated with horses and transport	24.8%
miscellaneous items	11.4%
objects used in the manufacture and working of textiles	9.9%
objects associated with domestic life	6.9%
weapons	3.5%

Items of personal adornment or dress represent approaching a half of the objects. These include clothes fasteners, cosmetic items and, most numerous, brooches. There are also eight complete and fragmentary torcs, from five separate locations. If the Snettisham torcs were added to these, this category of material would be easily the most prolific.

The second largest component, representing a quarter of the items, is that of horse-related material. These 44 items include terrets, horse bits, linch pins and a single harness strap union. Ten of the 36 terrets and horse bits are decorated with enamel.

There are very few weapons, with just seven items listed. This is perhaps surprising in view of the way that Iron Age people are portrayed as a warrior society. The star items are an iron anthropoid sword from Shouldham and a decorated bronze scabbard from Congham, while the remainder are fragments.

Compared to the more showy and prestigious items cited above, the percentage of non-ceramic objects that can be associated with everyday life is relatively very small. One component is that of vessels related to consumption and drinking. These include bowls, cups and tankard handles. There are also two bone weaving combs and numerous loomweights.

When the most prolific categories of material are considered together, including the Snettisham collection, horse-related objects and items related to dress, it can be seen that the overall collection is dominated by material of high quality. This reflects exceptional wealth and status, and not ordinary domestic activity.

Coins

The Iron Age numismatic collection (including Snettisham) currently totals approximately 900 items. It contains material from all across the county. The bulk of the collection is from hoards. Material from 6 Iron Age coin hoards is held in the collection, which are:

Fincham Hoard	140 silver units
Weybourne Hoard	13 Gallo-Belgic staters and quarter stater from a larger hoard of staters
Snettisham Hoard	145 potin coins
Honingham Hoard	338 silver units with pottery container
Thorpe, Norwich Hoard	4 silver units from larger silver hoard
Weston Longville Hoard	4 silver units from larger silver hoard

Coins from twelve individual sites are represented, including small groups from important pre-Roman settlements which subsequently developed into Romano-British towns, at Crownthorpe and Caistor St Edmund.

There are few non-Icenian coins in the collection. Of particular interest are two exotic silver units from Gaul, both discovered at a single location at Gayton, in west Norfolk. They were produced by the Santones, of western Gaul, and the Aedui, of central Gaul, and suggest some form of direct contact between Norfolk and the continent at that time.

Amanda Chadburn examined the range of tasks involved in the production of silver coins, in relation to the archaeology of the Iceni (Chadburn 1999). Coin manufacturing is evidenced from four locations in the county, all of which are represented in the Norwich collection. Clay moulds come from Fison Way Thetford, Saham Toney and Needham. The first two are sites which have produced much Iron Age material and have been put forward as prominent Iron Age centres (Davies 1996 and 1999). Needham is more problematic. There was an early Romano-British site there, which was excavated by Professor Sheppard Frere, much of which was removed by gravel quarrying (Frere 1941). Unfortunately, the full nature of the Iron Age presence there has been obliterated. In addition to evidence for coin production in the form of clay pellet moulds, discoveries of silver pellets, unstruck silver flans and bronze fragments, all apparently associated with coin production, have come from Fincham, in the west of the county, which were found at the same time as a major coin hoard from the same site.

The collection at Kings Lynn

The material held by King's Lynn Museum, in west Norfolk, comprises a much smaller collection but it does contain some important items. This is the only other significant collection in the county. It reflects a cluster of important sites in north west Norfolk, in the vicinity of Snettisham, at Sedgeford, Fring and Heacham. The site of Bawsey might be added to this group, although it is not reflected in the collection.

Important element is coin hoards:

Fring Hoard	184 silver units with pottery container and textile from the container mouth
Heacham Hoard	5 gold staters
Sedgeford Hoard	32 gold staters with cow bone container

There are just seven other non-ceramic items, although most of these are, once again, items of beauty, related to status. Three are related to horse equipment, including one beautifully enamelled harness strap union. There is also a drink-related item – a vessel spout – and another bone weaving comb.

What do the Norfolk museum collections tell us?

The variety of Iron Age object types increased sharply from the more restricted range of forms used during the Bronze Age. Although the whole of the Iron Age is represented within the collection, the overwhelming bulk belongs to the Late Iron Age, dating from the first centuries BC and AD.

The collection accordingly contains a greater range of artefact types than the preceding period, embracing the categories of functional items (ceramics, domestic and dress) and prestige objects (torcs and weapons). Some of this material is highly decorated, both with enamel inlay and Celtic style relief mouldings. As such, a more in-depth study and publication is required (Davies, forthcoming).

The nature of discovery and acquisition, particularly the objects acquired through metal-detection, has meant that it is not possible to tell the original method of deposition or context for much of the material. However, among that for which we do have a provenance, there is a significant amount which was clearly intentionally deposited or buried. There are many examples which exhibit circumstantial evidence of formal deposition. Some of these finds are associated with specific types of location, such as shafts, pits or watery places (rivers, springs, lakes, marshes) or ceramic containers. In this way, a whole range of material may be interpreted as offerings. They have been separated into three broad categories, below.

Items associated with ritual deposition

The following are examples where the Iron Age material was deliberately concealed, buried or deposited in a manner that may be associated with ritual behaviour.

Ashill Shaft

A substantial wooden construction was discovered in 1874 at Ashill, by workmen digging a railway cutting. This was subsequently found to be a deep lined shaft. This is now known to be adjacent to an area of recognised Iron Age activity and occupation. The shaft contained a distinct sequence of layers of ceramic and basketry containers and objects, embedded in layers of twigs and leaves (VCH Norfolk, p295; Gregory 1977). The pottery vessels are held in the Norwich collection.

Snettisham Treasure

This world famous site has been mentioned above. There are nine hoards of torcs and associated material from the site at Ken Hill, which are held in the collections of Norwich Castle and the British Museum (Stead 1991).

Fincham hoard

This hoard of silver coins has a highly unusual composition, distinct from that of other Icenian silver hoards (unpublished). It contains what appears to be a *selection* of very unusual fine coins coupled with very poor and base examples. These include gold, silver and non-Icenian types. This composition appears to be what one would expect to find at a shrine or as a collection of sacred offerings.

Sedgeford gold coin hoard

This hoard of 32 gold staters, discovered during excavations by Sedgeford Historical and Archaeological Research Project (SHARP) in 2003, had been hidden inside a cow bone container (Dennis and Faulkner 2005). This had been placed within a specially dug pit in a carefully chosen high location overlooking the nearby river. This most unusual choice of container and special location suggests a strong possibility of ritual deposition.

Items deposited in watery places

The following are unusual and potentially significant items and all were deposited in watery places.

Fragment from an equestrian statue

This fragment from a Roman equestrian statue, in the shape of a horse's knee, was found at Ashill (near to an area of known Iron Age occupation). Believed to have been part of the statue of the emperor Claudius at Colchester, that was destroyed by Boudica's army (Sealey 1997 pp28-9; Davies 2009 p9).

Slave shackles

A complete set of iron slave shackles deposited in the River Wensum at Worthing. (See Davies 2009 pp128-9).

Other intentionally buried material

There are many objects in the collection which comprise hoards. They contain a range of material but all were deliberately buried in the ground.

The Crownthorpe Hoard

Discovered in 1982 in the parish of Wicklewood. Seven bronze vessels comprising a drinking set. They include a strainer bowl, patera, two shallow bowls, saucepan and two drinking cups. The handles of the cups are decorated with Celtic-style swimming ducks (see Davies 2009 p10). They had been intentionally buried, all inside the largest bowl.

Carleton Rode terret hoard

Found in 2004. A hoard of seven pieces of horse furniture, including terrets, linch pins and an enamelled harness mount (see Davies 2009 p113).

Ringstead Hoard of horse equipment and associated metalwork

Discovered in 1950. Consists of twelve bronze objects and parts of objects. These include two magnificent bridle bits and two decorative plates from a shield (Clarke 1951).

Saham Toney/Ovington hoard of horse equipment

Found in 1838. Hoard of seven bronze enamelled horse trappings. Comprises five terrets, snaffle bit ring and strap union (Clarke 1939).

Quidney Farm, Saham Toney, Sites A and B, horse-related equipment

Terrets, bridle bits, linch pin and roundels (Bates 2000).

Coin hoards

There are nine coin hoards in the two Norfolk collections, as listed above. Five are silver hoards, three gold and one potin. Weybourne, Thorpe and Weston Longville are just small groups from larger hoards. Of the remaining six hoards, three were found with containers. The Sedgeford gold coins were buried inside an unusual container, in the form of a cow bone. The two silver hoards associated with containers, from Honingham and Fring, were both deposited in more conventional pottery containers.

Other themes identified within the collection

During the preparation of the Norwich Castle Iron Age Catalogue (Davies forthcoming), objects have been describes and grouped according to their function.

However, during this initial analysis of the collection, it became apparent that some of the material can be grouped in other ways. Some of these categories are outlined below. They may provide different insights into the society in which these objects were used.

Objects associated with drinking

Paul Sealey has argued that the use of drinking sets, such as that from Crownthorpe (see above), was associated with beer drinking (*pers comm*). These items collectively appear to reflect beer drinking and not wine consumption.

Drinking horn terminal
Discovered in 2007 at Needham. A cast bronze drinking horn mount, with a flaring open end and a bovine head at the terminal. Two similar examples were discovered at Snettisham in 1989, although their terminals were cast in the shapes of birds (Gurney 1990). (They were both acquired by the British Museum).

Tankard handles
The collection contains two bronze tankard handles, from Billingford and West Rudham.

The geographical association of rich deposits

A range of significant deposits reflect the importance and richness of west Norfolk and its sites:

Snettisham: Treasure hoards (Stead 1991).
Sedgeford: Hoard of gold coins, associated with a settlement with high status metalwork (Dennis and Faulkner 2005).
Fring: Silver coin hoard (Chadburn and Gurney 1991).
Heacham: Gold coin hoard (unpublished).
Fincham: Coin hoard, with metalworking debris (unpublished).
Bawsey: High status metalwork and torcs (unpublished). (Most finds are held by the British Museum).
Hockham: Electrum torc (unpublished).

The 'Celtic zoo'

A number of items in the collection are representations of animals and birds. These are all discussed in more detail in a separate contribution to this volume.

Boar figurine
In 1997 a Celtic style bronze boar figurine, measuring 87mm in length, was discovered at Ashamanhaugh in central Norfolk. A striking feature is a perforated crest which runs along its back. The angle of the feet suggests

that this may have been attached to the top of a warrior's helmet (see Davies 2009 pp 112 and 118).

Bovine drinking horn terminal
See above.

Duck handles from the Crownthorpe Hoard cups
See above.

Coins
It should also be noted that Icenian coins carry representations of animals. The horse if present on almost all types. A boar is represented on one of the larger silver issues, known as the 'boar-horse' type. The Norfolk Wolf is a particularly distinctive type of gold stater, which was produced during the first century BC.

Conclusions

The piecemeal methods of collection of the Norfolk museums' Iron Age collections means that they are possibly not fully representative of the original range of material culture of that time. Historically, they result from sporadic acquisition, often biased towards some of the more remarkable and important pieces. However, despite such biases, there are clear groupings and patterns in the material. Some observations can be made at this stage.

Firstly, the collection contains very few iron items. Reasons for this include the fact that iron does not survive as well as bronze, which accounts for the majority of objects. Secondly, the bronze items tend to be some of the finer and more collectable pieces. It is also the case that many iron objects were utilitarian everyday items and not easily dateable, unless recovered during excavation.

There are very few weapons. This is a surprising observation given the historically attested troubles within the region, including an armed rebellion and suppression in AD 47 and the Boudican uprising in AD 60-1. This may be partly because swords were treasured items of great value and not casually lost. However, it is likely that most warriors would have been armed with less fine weaponry, such as iron-tipped spears, which don't survive or are not readily recognised as being Iron Age.

The most common locations represented in this collection (excluding the site of Snettisham and also excluding coins) are Saham Toney, Swanton Morley, Thetford, Wicklewood (Crownthorpe), Brampton, Caistor St Edmund and Bawsey. All of these are locations of known activity either in the late Iron Age or early Roman period. It must be noted that there are other important Norfolk sites which are not represented in these collections. The largest individual site collection is that from Saham Toney, where material has been found over many years. Accessions from this location date from the 19th century through to the present day. The significance of this location has been discussed in Davies 1996 and 1999.

A notable proportion of the items and groups of material appear to have been intentionally buried in the ground as formal deposits, in particular ways and in significant locations. Where records exist, some of these can be seen to have been deposited in a carefully structured way. It appears that significant portions of the Iron Age material were not just casually lost. This observation can be contrasted with the situation for other archaeological periods, such as in the Roman and medieval years.

We may conclude that although the Norfolk collections may not be fully representative in many ways, they do give us some idea about the character of the people of the area. A number of traits can be defined and expressed in terms of how we may describe these people.

- the raising and use of horses played a major role in their society.
- they were not obviously romanised, nor did they choose to use Roman goods.
- they possessed great wealth, especially in the west of the area.
- many of their objects reflect people of high status and wealth.
- there is very little evidence for warfare in their society, with few weapons. Those weapons which do survive reflect the presence of high status individuals.
- they were very familiar with the use of gold and silver coinage and coin production.
- ritual behaviour was very important within their society.
- drinking, especially beer, was an important activity for them.
- specific animals were important in their iconography, in particular the horse, wolf and boar.

Perhaps these conclusions may appear rather obvious and predictable. Alternatively, this significant source of data may be considered an important starting point from which to derive the cultural indicators which can serve to define the distinctive identity of the Iceni. In this way, the museum collections remain an important, and expanding, resource from which we may better understand the people of Iron Age Norfolk, covering almost all aspects of their daily life.

Bibliography

Bates, S. 2000. Excavations at Quidney Farm, Saham Toney, Norfolk 1995. *Britannia* 31, 201-237.

Bradley, R. 1990. *The Passage of Arms.* , Cambridge, Cambridge University Press.

Chadburn, A. 1999. Tasking the Iron Age: The Iceni and minting. In J. Davies and T. Williamson (eds), *Land of the Iceni: the Iron Age in Northern East Anglia*, 162-172. Norwich, Centre of East Anglian Studies.

Chadburn, A. and Gurney, D. 1991. The Fring coin hoard. *Norfolk Archaeology* 41:2, 218-225.

Clarke, R. R. 1939. The Iron Age in Norfolk and Suffolk. *Archaeological Journal* 96, 1-113.

Clarke, R. R. 1951. A Hoard of Metalwork of the Early Iron Age from Ringstead, Norfolk. *Proceedings of the Prehistoric Society* 17, 214-225.

Clarke, R. R. 1954. The Early Iron Age Treasure from Snettisham, Norfolk. *Proceedings of the Prehistoric Society* 20, 27-86.

Collingridge, V. 2005. *Boudica*. London, Ebury Press.

Davies, J. A. 1996. Where Eagles Dare: the Iron Age of Norfolk. *Proceedings of the Prehistoric Society* 62, 63-92.

Davies, J.A. 1999. Patterns, Power and Political Progress in Iron Age Norfolk. In J. Davies and T. Williamson (eds), *Land of the Iceni: the Iron Age in Northern East Anglia*, 14-43. Norwich, Centre of East Anglian Studies.

Davies J. A. 2009. *The Land of Boudica: Prehistoric and Roman Norfolk*. Oxford, Oxbow Books.

Davies J. A. forthcoming. *A Catalogue of Iron Age Artefacts in Norwich Castle Museum*.

Davies J. and Williamson T. (eds) 1999. *Land of the Iceni: the Iron Age in Northern East Anglia*. Norwich, Centre of East Anglian Studies.

Dennis M. and Faulkner N. 2005. *The Sedgeford Hoard*. Stroud, Tempus.

Frere S. 1941. A Claudian site at Needham, Norfolk. *Antiquaries Journal* 21, 40-55.

Green, B. 1993. The Iron Age. In P. Wade-Martins (ed) *An Historical Atlas of Norfolk*, 32-33. Hunstanton, Norfolk Museums Service.

Gregory, T. 1977. The enclosure at Ashill. In P. Wade-Martins (ed), East Anglian Archaeology 5, 9-30. Gressenhall, Norfolk Archaeological Unit.

Gregory, T. 1991. *Excavations in Thetford, 1980-1982, Fison Way*. Norwich, East Anglian Archaeology 53.

Gurney, D. 1990. Archaeological Finds in Norfolk 1989. *Norfolk Archaeology* 41(i), 101.

Hutcheson, N. C. G. 2004. *Later Iron Age Norfolk: Metalwork, Landscape and Society*. Oxford, British Archaeological Report 361.

Robinson B. and Gregory T. 2003. *Celtic Fire and Roman Rule* (revised edition). North Walsham, Poppyland.

Sealey, P. 1997. *The Boudican Revolt Against Rome*. Princes Risborough, Shire.

Stead, I. 1991. The Snettisham Treasure: Excavations in 1990. *Antiquity* 65, 447-65.

Victoria County History Norfolk 1901. *The Victoria County History of the Counties of England: Norfolk*. Westminster, Archibald Constable.

Late Bronze Age and Early Iron Age pottery in Norfolk – a review

Matt Brudenell

Introduction

In northern East Anglia, and elsewhere, ceramics play a pivotal role in the phasing and dating of most later prehistoric sites. As a consequence, the precision of our pottery chronologies has a major impact on our ability to comprehend settlement sequences, at both a local and region scale. Until relatively recently, the lack of an Iron Age pottery chronology in Norfolk was a serious impediment to the sequencing and interpretation of first millennium BC settlement remains (Davies 1996, 64). This situation has improved, thanks largely to the work of Sarah Percival (1999), who has established a framework for the region's Iron Age ceramics. However, now that a decade has passed since this last review, it is time to take stock of what has been learnt in the intervening years, and assess our current state of knowledge.

The primary objective of this chapter is to provide an updated ceramic sequence for the Late Bronze Age and Early Iron Age in Norfolk; a ceramic 'horizon' only partially dealt with in the *Land of the Iceni* volume (Davies and Williamson 1999). As the number of relevant assemblages and radiocarbon dates has gradually accumulated in the last ten years, our understanding of the period's pottery has changed quite considerably. This is of broader concern to those working within the region as it alters the dating of some published sites, and affects current models of settlement distribution. The following account offers a synthesis of the typological and chronological evidence for ceramic change in the late second and early first millennium BC, based on a reassessment of later prehistoric pottery in Norwich Castle Museum, and a selective review of other published and unpublished assemblages from the county.

Problems with creating a ceramic sequence

There are a number of factors which make developing a regional ceramic sequence for the Late Bronze Age and Early Iron Age in northern East Anglia problematic. For a start, many of the forms and fabrics which characterise pottery traditions in this period can have long currencies which span the conventional Bronze Age-Iron Age divide, with some characteristics persisting from *c*. 1150-350 BC. As a result, very few pottery 'types' can be dated reliably within 200-300 year time-blocks, despite there being a relatively wide repertoire of vessels. This imprecision is difficult to resolve because we rarely encounter large stratified groups of pottery which would be useful for seriation or methods of gauging ceramic change. The ditched enclosures at Micklemoor Hill, West Harling (Clark and Fell 1953) potentially contained an informative sequence spanning the Bronze Age-Iron Age transition and Earliest Iron Age, in a similar manner to the Essex ringworks. However, since all the pottery from the original excavations was grouped together, and there is no detailed recording of stratification, only further investigations at the site could resolve this issue. Another hindrance is that there are few associations between ceramics and more closely datable objects of metalwork. Although northern East Anglia has yielded a vast quantity of Late Bronze Age metalwork, few hoards or individual objects have been recovered alongside pottery. Finally, our ability to refine pottery chronologies is further hampered by the fact that the Early Iron Age coincides with the infamous 'plateau' in the radiocarbon calibration curve between *c*. 800-400 BC.

Some of these obstacles are hard to overcome, as they are limitations imposed by the nature of the region's archaeology, or problems associated with independent dating methods. We can, however, re-think the way we conceptualise ceramic change in this period. In the last few decades, it has been widely accepted that the pottery traditions of the Late Bronze Age and Early Iron Age in northern East Anglia form an unbroken ceramic sequence with only subtle changes to fabrics, forms and decorative schemes, rather than wholesale changes in vessel class. Though this may be true, statements to this effect have tended to over-emphasise the degree of continuity between the two periods, creating the picture of a relatively static ceramic tradition. This consensus has probably inhibited our search for a refined sequence, and has encouraged the use of broad dating brackets encompassing the whole of the Late Bronze Age and Early Iron Age. Confronting this issue is by no means straightforward, partly because the models we use to frame our sequences are themselves defined very broadly.

In eastern England, the basic structure of the ceramic sequence is continues to be informed by Barrett's (1980) identification of a Late Bronze and Earliest Iron Age Post-Deverel Rimbury (PDR) ceramic tradition, and Cunliffe's chronological arrangement of various Early Iron Age pottery style-groups (1968; 1974, 34-40; 1978, 36-43; 1991; 67-77; 2005, 94-102). The two models are important reference points, though individually, they are each problematic. For example, Barrett's scheme is highly generalised, and the changes he identifies are mainly based on pottery sequences from Wessex and the Thames valley, not those from northern East Anglia. His distinction between *Plain* and *Decorated* phases of the PDR tradition has also lead to a misplaced dependence of the presence/absence of decoration as the primary criterion for phasing assemblages. Whilst Cunliffe's style-zones are more regionally specific, his groupings are essentially constructed on the basis of the form and decoration of fineware bowls, which in northern East Anglia, tend to constitute only a minor part of most pottery assemblages. We may also question to what extent some style-groups are regionally distinct. It is arguable that some pottery assemblages in Norfolk have more in common with the range of forms and decorative treatments now published as belonging to the Kimmeridge-Caburn, Staple Howe, or Ivinghoe-Sandy group, than they do with the newly formed West Harling-Fengate Group (Cunliffe 2005, 92-97). This inevitably creates problems when we come to categorise assemblages and discuss affinities.

Overall, it remains difficult to situate some of the region's late second and earlier first millennium BC assemblages within this typo-chorological framework. In some instances, this has resulted in pottery being mis-assigned, which not only has implications for the dating of sites where the pottery came from, but for our overall understanding of regional settlement patterns. It has also resulted in the emergence of a confusing and inconsistent terminology for describing pottery from the period. Non-specialists attempting to penetrate the literature are confronted with a diverse and sometimes ill-defined set of terms for cultural affinity or chronology of ceramics. Terms are often used with different meaning by different ceramicists, and dating brackets may vary between specialists by up to several centuries (Champion 2007, 296). The aim of this chapter is to help resolve some of these issues, and lay the foundations for a more detailed understanding of ceramic change.

Terms and traditions: new starting points

The ceramic record of the late second and early first millennium BC can essentially be split by a distinction between jars, bowls and cups. These basic vessel categories can be sub-divided into coarsewares and finewares, based on the nature of their fabrics and method of surface treatment. In northern East Anglia, the coarsewares are characterised by fabrics with ill-sorted burnt-flint inclusions, which regularly penetrate the surface of the sherds, giving the pottery a rough abrasive texture. By contrast the finewares are normally thin-walled vessels, with finely crushed, well-sorted burnt-flint inclusions, or gritless sandy wares; all of which have well-smoothed, burnished, or highly polished surfaces, and carefully executed rim mouldings. It is this combination of vessel categories which defines the PDR ceramic tradition (Barrett 1980), and differentiates it from the preceding urn-based traditions of the Earlier/ Middle Bronze Age, and the 'slack-shouldered' jar traditions of the Middle/ Later Iron Age. Though conventionally the term PDR is used to classify ceramics dating to the Late Bronze Age (c. 1150-800 BC) and Earliest Iron Age (c. 800-600 BC), it is suggest here that pottery of the 'full' Early Iron Age (c. 600-350 BC) be included in this tradition, which is united by the categorical distinction between coarse and fineware jars, bowls and cups.

By accepting a longer chronology for the PDR ceramic tradition, the term 'Post-Deverel Rimbury' becomes a convenient label for all pottery of the Late Bronze Age and Early Iron Age. It also becomes a base level classificatory term, whose use immediately conveys an affinity to a ceramic tradition, and places a given assemblage somewhere within a poor-resolution dating bracket of c. 1150-350 BC. In some circumstances, we may not be able to refine the dating of an assemblage any further than this, particularly when presented with small groups of plain, un-diagnostic body sherds. Unsurprisingly, this type of assemblage will always be difficult to date. Nevertheless, we may presume that where assemblages are dominated by hard sherds with burnt-flint inclusions, these *probably* belong to the PDR ceramic tradition. Though burnt-flint continues to be employed as a tempering agent during the Middle/Later Iron Age in Norfolk and Suffolk, the manner of its use is quite different after c. 350 BC. Not only do sand-tempered fabrics typically dominate later assemblages, but the use of flint is mainly restricted to larger coarsewares, as opposed to vessel of all size and class in the Late Bronze Age and Early Iron Age. The temper also tends not to be as thoroughly burnt as those in PDR ceramics, and in general, the fragments are crushed to a uniform size, and are evenly sorted throughout the clay matrix.

Inevitably, the resolution offered by typo-chronological dating will be dependent on the size and condition of the pottery assemblage recovered. Where groups contain numerous partial or complete vessel profiles, there is obviously a greater chance of dating precision than when presented with a handful of small, abraded body sherds. It would be useful, then, to describe chronological ranges at different levels, depending on the quality of the data. With small assemblages, we may only be able to recognise broad affinities to the PDR ceramic tradition; in which case, the pottery should be given wide dating bracket of c. 1150-350 BC, coving the Late Bronze Age *and* Early Iron Age. Where larger groups are available, we can move beyond this base-level category and, following Barrett (1980), identify assemblages belonging to the Plainware or Decorated phase of the PDR tradition. The conventional chronology of these ceramic phases has recently been revised by the back-dating of Late Bronze Age metalwork assemblages (Needham 1996; 2007; Needham *et al.* 1997). As a consequence, the currency of the Plainware phase is now thought to be broadly coeval with the Late Bronze Age (defined by the currency of the Wilburton/ Ewart Park metalwork complex), and is dated c. 1150-800 BC, whereas the main *floruit* of the Decorated phase is believed to post-date 800 BC, and is therefore aligned upon the Early Iron Age (Figure 1). In this chapter Decorated phase

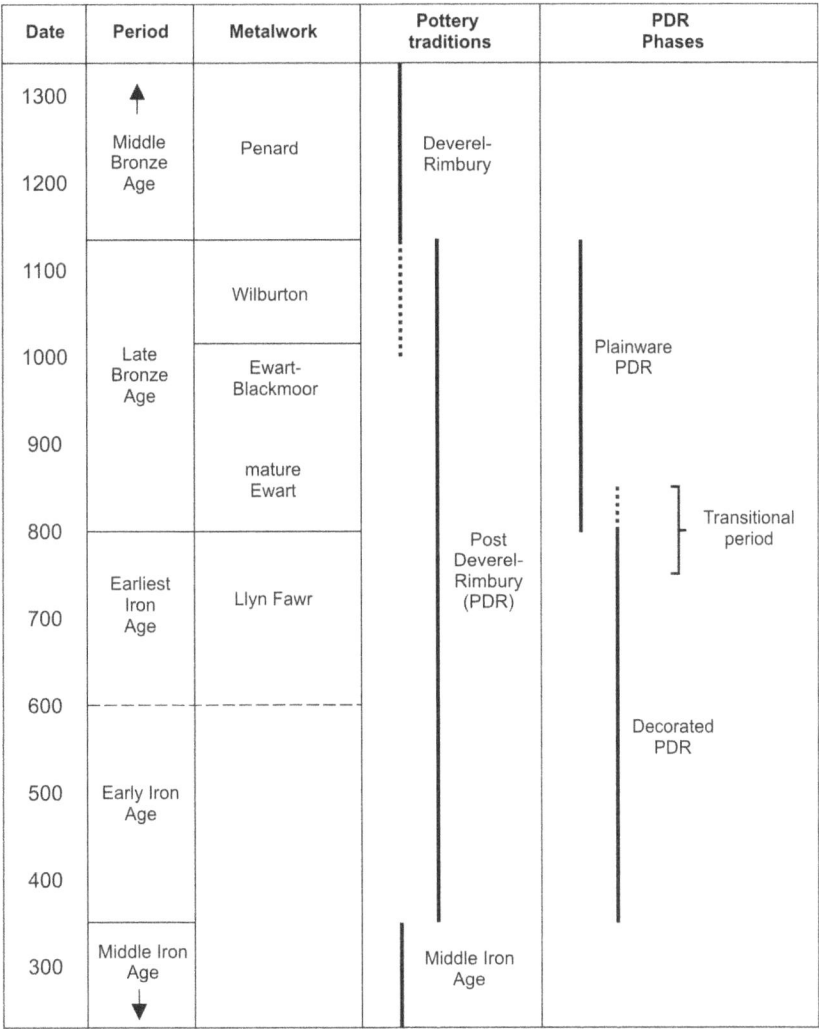

FIGURE 1. CHRONOLOGY AND TERMINOLOGY FOR LATE BRONZE AGE AND EARLY IRON AGE CERAMICS.

ceramics are dated c. 800-350 BC, with the proviso that some of the characteristic forms and decorative features of this phase may, on certain sites, begin to appear in the ceramic repertoire from the late ninth century BC, during the transitional period between the Bronze Age and Iron Age, c. 850-750 BC.

The two phases of the PDR ceramic tradition provide a simple framework for periodising pottery of the Late Bronze Age and Early Iron Age. In certain instances, it may prove possible to identify typologically 'early', 'mature' or 'late' groups within each phase (for example an early Plainware group). At this point we move into more detailed discussions surrounding the currency of individual vessels forms and decorative treatments. Although some features of the ceramic repertoire may be bracketed by radiocarbon determinations and/ or metalwork associations, we cannot yet be certain about the chronology of these sub-divisions. Nevertheless, we can outline sequences of development and provide tentative dates which may be refined and tested in the future.

Ceramics of the Late Bronze Age: Plainware phase pottery 1150-800 BC (Figures 2-3)

A comprehensive series of radiocarbon dates has yet to been obtained for the Plainware phase of the PDR tradition in Norfolk. An understanding of the ceramic sequence must therefore hinge upon typological comparison with better dated assemblages in neighbouring counties. Whilst acknowledging that changes to the ceramic repertoire will not necessarily be perfectly synchronised between different regions, it is unlikely that basic transformations in sequence will be significantly different in Norfolk to those found elsewhere. However, establishing a sound chronological framework for Late Bronze Age pottery, fixed by a series of reliable, high precision radiocarbon dates, remains a priority.

'Early' Plainware groups c. 1150-1000 BC

The early history of the PDR ceramic tradition is not fully understood in northern East Anglia. Though it is widely accepted that a new repertoire of pottery forms was adopted in parts of southern Britain during the second half

FIGURE 2. LOCATION OF SITES WITH LATE BRONZE AGE PLAINWARE PDR POTTERY (c1150-800 BC). 1. SNETTISHAM (SITE 1487); 2. GRIMES GRAVES (SITE 5640); 3. SNAREHILL, BRETTENHAM (SITE 5955); 4. HONEYPOTS PLANTATION SITE, SHROPHAM (SITE 36218); 5. WATTON ROAD, LITTLE MELTON (SITE 29057); 6. BEESTON REGIS (SITE 15534); 7. AYLSHAM BYPASS, ERPINGHAM (SITE 14940); 8. HARFORD FARM, CAISTOR ST. EDMUND (SITE 9794); 9. FRETTENHAM LIME CO. QUARRY (SITE 13350); 10. OS 171, WITTON (SITE 7128).

of the 12th century BC, the extent to which these new styles overlapped with Deverel-Rimbury type ceramics in still debatable. In Norfolk it is plausible that the earlier potting tradition continued to the end of the second millennium BC, given that some of the radiocarbon dates from the midden deposit in Grimes Graves, Shaft X, post-dated 1200 BC (particularly dates BM-1266, 2834 ± 53 BP; BM-1039, 2806 ± 54 BP; BM-1265, 2800 ± 79 BP). These dates, however, are not without their complications. As Needham (1996, 135) has noted, the charcoal from which they derived may not be contemporary with the Deverel-Rimbury pottery, and could have been introduced at a later point when pre-existing midden material was used to infill the top of the shaft. Moreover, the collection of later prehistoric pottery published from the site does seem to include a limited number of 'classic' Late Bronze Age Plainware PDR forms, namely the illustrated vessels LP7-9, and possibly LP3 and LP5 (Longworth et al. 1998, 110, fig. 44). Unfortunately, most of these vessels were not from particularly informative groups, though LP3 was stratified amongst Deverel-Rimbury type ceramics. This raises further questions about the sequence and chronology of the site, and hints at a more complex relationship between the two pottery traditions (Rigby 1988, 104).

Irrespective of whether the Deverel-Rimbury potting tradition continued beyond c. 1150 BC, it is evident that some of the earliest PDR Plainware forms develop from the bucket-shaped urns of the Middle Bronze Age.

Typologically, the earliest groups of Plainware PDR pottery tend to be dominated by a restricted range of coarsely-tempered convex-walled and barrel-shaped jars. These have upright, in-turned, or 'hooked' rims, infrequently embellished with finger-tip or finger-nail impressions on the rim-top, or a by a row of small pre-fired perforations below the vessel mouth. In both form and decoration, these vessels clearly derive from the Deverel-Rimbury tradition, representing one of the few discernable points of continuity between ceramics of the Middle and Late Bronze Age. In Norfolk, pottery potentially belonging to an early Plainware group has been published from site OS 171, Witton (NHER 7028; Lawson 1983)[1] and Watton Road, Little Melton (NHER 29057, excluding Pit 302; Ashwin and Bates 2000, 212-215). Charcoal from Pit 300 at Watton Road was radiocarbon dated 1520-1220 cal BC (GU-5290; 3110±60); though this determination is too early for the pottery it was associated with. A more realistic dating bracket for both assemblages would be c. 1150-1000/950 BC. This range probably spans the main currency of forms and decorative schemes which developed from Middle Bronze Age antecedents. It also accords well with the 1130-920 cal BC (Beta-220350; 2860 ± 40 BP) date from Earith, Cambridgeshire, associated with a comparable group of convex-walled jars (Brudenell and Evans 2006).

---

[1] The NHER references relate to the Norfolk Historic Environment Record numbers

'Mature' and 'late' Plainware groups c. 1000-800 BC

Shouldered vessels tend to be rare amongst the earliest Plainware groups, but are the dominant component of most assemblages dating to c. 1000-800 BC. These comprise a wide assortment of round and slack-shouldered jars, divisible into a number of different types according to the morphology of the neck and rim. Their appearance signifies a broadening of the ceramic repertoire, and a new emphasis on forms not represented in the local Deverel-Rimbury tradition. Common varieties include jars with high rounded-shoulders and upright or concave necks; vessels with long in-sloped necks and short upright or out-turned rims, and bipartite or biconical jars. Collectively, these vessels display a range of rim forms, most of which have flat, rounded, or slightly expanded lips. The distinctive types include rims with internal bevels or sharp internal neck angles. Some even had an internal hollowing to the neck which may have been used to support a lid. The finewares in Late Bronze Age assemblages were normally bowls and cups, though a small number of jars may also be present. The typical forms were plain round bodied bowls with short upright necks, and hemispherical bowls and cups; most of which have rounded, tapered, or carefully bevelled rims. These vessels may have a currency spanning the entire Plainware phase, but may be more prevalent in assemblages post-dating c. 1000 BC.

Decoration was intermittently applied to vessels in the Late Bronze Age, and was normally restricted to the coarsewares. These were sporadically embellished with a single row of fingertip or fingernail impressions, normally positioned along the rim-top, or on occasions, across the edges of the rim, the neck or the shoulder. In addition, cordons were sometimes applied to the girth of vessels, or to a zone above the shoulder. These may be present in the early Plainware groups, and represent another continuation of decorative schemes from the Deverel-Rimbury tradition. However, the application of cordons to the neck of tripartite jars only occurs at the very end of the Plainware sequence (during the Bronze Age-Iron Age transition), and is a form of embellishment which continues into the Earliest Iron Age and beyond.

Norfolk now contains a number of Late Bronze Age assemblages which, on the basis of typology, are assignable to a 'mature' phase of the Plainware PDR sequence, dating c. 1000-800 BC (Figure 3). Published assemblages include those from Frettenham Lime Co. Quarry (*NHER* 13350; Ashwin and Bates 2000) and Harford Farm, Caistor St. Edmund (*NHER* 9794; ibid). Though pottery from the latter was previously dated to the Iron Age (Percival 2000, 112), with hindsight this assemblages is now better placed within the Late Bronze Age (S. Percival pers comm.). An important Plainware vessel has also been published from Beeston Regis, where a hoard of Ewart Park-type socketed axes was found within a shouldered coarseware jar/bowl (*NHER* 15534; Lawson 1980a). This is one of only a handful of sites in eastern England where pottery and metalwork have been found in direct association. In this instance, we can be confident that the vessel belongs to the 'mature' Plainware phase as the chronology of this metalworking tradition centres upon 1020-800 BC (Needham et al 1997, 93-98). Other unpublished assemblages assignable to this group include pottery from pits uncovered in the Aylsham Bypass excavations, Erpingham (*NHER* 14940), and a jar found at Snettisham (*NHER* 1487). To this list we can also add a small but important group of Late Bronze Age pottery recently excavated by at Honeypots Plantation site, Shropham (*NHER* 36218; S. Percival pers comm.). The assemblages contained a range of shouldered jars associated with a radiocarbon determination of 930-800 cal BC (Wk-16704; 2716 ± 37 BP).

Towards the close of the Late Bronze Age, the basic range of Plainware forms was supplemented by a new and distinctive series of angular-profiled vessels. The enlarged repertoire of this 'late' Plainware group incorporated a variety of different carinated bowls, including vessels with pronounced shoulders and hollowed necks; angular tripartite bowls with a short everted rim, and bi-partite bowls with an in-sloped neck and a tapered or beaded lip. The vessels in this series had thin-walls and burnished exterior surfaces; commonly dark grey or back in colour. Some were also equipped with a distinctive *omphalos* base (a dished base), and were occasionally decorated with furrows or grooves on, or above, the carination.

In Norfolk, the only assemblage potentially belonging to this late Plainware group is from the unpublished site at Snarehill, Brettenham (*NHER* 5955; Shand 1985a). This contains a range of carinated fineware bowls with omphalos bases; some of which carried horizontal groves and furrows above the shoulder, or groups of incised diagonal lines. These decorative treatments have parallels in other published Late Bronze Age assemblages in northern East Anglia, including Game Farm (Gibson *et al.* 2004) and Maidscroft, Suffolk (Needham 1995). In Essex, vessels with these features were stratified in the middle-upper fills of the ringwork enclosures (Barrett and Bond 1988; Brown in prep; Brudenell in prep), suggesting they were grafted into the Plainware repertoire during the (late?) ninth century BC. Their makers may even have been influenced by contemporary metalworking traditions, as strong parallels are evident between the 'late' Plainware bowls and the well-known Ewart Park phase bronze cup from Welby, Leicestershire (Powell 1948). Further support for a ninth century BC date comes from a recently investigated crannog-type timber platform at Must Farm, Whittlesey, Peterborough (M. Knight pers comm.). This yielded a large group of 'late' Plainware pottery, associated with objects of Ewart Park-type metalwork. The assemblage incorporated a range of carinated fineware bowls with omphalos bases, including two vessels with incised decoration and an unusual furrowed cup with a pedestal foot. Importantly, carbonised food residue preserved within one of the complete bowls produced a radiocarbon date of 920-800 cal BC (Beta-243230; 2700 ± 40 BP).

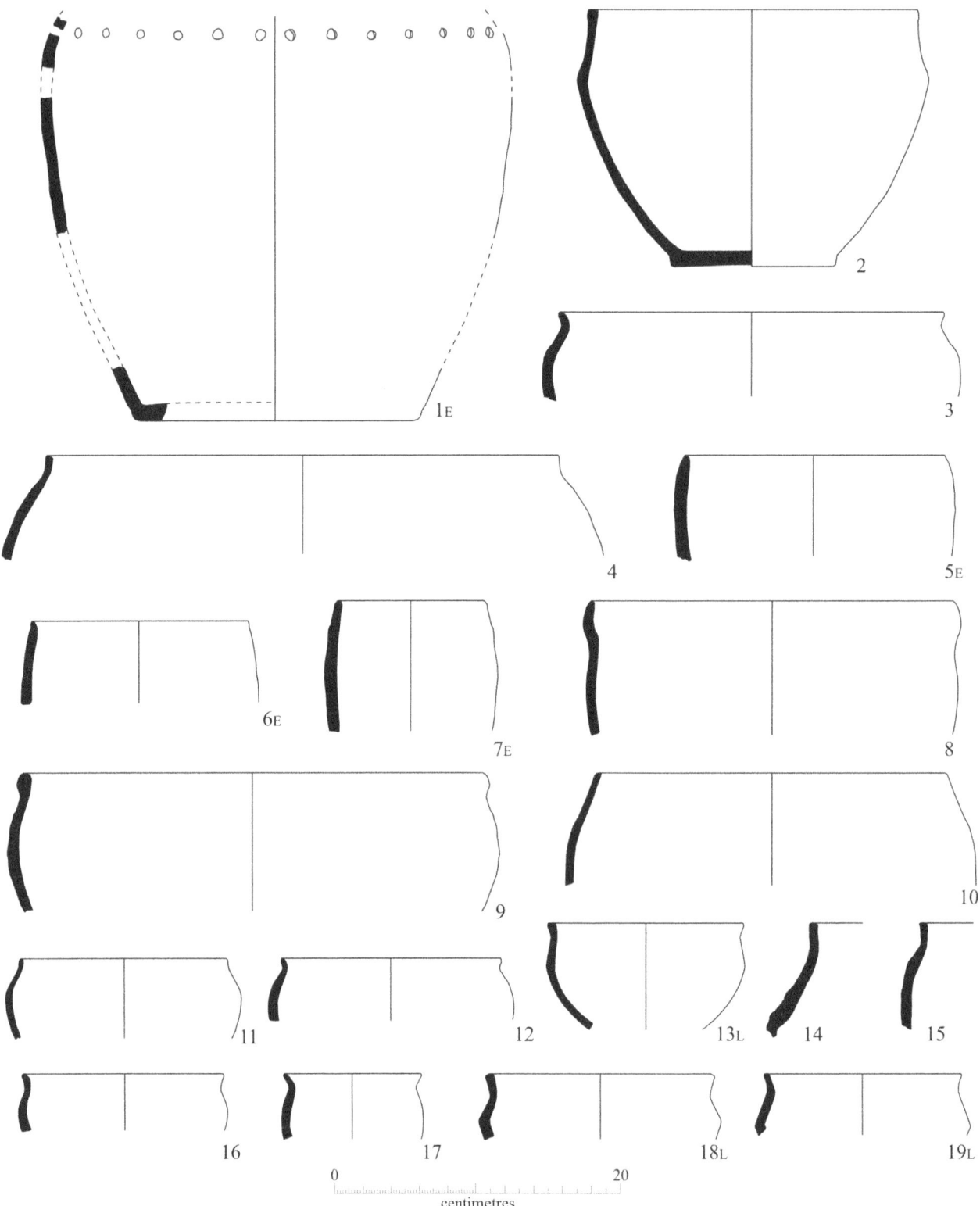

FIGURE 3. FORMS CHARACTERISTIC OF LATE BRONZE AGE PLAINWARE PDR ASSEMBLAGES (c1150-800 BC). 1., 6-7. OS171, WITTON (AFTER LAWSON 1983, 43, FIG.39); 2. BEESTON REGIS (AFTER LAWSON 1980, 218, FIG. 1); 3.. 9., 15. HARFORD FARM, CAISTOR ST EDMUND (AFTER ASHWIN AND BATES, 113-114 FIGS 92-93); 4., 11. FRETTENHAM LIME CO. QUARRY (AFTER ASHWIN AND BATES, 207, FIG. 169); 5., 14. WATTON ROAD, LITTLE MELTON (AFTER ASHWIN AND BATES, 314, FIG. 175); 8. SNETTISHAM (SITE 1487); 10., 12., 16. AYLSHAM BYPASS, ERPINGHAM; 13., 17., 18., 19. SNAREHILL, BRETTENHAM (AFTER SHAND 1985, FIGS 9, 10, 13). 'E' DENOTES FORMS COMMON AMONGST 'EARLY' PLAINWARE GROUPS; 'L', FORMS OCCURRING IN 'LATE' PLAINWARE GROUPS.

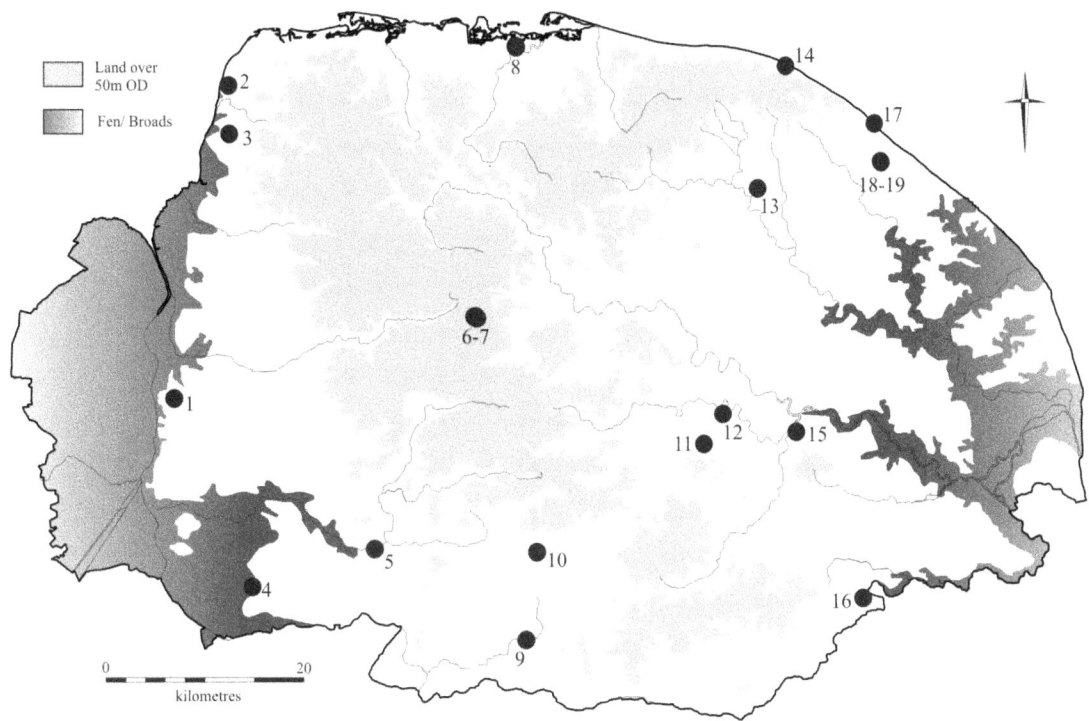

FIGURE 4. LOCATIONS OF SITES WITH EARLY IRON AGE DECORATED PDR POTYTERY (C800-350 BC). 1. RUNCTON HOLME (SITE 2398); 2. REDGATE HILL, HUNSTANTON (SITE 1396); 3. SNETTISHAM (SITE 1487); 4. CAULDRON FIELD, FELTWELL (SITE 5188); 5. LYNFORD QUARRY, STANFORS (SITE 35165); 6. BITTERING QUARRY, BEESTON WITH BITTERING (SITE 13023; 15910); 7. 'LONGHAM MOUND' SITE, LONGHAM (SITE 7239); 8. WARBOROUGH HILL, STIFFKEY (SITE 1863; 11327); 9. MICKLEMOOR HILL, WEST HARLING (SITE 6019); 10. HONEYPOTS PLANTATION SITE, SHROPHAM (SITE 36218); 11. HETHERSETT (SITE 9423); 12. LAND OFF WATTON ROAD, LITTLE MELTON (SITE 50209); 13. AYLSHAM BYPASS, ERPINGHAM (SITE 14940); 14. CROMER (SITE 6452); 15. VALLEY BELT, TROWSE (SITE 9589); 16. PASTON (SITE 6879?); 17. OS 3 SITE II, WITTON (SITE 16641); 18. OS 91, WITTON (SITE 6969).

Ceramics of the Early Iron Age: Decorated phase pottery c. 800-350 BC (Figure 4)

The Bronze Age-Iron Age transition was accompanied by a broadening of the ceramic repertoire and a renewed emphasis on decoration. These changes define Decorated phase assemblages, to which we conventionally assign a start date of c. 800 BC, so as to coincide with the beginning of the Early Iron Age. In reality, it is unlikely that there was a single moment when one ceramic phase switched to the next. Changes may not have been perfectly synchronised between regions, or between sites *within* regions. Instead we should envisage a period of transition, occurring over a few generations, where new vessel forms and decorative schemes were gradually incorporated into the traditional practices of potting. This process was probably underway in the closing decades of the ninth century BC, with changes becoming formalised/institutionalised in the period *after* 800 BC, during the Earliest Iron Age. In the absence of stratified deposits, these sequences of transformation are almost impossible to observe. In most cases we encounter groups which represent a 'before and after' snap-shot of the ceramic repertoire on either side of the transition. In the future it may be possible to unpick this process with more precision. However, for now we must aim to characterise Decorated phase PDR pottery, and identify the changes which occur during the course of the Early Iron Age.

'Early' Decorated groups c. 800-600/500 BC (Figure 5)

With a few exceptions, most of the shouldered jar types which emerged in the Plainware phase had currencies extending into the Earliest Iron Age (c. 800-600 BC). However, the new and distinct forms of this period included an array of angular-shouldered jars of bipartite or tripartite profile. Common varieties included carinated jars with concave necks; angular tripartite jars with everted and flared rims, and bipartite jars with a high angular shoulder and short in-turned neck. Most of these forms belong to the coarseware category, which continues to be characterised by fabrics with poorly-sorted burnt-flint inclusions. There are, however, some differences in the surfaces texture of coarsewares in the Early Iron Age. The rough, vertical 'finger-fluting' which appears on the lower body of some Late Bronze Age vessel is not a features of later ceramics. Overall, the surfaces of Early Iron Age coarsewares tend to be slightly smoother than their Late Bronze Age counterparts, suggesting an adjustment in finishing techniques, and perhaps a new sense of tactile aesthetics.

The Iron Age in Northern East Anglia: New Work in the Land of the Iceni

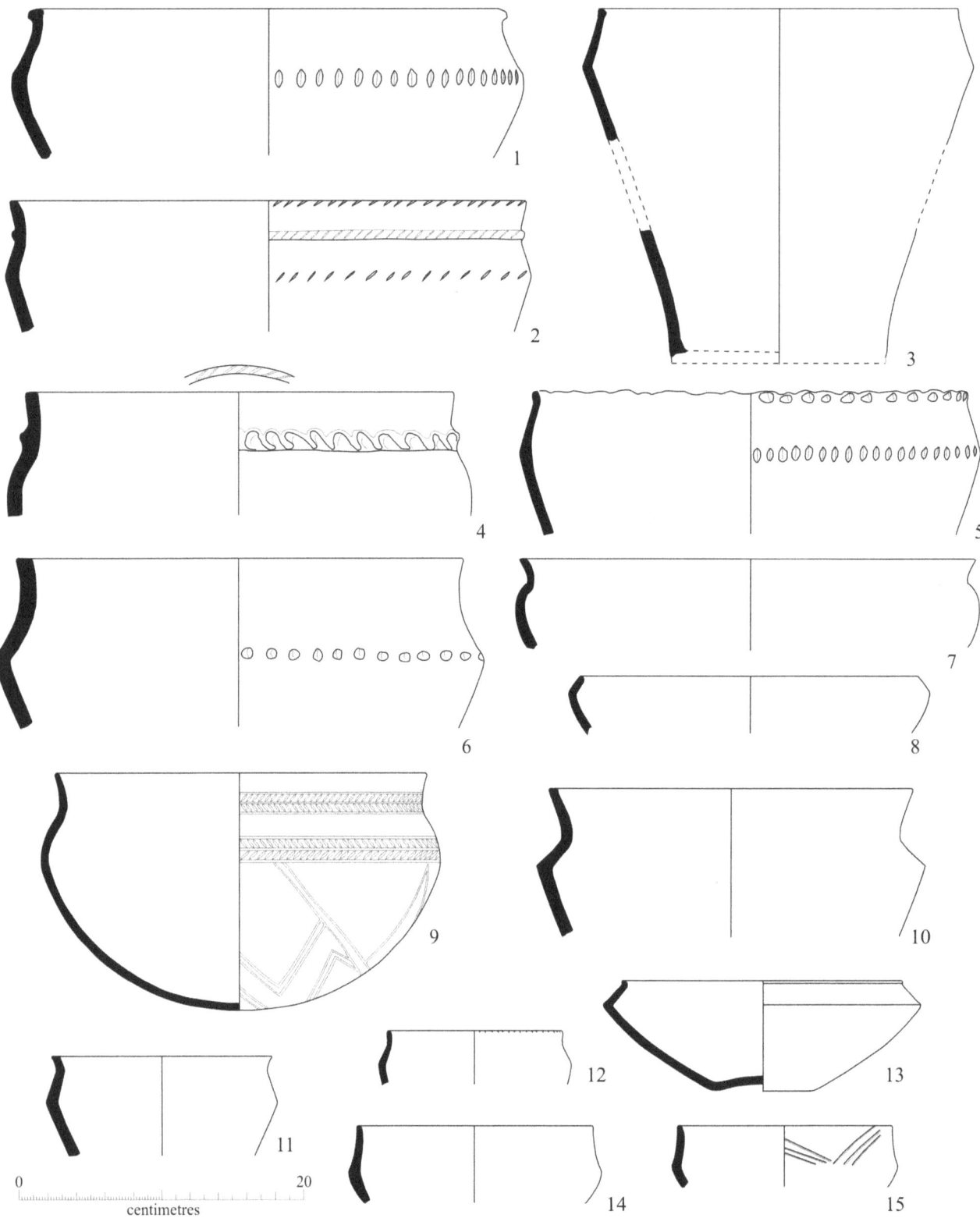

Figure 5. Forms and decorative styles characteristic of Earliest Iron Age, 'early' Decorated PDR assemblages (c800–600 BC). 1., 3., 5., 7-8. OS 3 site II, Witton (after Lawson 1983, 39, fig. 32). 2., 4., 6., 10-11., 13., 15. Micklemoor Hill, West Harling (after Clarke and Fell 1953, 16., 19., 21., figs 10, 13, 15); 9. Cromer (after Cunliffe 2005, 616, fig. A:5). 12, 14. Warborough Hill, Stiffkey.

The visual appearance of the coarsewares was also transformed in the Earliest Iron Age by the more regular use of decoration. Meaningful figures on decorative frequency are difficult to come by, but a brief review of published and unpublished literature from eastern England suggests that around 20% of coarseware vessel rims were normally decorated in Earliest Iron Age assemblages, as opposed to figures around the 10% mark in the Late Bronze Age. Furthermore, decoration was often found on multiple vessel zones after c. 800 BC, such as the rim and shoulder. Rim-tops, rim-exteriors, and shoulders were all commonly embellished in this period, whilst the rim-interior, neck and body were also intermittently treated. In some instances double rows of decoration were used to adorn the girth of jars, and on rare occasions, columns of impressions were made along the body of vessels. By varying the manner of execution, potters were able to achieve a surprisingly diverse range of visual and tactile effects from a limited 'decorative grammar'. This was implemented by various fingertip treatments, or by simple edged-tools which were used to impress, nick or stab the surfaces of the clay. Slashed and finger-tipped cordons were also applied to the neck of large, tripartite coarseware jars, and were a common feature of 'early' Decorated assemblages.

The bowl forms of the Earliest Iron Age descended from the carinated series which emerged during the ninth century BC. Some of these types spanned the Bronze Age-Iron Age divide, and probably remained in circulation until at least the end of the seventh century BC (as does the omphalos base). The new bowl types of the Earliest Iron Age are generally distinguished by their sharp shoulder angles. Variations in the morphology of the rim, neck, and height of the carination created an array of subtly different profiled bowls, each generated from a basic bipartite or tripartite 'theme'. In Norfolk, the commonest form appears to be the bipartite bowl with a sharply angled shoulder. These were sometimes embellished with either a plain or decorated cordon on the neck; a short ledge on the carination, and/ or a tooled chevron pattern above the girth. Other fineware decorative styles of this period included bands of parallel grooves on or immediately above the shoulder, simple geometric motifs such as incised triangles, chevrons, and punched dots, or 'herringbone' incisions between parallel grooves.

The large assemblage from Micklemoor Hill, West Harling (*NHER* 6019; Clarke and Fell 1953) contains many of the vessels forms and decorative treatments which characterise Earliest Iron Age ceramics in Norfolk. The term 'Harling-type' or 'Harling-style' is therefore an appropriate short-hand for early Decoarted phase assemblages in this region. Other published groups which may be assigned to this period include assemblages from OS3 Site II, Witton (*NHER* 1664; Lawson 1983); Valley Belt, Trowse (*NHER* 9589; Ashwin and Bates 2000); Warborough Hill, Stiffkey (*NHER* 1863, 11327; Clarke and Apling 1935); the 'Longham mound' site, Longham (*NHER* 7239; Ashwin and Flintcroft 1999), and Bittering Quarry, Beeston with Bittering (*NHER* 15910; ibid). Moreover, in recent years three other large assemblages of Early Iron Age pottery have been recovered from Pheasnat's Walk, Earsham (*NHER* 44609) the Honeypots Plantation site, Shropham (*NHER* 36218); and Land off Watton Road, Little Melton (*NHER* 50209). All three yielded important groups of 'Harling-type' pottery (S. Percival and P. Thomson pers comm.), with decorated finewares paralleled in the Pre-War gravel pit assemblage from Fengate, Peterborough (Hawkes and Fell 1945). Significantly, the pottery from the Honeypots Plantation site is associated with radiocarbon determinations of 820-550 cal. BC (Wk-16703; 2574 ± 37 BP) and 800-420 cal. BC (Wk-16705; 2519 ± 44 BP).

'Late' Decorated groups c. 600/500-350 BC (Figure 6)

The later history of Decorated phase pottery is poorly understood (Knight 2002, 127). In northern East Anglia is seems likely that styles associated with this phase may have continued, with some modifications, into the mid to late fourth century BC. In some areas the 'Harling- type' pottery described above may have remained in vogue throughout parts of the the sixth and possibly early fifth centuries BC. A late continuation of this 'style' is now suggested by a radiocarbon date of 510-380 Cal. BC (Beta-286573; 2350±40 BP), recently obtained from carbonised residue adhering to a decorated jar from enclosure II, Micklemoor Hill, West Harling (for an illustration of this vessel see Clark and Fell 1953, 16, fig. 10.8).[2] As a site conventionally placed in the Earliest Iron Age, this determination is unexpectedly 'late' and demonstrates how vaguely we understand the settlement or its ceramics.

Unfortunately, we cannot always depend wholeheartedly on radiocarbon dating to refine our Early Iron Age ceramic sequences, as the period overlaps with the C14 calibration plateau of c. 800-400 BC. As other helpful sources of dating evidence are seldom encountered, such as metalwork associations or stratigraphic relationships, our knowledge of ceramic change must continued to be gauged/guestimated by imperfect typological means. In Norfolk there are currently few pottery groups which may be positioned between 'Harling-type' assemblages, and ceramic styles typifying the Middle Iron Age. Where encountered, these 'late' Decorated PDR groups continue to display some of the form traits and decorative features which emerged at the beginning of the Early Iron Age, but are otherwise dominated by a new series of sinuous profiled jars and bowls; some of which anticipate vessel forms of the Middle Iron Age.

The diagnostic jars in this group have tall, upright or hollowed necks which end in a thickened rim, often expanded or flanged internally. Examples from the Alysham Bypass (*NHER* 14940) and Bittering Quarry (*NHER* 13023; Ashwin and Flitcroft 1999, 241, fig. 20, P10) have rounded shoulders, though a related form from

---

[2] This sample was taken by the author with permission of the staff at Norwich Castle Museum. The date itself was funded by the Cambridge Archaeological Unit, courtesy of Chris Evans.

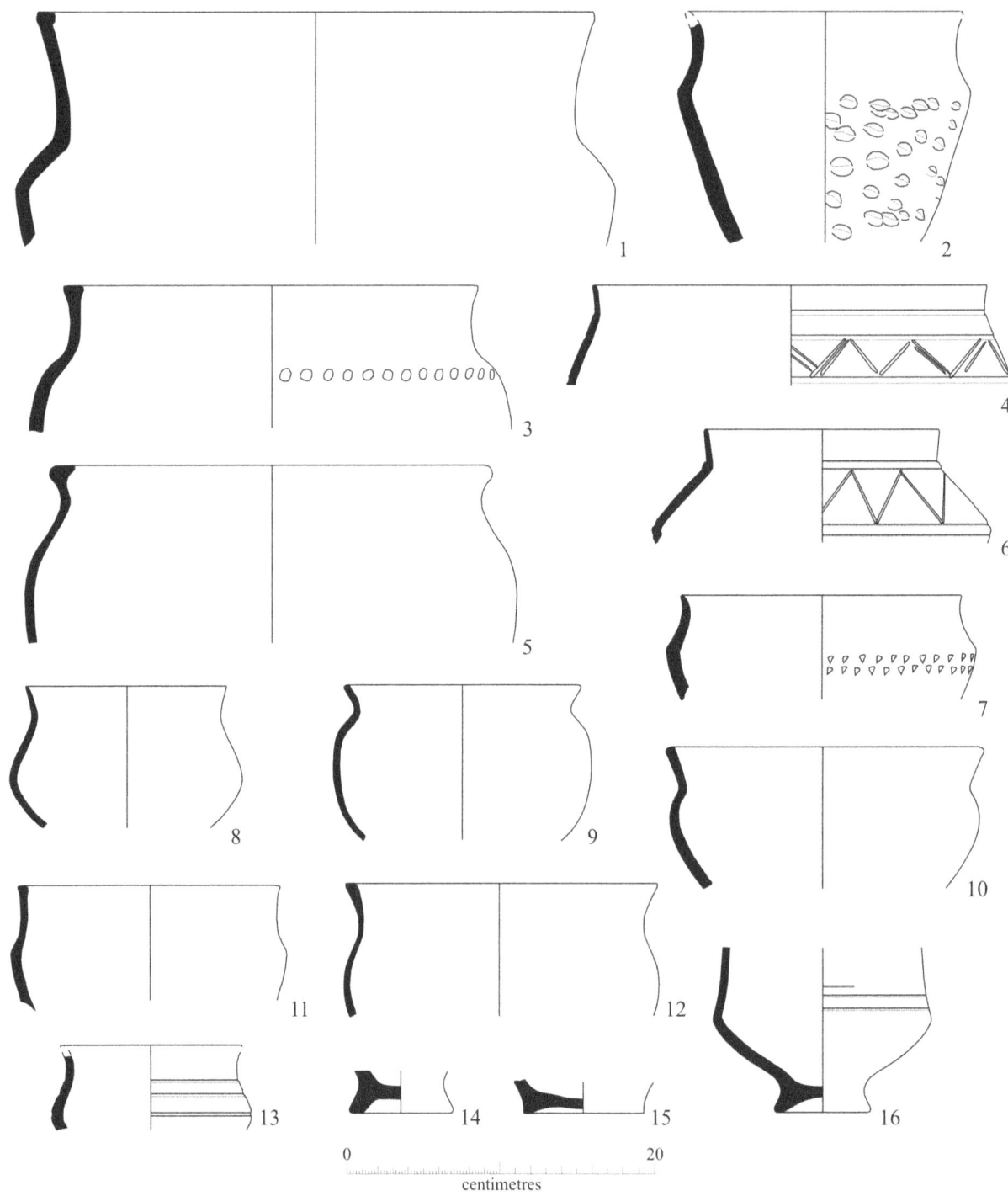

FIGURE 6. FORMS AND DECORATIVE STYLES CHARACTERISTIC OF EARLY IRON, 'LATE' DECORATED PDR ASSEMBLAGES (C600-350 BC). 1. RUNCTON HOLME; 2. BITTERING QUARRY, BEESTON WITH BITTERING (AFTER ASHWIN AND FITCROFT 1999, 244, FIG. 23); 3-9. AYLSHAM BYPASS, ERPINGHAM; 10-11. OS 91, WITTON (AFTER LAWSON 1983, 41, FIG. 38); 12-16. CAULDRON FIELD, FELTWELL (SHAND 1985, FIG. 5,7,10,12).

Runcton Holme (*NHER* 2398; Hawkes 1933) retains an angular profile. Jars of this type tend not be decorated on the rim, but may display a row of carefully placed fingertip impressions on the shoulder. In general, coarseware ornamentation tends to decline towards the end of the Early Iron Age, and various elements of the decorative repertoire, such as cordoning and tooled slashing, appear to disappear altogether (as do omphalos bases). The finewares, on the other hand, may still be embellished with bands of horizontal grooves or chevrons patterns between the base of the neck and the shoulder. The range of 'late' fineware motifs is best exemplified by pottery from Cauldron Field (*NHER 5188*; Shand 1985b) which contains an array of decorated S-profiled bowls with flared rims. Other sites have yielded rounded and angular-shoulder jars decorated with chevron patterns, namely Lynford Quarry, Stanford

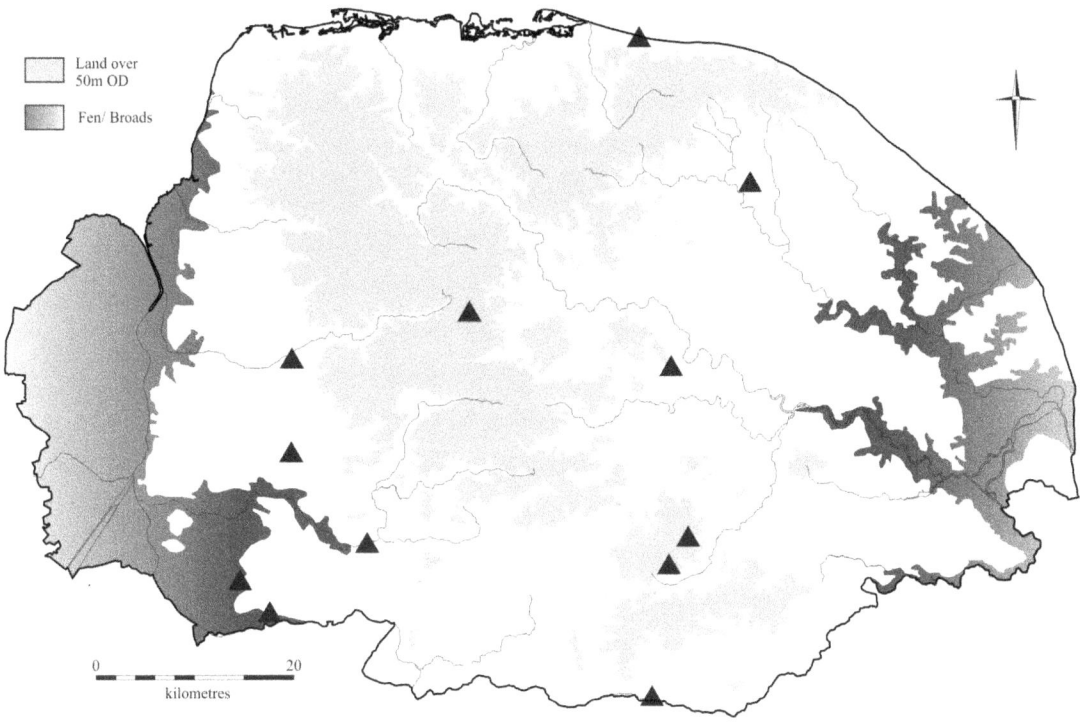

FIGURE 7. LOCATION OF SITES WITH RUSTICATION EARLY IRON AGE SHERDS.

(*NHER* 35165; Birks and Robertson 2005, 691, fig. 11, C- E) and the Alysham Bypass, Erpingham (*NHER* 1494). These are reminiscent of some forms recovered the gravel pits at Fengate, Peterborough, particularly those illustrated from Pit D and E (Hawkes and Fell 1945, 200, fig. 2).

The most distinctive ceramics of the late Early Iron Age are jars with marked shoulders and hollowed necks, whose body is rusticated by rows of fingertip impressions bearing nail marks. The decoration, which covers the entire body of the vessels was either haphazardly applied, or was very regular, occurring in close-set horizontal or diagonal bands. The rustication always occurs below the shoulder, and on several instances, the neck above was carefully smoothed or burnished. The best published example of one of these jars comes from Bittering Quarry (*NHER* 13023; Ashwin and Flitcroft 1999, 244, fig. 23, P34), although several unpublished profiles are present in assemblages from the Aylsham Bypass, Erpingham (NHER 14940) and Ken Hill, Snettisham (*NHER* 1487). A whole range of other Iron Age sites in Norfolk have yielded rusticated sherds presumably belonging to jars of this type (Figure 7). Among the better known are Lynford Quarry, Stanford (*NHER* 35165; Birks and Robertson 2005, 691, fig. 11, H) and Cauldron Field, Feltwell (*NHER* 5188; Shand 1985b, figs. 11, nos. 7-10) Intriguingly, they seldom occur elsewhere in northern East Anglia. Single sherds have been published from Darmsden (Cunliffe 1968, 187, fig. 3, no. 51) and Barham in Suffolk (Martin 1993, 39, fig. 23, no. 70), and Linton in Cambridgeshire (Fell 1953, 37, fig. 5, 34), but are otherwise all but absent from Iron Age assemblages in these counties. It is possible then,

that this form of treatment constitutes a regionally distinct decorative style whose distribution centres upon Norfolk.

The manner of rustication on the Norfolk jars differs from the deep finger-pinching which covers some vessels assignable to the Darmsden-Linton group (Cunliffe 1968, 178-181; 1974, 39; 1978, 42; 1991, 76; 2005, 102); for example those illustrated from Lofts Farm, Essex (Brown 1988, 268, fig. 17, no. 83), and Linton, Cambridgeshire (Fell 1953, 37, fig. 5, no. 33). Conventionally, pottery belonging to the Darmsden-Linton style-zone is found over a large area of eastern England, stretching from the Thames to the Wash. However, its presence in Norfolk is now is highly questionable. When the style-zone was first defined, Cunliffe (1968, 178-181) listed six sites in Norfolk belonging to the group (including Snarehill, Brettenham, which in this review is dated to the end of the Late Bronze Age). Since then, no further sites have been added to the original catalogue for Norfolk, and in fact, the Darmsden-Linton distribution maps which appear throughout the various editions of *Iron Age Communities*, only display five find-spots for the county. Having reassessed these assemblages, it is now apparent that none of these sites, or any others in Norfolk, has yielded ceramics which irrefutably belong to the Darmsden-Linton group. Most importantly, the distinctive tripartite bowls which characterise this style are entirely absent from the county. Instead, their distribution centres upon Essex, south Suffolk, and south east Cambridgeshire; a zone excluding the area which would later become the 'land of the Iceni'.

In the future it may prove possible to define a discrete Early Iron Age potting tradition in northern East Anglia, whose 'identity' is distinct from the Darmsden-Linton groups further to the south. The date range of these 'late' Decorated PDR groups in Norfolk is still uncertain, though there is some indication that their currency is broadly coeval with Darmsden-Linton pottery. This evidence comes in the form of foot-ring and pedestal bases, which occur in assemblages from Bittering Quarry (*NHER*13023; Ashwin and Flitcroft 1999, 241, fig. 20, P17); Cauldron Field, Feltwell (*NHER* 5188; Shand 1985b, fig. 5, nos. 8-9; fig. 10, no. 4; fig. 11, no. 2; Cunliffe 2005, 624, fig. A:13, no. 24) and Lynford Quarry, Stanford (Percival 2005, 691; un-illustrated). These bases were modelled on continental prototypes of the sixth century BC and later (Hodson 1962, 142; Barrett 1978, 286-287), and commonly occur on bowls in the Darmsden-Linton and Chinnor-Wandlebury group (and indeed on other Early Iron Age ceramics in southern England). A date no earlier than the sixth century BC is therefore suggested for the 'late' Decorated PDR assemblages in Norfolk, though a fifth or fourth century date may be more appropriate.

Discussion

This chapter demonstrates that Norfolk holds a rich Late Bronze Age and Early Iron Age ceramic resource, which we are now capable of arranging into a coherent sequence. Though the details of chronology will undoubtedly require modification as further radiocarbon dates are obtained, we now have a basic framework which will facilitate the classification and comparison of newly excavated material. This reassessment of published and unpublished assemblages also feeds into broader discussions about regional settlement patterns. Assuming that pottery distributions mark the location of settlement sites (Rogerson 1999, 125), this (partial) survey of Norfolk's PDR pottery collections reveals evidence for Late Bronze Age and Early Iron Age occupation across most parts of the county. Although the majority of sherds from these find-spots cannot be closely dated within the PDR tradition, they nonetheless indicate a widespread 'presence' during the late second or earlier first millennium BC, with over 90% of locatable 'sites' falling within 2 km of a watercourse - a distribution paralleled by Iron Age sites in Suffolk (Martin 1988, 68). Year-round access to water would have been essential for sustaining livestock, and as wells and waterholes appear to be absent from Norfolk's Late Bronze Age and Early Iron Age settlement record,[3] we must assume that rivers, streams and springs served as the main water source for both humans and animals throughout this period. This will have limited the number of locations suitable for permanent settlement, and could help us predict where dense areas of occupation might be in the landscape.

---

[3] These features which are regularly encouraged on settlement site in Cambridgeshire and Essex but appear to be absent from Norfolk and Suffolk.

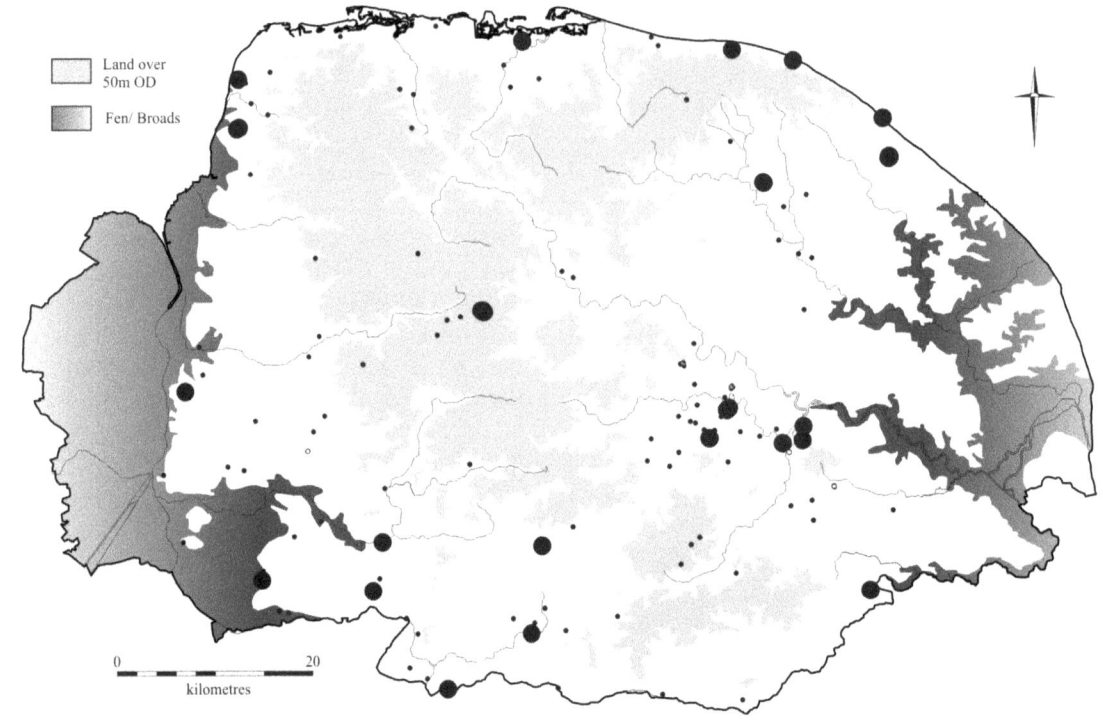

FIGURE 8. LOCATION OF PDR POTTERY FIND-SPOTS. LARGE DOTS: PHASED PDR ASSEMBLAGES FROM FIGURES 2 AND 4. SMALL DOTS: UN-PHASED PDR ASSEMBLAGES RECORDED IN NORWICH CASTLE MUSEUM.

In the past, regional surveys have tended to stress how elusive the evidence is for Late Bronze Age settlement in Norfolk (Ashwin 1996; Davies 1996; Lawson 1980b; 1984). With the re-dating of some pottery collections we are now presented with a rather different picture; but one which begins to complement the pattern of Bronze Age metalwork finds (Lawson 1984; Ashwin 1996). These new pottery distributions also cast doubt over the validity of some models of Iron Age settlement expansion/colonisation (Davies 1996; Hill 1999), and suggest we may have seriously underestimated how 'full' our later prehistoric landscapes might have been. However, before we can confidently approach the issue of population dynamics and regional settlement patterns, we must firstly tackle the outstanding problems of chronology, so that the relevant remains are correctly ordered. This survey has gone some way towards achieving this goal, but further gains will only be made if we continue to invest in absolute dating programmes, and 'test' the ceramic sequences forwarded.

Until the finer details of ceramic sequence are adequately resolved, radiocarbon dating should be mandatory for Late Bronze Age and Early Iron Age assemblages in excess of one thousand sherds or 10 Kg, and encouraged for smaller groups. The relative cost of this procedure is not the same as it was 20 years ago, and obtaining dates should no longer be a publication luxury, but a standard practice insisted upon at assessment level. Retrospective dating programmes for 'old' published assemblages are also needed, particularly as our typological schemes are founded on these type-site groups. The date recently achieved for the West Harling assemblage demonstrates the importance of going back to the material from old excavations, and highlights the potential of targeting surviving carbonised residues. With any luck, the next time a similar review is attempted, the author will be able to draw upon tens of absolute dates rather than the handful which Norfolk currently boasts.

Acknowledgements

I would like to thank John Davies and the staff at Norwich Castle Museum for allowing me access to the pottery collections, and for giving me the opportunity to write this paper. My thanks also go out to Sarah Percival (NAU Archaeology) for guiding me through the county's published and unpublished assemblages, and providing me with information on the radiocarbon dates from the Honeypots Plantation site. I am grateful too for the help of Peter Thompson (Archaeological Solutions), who allowed me to view the unpublished assemblage from Pheasant's Walk, Earsham. I would also like to thank Mark Edmonds, Mark Knight, Sarah Percival and Paul Sealey for reading and commenting on drafts of this report, as well as Katie Anderson for her usual patience and encouragement. The analysis of the pottery from Norwich Castle Museum was funded by the Arts and Humanities Research Council, and was conducted as part of my Ph.D thesis on the Late Bronze Age and Early Iron Age ceramics of East Anglia.

Bibliography

Ashwin, T. 1996. Neolithic and Bronze Age Norfolk. *Proceedings of the Prehistoric Society* 62, 41-62.

Ashwin, T. and Bates, S. 2000. *Excavations on the Norwich southern bypass, 1989-91: Part I, Excavations at Bixley, Caistor St Edmund, Trowse, Cringleford and Little Melton.* Dereham, East Anglian Archaeology 91.

Ashwin, T. and Flitcroft, M. 1999. The Launditch and its setting: excavations at the Launditch, Beeston with Bittering, and Iron Age features and finds from its vicinity. *Norfolk Archaeology* 43, 217-256.

Barrett, J. 1978. The EPRIA prehistoric pottery. In J. D Hedges and D. G. Buckley, Excavations at a Neolithic causewayed enclosure, Orsett, Essex, 1975. *Proceedings of the Prehistoric Society* 44, 268-288.

Barrett, J. 1980. The pottery of the later Bronze Age in lowland England. *Proceedings of the Prehistoric Society* 46, 297-319.

Birks, C., and Robertson, D. 2005. Prehistoric settlement at Stanford: excavations at Lynford quarry, Norfolk 2000-2001. *Norfolk Archaeology* 44, 676-701.

Bond, D. 1988. *Excavations at the North Ring, Mucking, Essex: a Late Bronze Age enclosure.* Chelmsford: East Anglian Archaeology 43.

Brown, N. 1988. A Late Bronze Age enclosure at Lofts Farm, Essex. *Proceedings of the Prehistoric Society* 38, 249-302.

Brown, N. in prep. Springfield Lyons Late Bronze Age Pottery.

Brudenell, M. in prep. Mucking Late Bronze Age Pottery.

Brudenell, M. and Evans, C. 2006. *Rhee Lakeside South: archaeological excavations at Colne Fen, Earith.* Unpublished Cambridge Archaeological Unit report.

Champion, T. C. 2007. Settlement in Kent 1500 to 300 BC. In C. Haselgrove and R. Pope (eds), *The Earlier Iron Age in Britain and the near continent*, 293-305. Oxford, Oxbow.

Clark, J. G. D. and Fell, C. I. 1953. The Early Iron Age site at Micklemoor Hill, West Harling, Norfolk, and its pottery. *Proceedings of the Prehistoric Society* 24, 1-40.

Clarke, R. R. and Apling, H. 1935. An Iron Age tumulus on Warborough Hill, Stiffkey, Norfolk. *Norfolk Archaeology* 25, 408-428.

Cunliffe, B. 1968. Early pre-Roman Iron Age communities in eastern England, *Antiquaries Journal* 48, 175-191.

Cunliffe, B. 1974. *Iron Age communities in Britain: an account of England, Scotland and Wales from the seventh century BC until the Roman Conquest.* London, Routledge and Kegan Paul.

Cunliffe, B. 1978. *Iron Age communities in Britain: an account of England, Scotland and Wales from the seventh century BC until the Roman Conquest* (second edition). London, Routledge and Kegan Paul.

Cunliffe, B. 1991. *Iron Age communities in Britain: an account of England, Scotland and Wales from the seventh century BC until the Roman Conquest* (third edition). London, Routledge.

Cunliffe, B. 2005. *Iron Age communities in Britain: an account of England, Scotland and Wales from the seventh century BC until the Roman Conquest* (fourth edition). London, Routledge.

Davies, J. 1996. Where eagles dare: the Iron Age of Norfolk. *Proceedings of the Prehistoric Society* 62, 63-99.

Davies, J., and Williamson, T (eds). 1999. *Land of the Iceni: the Iron Age in Northern East Anglia.* Norwich, Studies in East Anglian History 4.

Fell, C. I. 1953. An Early Iron Age settlement at Linton, Cambridgeshire. *Proceedings of the Cambridge Antiquarian Society* 46, 31-42.

Gibson, C., with Last, J., McDonald, T. and Murray, J. 2004. *Lines in the sand: Middle to Late Bronze Age settlement at Game Farm, Brandon.* Hertford, East Anglian Archaeology Occasional Paper 19.

Hawkes, C. F. C. 1933. An Early Iron Age settlement at Runcton Holme - the second occupation - a peasant settlement of the Iceni. *Proceedings of the Prehistoric Society of East Anglia* 7, 231-62.

Hawkes, C. F. C. and Fell, C. 1945. The early Iron Age settlement at Fengate, Peterborough. *Archaeological Journal* 100, 188-223.

Hill, J. D. 1999. Settlement, landscape and regionality: Norfolk and Suffolk in the pre-Roman Iron Age of Britain and beyond. In J. Davies and T. Williamson (eds), *Land of the Iceni: the Iron Age in Northern East Anglia,* 185-207. Norwich, Studies in East Anglian History 4.

Hodson, R. 1962. Some pottery from Eastbourne, the 'Marnians' and the pre-Roman Iron Age in southern England. *Proceedings of the Prehistoric Society* 28, 140-155.

Knight, D. 2002. A regional ceramic sequence: pottery of the first millennium BC between the Humber and the Nene. In J.D. Hill and A. Woodward (eds), *Prehistoric Britain: the ceramic basis,* 119-142. Oxford, Prehistoric Ceramic Research Group Occasional Publication 3.

Lawson, A. J. 1980a. A Late Bronze Age hoard from Beeston Regis, Norfolk. *Antiquity* 54, 217-219.

Lawson, A.J. 1980b. The evidence for later Bronze Age settlement and burial in Norfolk. In J. Barrett and R. Bradley (eds), *Settlement and society in the British later Bronze Age,* 271-294. Oxford, British Archaeological Reports (British Series) 83.

Lawson, A. J. 1983. *The archaeology of Witton, near North Walsham, Norfolk.* Dereham, East Anglian Archaeology 18.

Lawson, A. J. 1984. The Bronze Age in East Anglia with particular reference to Norfolk. In C. Barringer (ed), *Aspects of East Anglian prehistory,* 141-177. Norwich, Geo Books.

Longworth, I., Ellison, A., and Rigby, V. 1988. *Excavations at Grimes Graves Norfolk 1972-1976: Fascicule 2, The Neolithic, Bronze Age and later pottery.* London, British Museum Press.

Martin, E. 1988. *Burgh: Iron Age and Roman Enclosure.* Ipswich, East Anglian Archaeology 40.

Martin, E. 1993. *Settlements on hill-tops; seven prehistoric sites in Suffolk.* Ipswich, East Anglian Archaeology 65.

Needham, S. P. 1995. A bowl from Maidscross, Suffolk; burials with pottery in the Post Deverel-Rimbury period. In I. Kinnes and G. Varndell (eds), *'Unbaked urns of rudely shape': essays on British and Irish pottery for Ian Longworth,* 159-171. Oxford, Oxbow Monograph 5.

Needham, S. P. 1996. Chronology and periodisation in the British Bronze Age. *Acta Archaeologica* 67, 121-140.

Needham, S. P., Ramsey, C. B., Coombs, D., Cartwright, C., and Pettitt, P. 1997. An independent chronology for British Bronze Age metalwork: the results of the Oxford radiocarbon accelerator programme. *Archaeological Journal* 154, 55-107.

Needham, S. P. 2007. 800 BC, the great divide. In C. Haselgrove and R. Pope (eds), *The Earlier Iron Age in Britain and the near continent,* 39-63. Oxford, Oxbow.

Percival, S. 1999. Iron Age pottery in Norfolk. In J. Davies and T. Williamson (eds), *Land of the Iceni: the Iron Age in Northern East Anglia,* 173-184. Norwich, Studies in East Anglian History 4.

Percival, S, 2000. Pottery. In T. Ashwin and S. Bates, *Excavations on the Norwich southern bypass, 1989-91: Part I, Excavations at Bixley, Caistor St Edmund, Trowse, Cringleford and Little Melton.* Dereham, East Anglian Archaeology 91, 108-114.

Percival, 2005, Prehistoric pottery. In C. Birks and D. Robertson, Prehistoric settlement at Stanford: excavations at Lynford quarry, Norfolk 2000-2001. *Norfolk Archaeology* 44, 689-692.

Powell, T. G. E. 1948. The Late Bronze Age hoard from Welby, Leicestershire. *Archaeological Journal* 105, 27-40.

Rigby, V. 1988. The late prehistoric, Roman and later wares. In I. Longworth, A. Ellison, and V. Rigby. 1988. *Excavations at Grimes Graves Norfolk 1972-1976: Fascicule 2, The Neolithic, Bronze Age and later pottery.* London, British Museum Press, 100-110.

Rogerson, A. 1999. Arable and pasture in two Norfolk parishes: Barton Bendish and Fransham in the Iron Age. In J. Davies and T. Williamson (eds), *Land of the Iceni: the Iron Age in Northern East Anglia,* 125-131. Norwich, Studies in East Anglian History 4.

Shand, P. 1985a. *Snarehill urnfiled, Brettenham: excavations of a Late Bronze Age settlement near Thetford, Norfolk, 1959.* Unpublished Report, Norfolk HER.

Shand, P. 1985b. *Cauldron field, Feltwell: excavations of an Early Iron Age settlement on the fen edge, 1962.* Unpublished Report, Norfolk HER.

Iron Age landscapes from the air: results from the Norfolk National Mapping Programme

Sophie Tremlett

with James Albone and Sarah Horlock

The National Mapping Programme (NMP) is a national, English Heritage sponsored programme that uses aerial photographs to identify, map and interpret earthworks, cropmarks and structures ranging in date from the Neolithic to World War Two. Since 2001 this systematic survey has been completed for *c* 28% of Norfolk. Not only is new information now available for previously known sites, but the majority (*c* 60%) of the archaeological sites encountered have been new discoveries. Clearly, in a county and region where aerial photography plays such a significant role in archaeological research and curation (see Wade and Brown 2000, 54), the impact of the NMP survey is considerable. It has the potential to radically alter perceptions of the density and character of archaeological sites in the areas it covers.

By April 2008, the NMP had been completed for Norfolk's coastal and Broads landscape zones, and for sample areas of the county's main aggregate-bearing geologies. Within these areas, the survey recorded more than 6,000 archaeological sites, including 640 of known or potential Iron Age date (Figure 1). A considerable degree of synthesis of the results for specific areas had been undertaken for the project's reports (Albone *et al* 2007a; 2007b; in prep) and interim publications (Massey et al 2003; Albone *et al* 2004; Horlock *et al* 2008). The prospect of speaking at the 2008 *Land of the Iceni* conference, and in the same year contributing to the revised Regional Research Frameworks (Medlycott and Brown *in prep*), provided an opportunity to evaluate the NMP results for the period as a totality, and to assess their significance in the context of Iron Age studies in Norfolk and the wider region. The results of ongoing work covering Norwich, Thetford and the A11 corridor are for the most part too recent for inclusion in the following discussion. It should be kept in mind, therefore, that this is an ever-growing dataset, subject to constant reappraisal

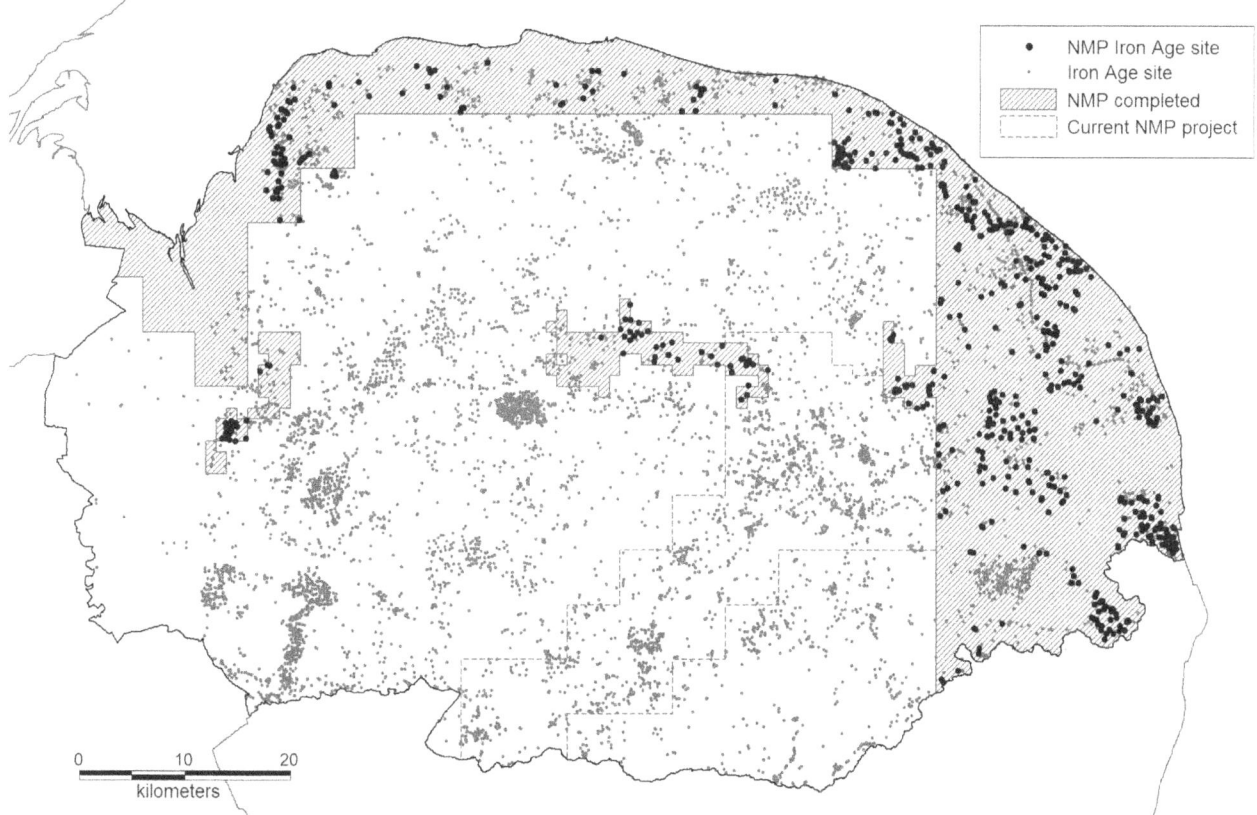

FIGURE 1. THE DISTRIBUTION OF NMP AND NON-NMP IRON AGE SITES, IN RELATION TO THE AREAS FOR WHICH NMP HAS BEEN COMPLETED (SITE DISTRIBUTIONS DERIVED FROM NORFOLK HISTORIC ENVIRONMENT RECORD).

in light of new discoveries or newly revealed facets of previously known sites. Furthermore, Norfolk is not the only county within the Icenian 'territory', or within the wider region, to be the subject of an NMP survey. While the discussion below will touch upon results from other areas, a full integration of such data has been beyond the scope of the present study.

The Nature of the Evidence

The 640 Iron Age sites recorded by the NMP are, by their very nature, confined to those types of site that can be recognised from the air, namely enclosures, fields, trackways and boundaries. Sites not represented in the archaeological record in a way that is readily identifiable on aerial photographs, whether because they lack features substantial and regular enough to be recognised from cropmarks or earthworks, or because they occur in areas where geology, soils or vegetation cover leads to their 'invisibility', are inevitably scarce within the NMP dataset. Thus, while this paper focuses specifically on the results of the NMP survey, it does so while recognising that its dataset represents only a sample – and an unrepresentative one at that – of the archaeological record for Norfolk's Iron Age. Similarly, while it does not deal with a considerable part of the archaeological record, the interpretation of individual sites has been made using all available complementary information.

The vast majority of the NMP Iron Age sites are known from aerial photography alone. In the absence of additional forms of evidence, as at those few sites that have been subject to other forms of investigation, any interpretation must by necessity be crude. Such interpretations generally lack the nuances of chronology and characterisation possible at sites where a wider range of evidence is available. Much of the interpretation is based on site morphology, through comparison with other sites or reasoning and speculation upon how such a morphology might have developed (see Palmer 2007, 98–100, for a description of the processes involved). Such interpretations are generally tentative, left open to question until corroborative evidence can be found. This is particularly true for the dating of sites and highlights the principal problem with the NMP data for the period. With the exception of a few classes of site, on the basis of their morphology alone, Iron Age sites (and particularly later Iron Age sites) are for the most part indistinguishable from those dating to the Roman period. This is exacerbated by those sites, such as Spong Hill (Rickett 1995) and Watlington (Town 2004) where excavation has demonstrated continuity from the Iron Age into the Roman period. Thus, most of the NMP's Iron Age sites have in fact been assigned only a broad Iron Age (often later Iron Age) to Roman date.

It is also the case that there is a tendency to assign this date to most of the otherwise undated rectilinear enclosure complexes and field systems encountered by the project. While physical dating evidence, where it exists, tends to confirm such an interpretation, results from a number of excavations suggest that at least some of these enclosures and fields probably originated in the period spanning the Bronze Age to Middle Iron Age (Albone et al 2007a). Thus the interpretative frameworks commonly employed in the analysis of NMP data almost certainly mask important chronological distinctions. Such problems are made worse by the tendency of aerial photographs to reduce chronological depth, by recording a palimpsest of archaeological features that do not necessarily represent contemporary events. Where possible, air photo interpreters endeavour to make chronological distinctions, whether between different elements of a 'site' (where features slight or respect other features, or are slighted/respected by them), or through comparison with excavated sites. Within Norfolk, further work to 'ground truth' the dating of those sites where such distinctions have been made is vital if these interpretative models are to be refined.

Figure 1 shows the distribution of the NMP Iron Age sites in relation to that of Iron Age sites across the county as a whole. Unsurprisingly, the distribution is not uniform for either group. Dense clusters of NMP sites are evident, particularly in the east and northeast of the county and along its western fen edge. These reflect a variety of factors, not least the favourability of soils for cropmark formation, and the concomitant tendency of aerial photographers to target such soils. The availability of excavated evidence is also a significant factor, as it provides an opportunity to date sites more closely and more certainly than might otherwise be the case. The mass of sites on the Tottenhill Gravels at Watlington, where good conditions for cropmark formation coincide with extensive excavations undertaken in advance of aggregate extraction, are a case in point. This is not to say, however, that the site distribution may not also reflect a genuine preference for certain areas in the past. Only further work, both in terms of extending the NMP survey and more intensive investigation of those areas already covered, can elucidate the significance or otherwise of such patterns.

The NMP Iron Age sites can be grouped into a number of broad categories: fortified sites; enclosures and settlements; fields systems; linear boundaries; and funerary sites. While these categories are used in the discussion that follows, it should be recognised that such classifications are not rigid or definitive. Many of the sites have been interpreted only tentatively as representing a particular type, and a considerable number fall into more than one category - a trait also evident amongst many non-NMP sites. Norfolk's Iron Age forts are excluded from the more detailed analysis below, as the impact of the NMP mapping on those two sites it has covered (Holkham, Norfolk Historic Environment Record 1776, and Warham, NHER 1828) has been relatively minor.

NMP Results

Enclosures and Settlement

The character of Iron Age settlement in East Anglia is poorly understood when compared to other regions in southern England, particularly Wessex and the Thames

Valley (Bryant 2000, 14). While considerable progress has been made in the last decade, many aspects of the chronology, form, density and nature of settlement during the period remain enigmatic (Medlycott and Brown *in prep*). Within Norfolk (and presumably elsewhere), the need to investigate 'mundane' sites and those without substantial remains, rather than focussing on more unusual sites such as the forts, has to some extent been alleviated by work undertaken in advance of development (Ashwin 1999, 104–6).

The NMP can provide the broad-based, landscape-scale information, which is often beyond the scope of developer-led excavations. In the context of Iron Age settlement within Norfolk, however, the full potential of the aerial photographic evidence appears to have been overlooked. A perceived preference for unenclosed settlement and the likelihood that a significant number of sites were located on unresponsive clayland soils have been seen as restricting factors, limiting the number of such sites recognised from the air (Bryant 2000, 14). Ashwin (1999, 105) implies that only sites 'enclosed by major defences' or 'featuring deep ditches and other features which are not found on the undefended living sites' are visible from the air. The NMP has demonstrated that this is not necessarily the case; many of the enclosures and other features recorded for all periods, including the Iron Age, are relatively slight. While no claims can be made to record the totality of the buried archaeological record, the project's results are not dominated overwhelmingly by fortified sites or those with particularly substantial ditches. Very recent mapping (during March 2009), as part of the Thetford-Norwich-A11 project, has included an enclosure complex at Trowse, near Norwich, part of which has been excavated and found to be of Early to Middle Iron Age date (Ashwin and Bates 2000b). Cited as an exemplar of a 'hidden' settlement (Ashwin 1999, 105–6), its enclosed elements are in fact visible on a number of aerial photographs, with narrow gullies as well as substantial ditches being recognisable (although see below). This and other sites have undoubtedly benefited from the systematic and comprehensive nature of the NMP survey (although it should be noted that part of the enclosure complex at Trowse, if not its full extent, had been recognised prior to the excavations; Ashwin and Bates 2000b, 141, fig 113). At other sites, however, it has perhaps been the absence of an interpretative framework within which to view these technically undated enclosures, and a consequent failure to recognise their potential Iron Age date or their relationship to settlement, that has led to their being overlooked by previous overviews of Norfolk's Iron Age.

Iron Age settlement within Norfolk, and, to an extent, the wider region, has been characterised as typically unenclosed (Hill 1999, 189; Bryant 2000, 14). However, perceptions vary as to the nature of this 'unenclosure', and of those enclosed sites that did exist. Bradley (1993) and Ashwin (1999) emphasise the scarcity of large defended sites, or of settlements with major defences, while noting the prevalence of extensive unenclosed settlements. Hill (1999; 2007, 19–21) characterises Norfolk's settlement pattern as 'spurgy', with activity and occupation spread over extensive areas and shifting over time. Such areas could incorporate enclosure elements, but these were not necessarily used for settlement, and were part of the larger spread of settlement/activity, rather than containing it. Certainly, the settlement pattern of northern East Anglia differs from the distinct hamlets and farmsteads – Hill's 'spotty' landscape (1999) – seen elsewhere. It is also the case that large unenclosed sites undoubtedly existed within the county, as at Park Farm, Wymondham (Ashwin 1996), and that such sites might be difficult to recognise on aerial photographs. The excavations at Trowse recorded small features and material spread across an extensive area, much of it outside of the enclosure group visible on the aerial photographs (Ashwin and Bates 2000b). At the same time, the large numbers of enclosures of possible Iron Age date recorded by the NMP, together with those recorded by other methods, means that the 'enclosed' aspect of Norfolk's Iron Age landscape cannot simply be ignored.

The NMP's most significant recent finding in this context has been the identification of two enclosures at Rackheath, northeast of Norwich, both of which may relate to prehistoric settlement (Figure 2). These were not new discoveries – Derek Edwards photographed both in 1986 from the air – but their potential significance had not been appreciated. The enclosures, both visible as cropmarks, lie approximately 50m apart. That to the northeast is circular and measures approximately 40m in diameter. It has an entrance to the east and contains the cropmark of a possible round house measuring 11m in diameter (NHER 50758). In plan the site is strongly reminiscent of the eastern enclosure belonging to the Early Iron Age farmstead excavated at Micklemoor Hill, West Harling (Clark and Fell 1953). This too contained a round house, although larger and positioned more centrally than the possible Rackheath example. At the same time, the circular Rackheath enclosure also compares well with the later Bronze Age site of North Ring, Mucking (Jones and Bond 1980, 479).

The southwestern enclosure at Rackheath is larger (nearly 100m long and *c* 85m wide), with a rather irregular oval or sub-circular plan. It has a narrow, slanted entrance, defined by opposed inward/outward-turning terminals, and no visible internal features. Although no clear parallels have yet been identified within Norfolk, it has been suggested as being of Little Woodbury type (J D Hill *pers comm*). This would indicate a Middle Iron Age date, and that it was perhaps a successor to the earlier circular enclosure. However, it is worth noting that a second enclosure at Micklemoor Hill, which finds evidence suggested was contemporary with the first, also exhibits an irregular oval plan form (Clark and Fell 1953, 38, figure 6), although this is less pronounced and the enclosure is smaller than at Rackheath. Finds from the area surrounding the Rackheath site are dominated by dense clusters of Mesolithic and Neolithic to Bronze Age flints. No Iron Age material has been recovered.

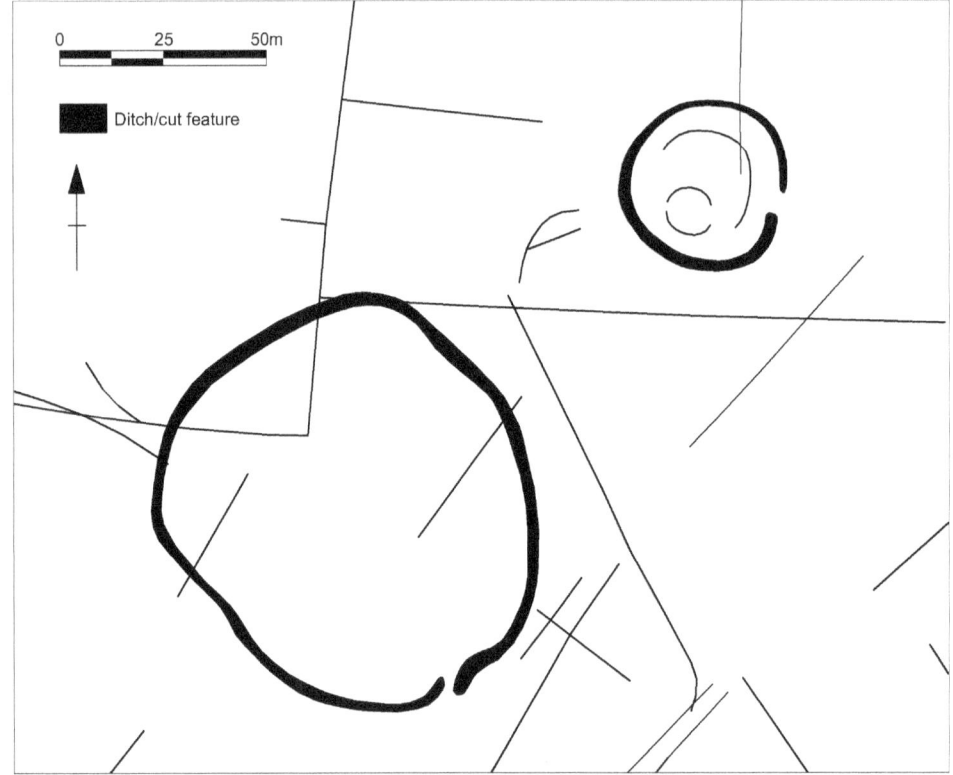

FIGURE 2. POSSIBLE SETTLEMENT ENCLOSURES AT RACKHEATH (COPYRIGHT ENGLISH HERITAGE/ NORFOLK MUSEUMS & ARCHAEOLOGY SERVICE).

FIGURE 3. A PROBABLE SETTLEMENT OR FARMSTEAD AT HEACHAM (PHOTOGRAPH BY D. EDWARDS. NORFOLK AIR PHOTO LIBRARY REFERENCE NHER 6638Q 5 JULY 1989. COPYRIGHT NORFOLK MUSEUMS & ARCHAEOLOGY SERVICE).

The Rackheath enclosures are unusual not only in their rarity as a form of site within Norfolk, but also in the context of the potentially Iron Age enclosures mapped by the NMP. A specifically Early or Middle Iron Age date can be suggested for few of those. The majority are postulated to be of Late Iron Age to Roman date, characterised by their rectilinear and relatively regular morphology, although a small number of polygonal and curvilinear enclosures are also known. Such simple interpretative frameworks, however, based almost entirely on morphology and perceived relationships with other features, are only adequate for an initial, basic analysis. The enclosure group at Trowse, for example, which is of Middle Iron Age date, is also rectilinear in plan.

Putting such reservations aside, the Late Iron Age to Roman enclosures and settlements mapped by the NMP can be grouped or differentiated according to a wide range of characteristics These are: single or multiple enclosures; enclosure morphology (rectangular, square, trapezoidal, single- or double-ditched); their isolation or integration into the surrounding landscape; and the presence or absence of round houses (see Albone *et al* 2007a). There is considerable variation, ranging from relatively small, plain, isolated enclosures, perhaps best interpreted as having an agricultural function, through to extensive complexes extending for a kilometre or more and incorporating fields and trackways as well as various forms of enclosure. One of the best examples of a smaller farmstead, and one where a domestic function seems difficult to dispute, lies at Heacham in northwest Norfolk (Figure 3; Wade-Martins 1999, 28; Massey *et al* 2005; NHER 13032). The site is complex, the NMP plot representing a palimpsest of several phases. It may

FIGURE 4. A PROBABLE SETTLEMENT AT HOPTON-ON-SEA
(COPYRIGHT ENGLISH HERITAGE/NORFOLK MUSEUMS & ARCHAEOLOGY SERVICE).

be associated with Iron Age pottery and an origin in the later Iron Age is certainly plausible, although it may have remained in use into the Roman period. The principal enclosure is square, defined by a bank and ditch, and contains three circular structures, which are presumably round houses. The site is distinctive for possessing what appears to be a highly elaborate and formalised entrance, with movement seemingly restricted to narrow corridors or pathways through and across ancillary enclosures and barriers. The surrounding area is heavily enclosed, with at least two 'styles' being evident, perhaps representing different areas for stock and cultivation.

Larger settlements have also been mapped. One of the best examples is at Hopton-on-Sea, in the east of the county (Figure 4; NHER 43494). The settlement lies within an extensive landscape of fields and paddocks, and exhibits a high degree of nucleation, focussed around several conjoined enclosures. The degree of internal subdivision is markedly high, perhaps separating domestic space from industrial or agricultural activities. Several probable round houses are evident. As at Heacham, a trackway leads into what may have been the main domestic area. This could have linked to one of the major long-distance trackways of postulated Late Bronze Age or Early Iron Age date discussed below. The enclosure itself appears to be overlain by a 'planned' field system of Roman (possibly mid to late Roman) date, providing a potential *terminus ante quem* for the settlement.

Mention should also be made of a postulated group of Late Iron Age rectangular enclosures, known as 'Thornham-type' enclosures, found in west and north Norfolk. Thus far, the NMP mapping has failed to support the coherence of this group, first identified by Gregory (1986), and subsequently discussed by Davies (1996, 77; 1999, 32–3). The NMP has recorded a wide variety of square, rectangular and trapezoidal plan forms, in a range of dimensions. The purpose of many such sites is unclear. At some, a settlement function seems most likely while at others, typically those which are least complex, stock management or other agricultural activity seems more probable.

The extent to which the enclosures recorded by the NMP (and by excavation) represent 'enclosed settlement' or 'enclosed components' of more extensive open settlements is unclear. Hill has suggested that Micklemoor Hill, often cited as a rare example in the county of enclosed settlement (Bryant 1997, 25–6; Hutcheson and Ashwin 2005, 23), might represent just such an enclosed component, rather than an isolated farmstead (Hill 1999, 192). Clearer definitions, coupled with more detailed analysis of the NMP and non-NMP data, will undoubtedly lead to a more nuanced characterisation of the material than the simple enclosed/non-enclosed dichotomy currently employed.

Field Systems

Perhaps the most dramatic aspect of the NMP mapping for the period is the recognition of the coherent systems of fields and trackways identified across extensive areas of eastern and northeast Norfolk, and across a more limited area of west Norfolk. As with many other NMP sites, these have been broadly dated to the Iron Age (usually later Iron Age) and/or Roman period. This is most often on the basis of their morphology, or their postulated relationship with other sites, rather than physical dating evidence. While fragments of these field systems had been recorded prior to the NMP, their true extent and overall coherence had not been recognised previously, nor their defining characteristics identified.

The majority of the field systems have a rectilinear, broadly coaxial, pattern and a northeast–southwest and northwest–southeast orientation. More distinctively, they are often articulated by numerous trackways, which usually form the major boundaries between fields. In the east of the county, some of the principal boundaries may have been established in the Bronze Age (see below and Albone *et al* 2007a). Enclosures and possible settlements and farmsteads, including those at Heacham and Hopton-on-Sea (described above), often form a seemingly integral part of these larger systems of land division. Some areas have a distinctly 'planned' appearance, with regularly sized fields laid out on a consistent alignment, extending for many hundreds of metres.

The most striking, and most extensive, areas of 'planned' field system were identified on the interfluves of Norfolk's Broads 'landscape zone' (Figure 5; Albone *et al* 2007b, 36–44). Here groups of rectilinear, coaxial fields, their primary alignment defined by parallel double-ditched boundaries or trackways, were identified running along four of the Broadland peninsulas or interfluves. The greatest concentration was identified on the Yare-Bure interfluve, with three main groups of discontinuous but seemingly related cropmarks covering an area of c13 sq km. The main alignments perhaps linked the upland heaths around Norwich to the grazing land surrounding the low-lying wetlands to the east. Small, often trapezoidal enclosures, attached to the field boundaries and trackways, are characteristic. These may relate to settlement or other specialised activities. The fields have parallels with similar patterns of cropmarks in northeast Suffolk, and with the 'brickwork pattern' fields identified in north Nottinghamshire/South Yorkshire (Riley 1980; Knight *et al* 2004), where an Iron Age and/or Roman date is certain for some elements. The Norfolk evidence is still inconclusive, but the NMP has identified instances of parts of the field systems being overlain by sites of probable Roman date.

Inevitably, the Broads field systems invite comparison with the large-scale, prehistoric coaxial system of land-division identified by Williamson (1987) in south Norfolk. The validity of Williamson's original study is now questioned

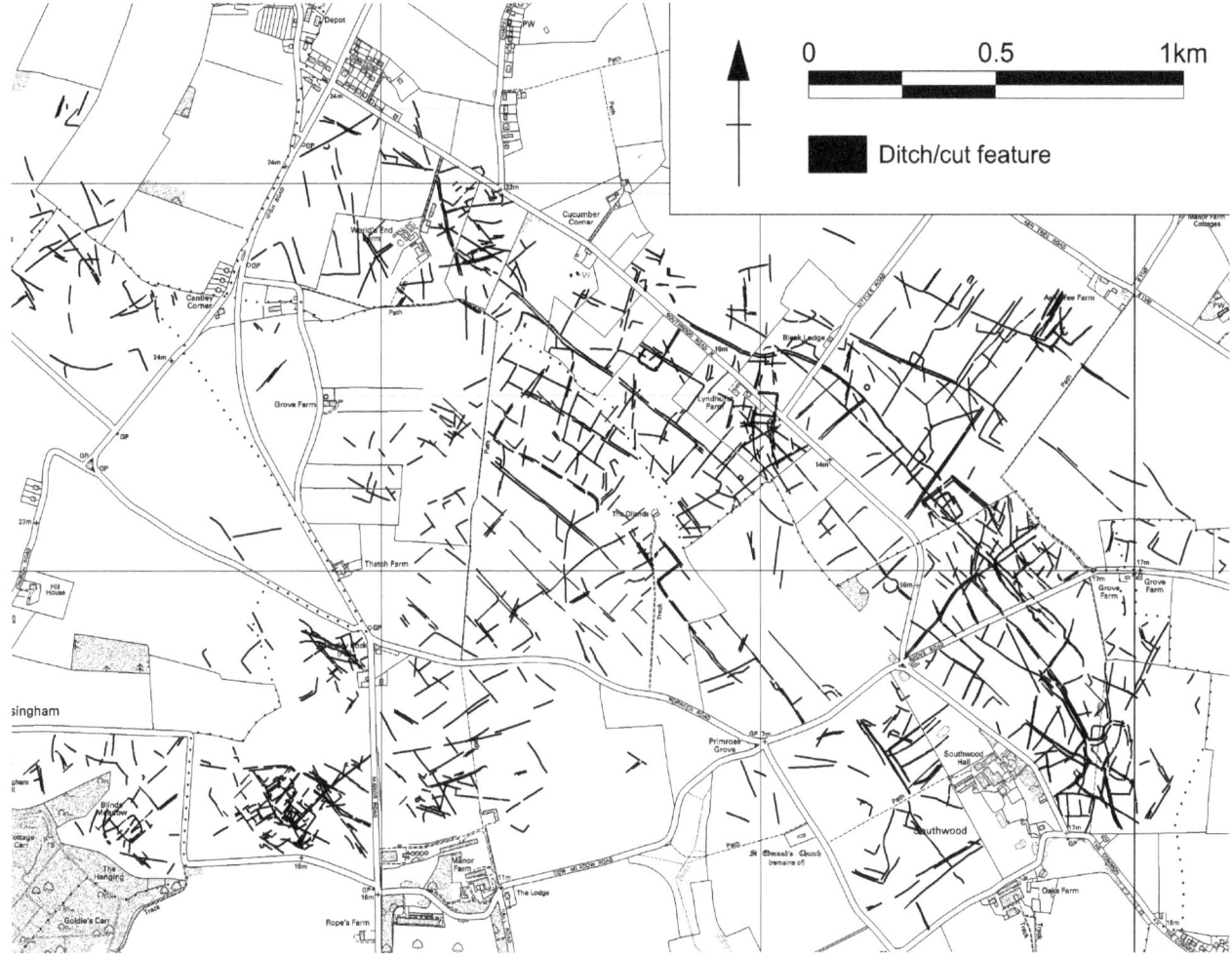

FIGURE 5. PART OF A COAXIAL FIELD SYSTEM VISIBLE ON THE SOUTHERN PART OF THE YARE-BURE INTERFLUVE (NMP MAPPING; COPYRIGHT ENGLISH HERITAGE/NORFOLK MUSEUMS & ARCHAEOLOGY SERVICE; BASE MAP REPRODUCED FROM AN ORDNANCE SURVEY MAP WITH THE PERMISSION OF THE CONTROLLER OF HMSO, CROWN COPYRIGHT. LICENCE NO. 100019340).

(eg Hinton 1997), and not least by Williamson himself, but the potential for further coherent 'planned' field systems in Norfolk (and to be identified by the NMP) remains. The presence of similar cropmarks in Suffolk, on the southern portion of the Lothingland peninsula, further highlights the great potential for further research.

Space here precludes a more detailed description and analysis of all the NMP field system sites, which collectively cover many hectares of the Norfolk landscape, and exhibit many different nuances of alignment and morphology. Some have been described in part elsewhere (Massey *et al* 2003, 339-41; Albone *et al* 2004, 552; Brennand 2004). Others, as at Hopton-on-Sea and around the Broads, warrant more detailed analysis and publication in their own right. The principal challenge in the interpretation of the NMP field systems is the paucity of dating evidence, which hinder our understanding of how – and when – these systems of land division developed.

Where physical dating evidence exists, often derived from pipeline excavations or similar work (eg Bates *in prep*), this has informed the NMP interpretation. However, the scarcity of finds at most such 'rural' sites, and the tiny proportion of these vast landscapes that have been investigated, means that the information is at best limited, and many questions remain. In some parts of southern Britain, enclosed landscapes increasingly appear to be a feature of the Middle to Late Iron Age (Medlycott and Brown in prep.). While a later Iron Age date is suspected for many of the Norfolk field systems, evidence from excavations combined with NMP mapping has identified several areas where some elements may have originated in the Bronze Age (Albone *et al* 2007a). The excavation in 2007 of a less rectilinear pattern of fields or stock enclosures of Early Iron Age date at Little Melton (Watkins 2008; NHER 50209), serves to highlight the huge gaps in our existing chronology of landscape development. There is consequently a pressing need for more extensive, targeted forms of investigation, incorporating scientific dating methods, to elucidate when, how and why such systems developed.

Linear Boundaries

A number of major linear earthworks are recorded in Norfolk. Traditionally, these have been held to be of post-Roman date, perhaps belonging to the 5th–7th century

(Clarke 1955; Wade-Martins 1974). More recently, an Iron Age date has been suggested for at least some of the sites, and parallels drawn with the prehistoric earthwork boundaries known from elsewhere in southern England (Davies 1996, 75–77; Ashwin *et al* 1999; Bates *et al* 2008). Unfortunately, the Norfolk NMP has been unable as yet to contribute to the ongoing debate concerning the date and nature of these earthworks. All of the known examples lie outside the area completed by the survey, and no definite evidence of any new examples has been recorded.

The project has, however, mapped two probable examples of multiple-ditched linear boundaries; one at Gimingham in northeast Norfolk (Figure 6; NHER 31746), and the other at Earsham on the Norfolk-Suffolk border (NHER 11676). These are comparable to those identified in Lincolnshire (Boutwood 1998) and on the Yorkshire Wolds (Stoertz 1997), where they are generally considered to be of Late Bronze Age to Iron Age date. In common with the linear earthworks already described, both of the Norfolk sites occupy distinctive topographic locations. The Gimingham site cuts across the narrowest point of the watershed between two minor watercourses, while the Earsham boundary stretches between the north bank of the River Waveney and a large, possibly natural, pond known as The Lay. The Earsham boundary also cuts across a substantial group of ring ditches, almost certainly representing the remains of a dispersed Bronze Age barrow cemetery (NHER 43610–2). Although the relationship between the two sites is not certain, linear earthworks are generally thought to post-date round barrows, with the barrows often acting as *foci* in the alignment of the boundary (Stoertz

FIGURE 6. A POSSIBLE MULTIPLE-DITCHED BOUNDARY AT GIMINGHAM (COPYRIGHT ENGLISH HERITAGE/ NORFOLK MUSEUMS & ARCHAEOLOGY SERVICE).

FIGURE 7. A PROBABLE MULTI-DITCHED BOUNDARY AT SCOTTOW; THE ROMAN ROAD THAT CROSSES IT CAN ALSO BE SEEN, APPROACHING IT FROM THE LEFT AT A PERPENDICULAR ANGLE (PHOTOGRAPH BY D. EDWARDS. NORFOLK AIR PHOTO LIBRARY REFERENCE NHER TG 2723D 18 JULY 1996. COPYRIGHT NORFOLK MUSEUMS & ARCHAEOLOGY SERVICE).

1997, 65). In Norfolk, the linear earthwork known as the Devil's Ditch is known to cut a Bronze Age ring ditch (Bates *et al* 2008, 4).

The Gimingham and Earsham sites exhibit considerable variation in form. The latter comprises three near-parallel curvilinear ditches, visible for some 300m. The easternmost ditch encompasses an apparent 'entrance' along its length, while the central ditch is interrupted, being composed of nine separate segments. Whether it was deliberately constructed in this way, or whether an originally more continuous ditch was partially removed by ploughing is not clear. The Gimingham boundary comprises up to four ditches, visible for a length of approximately 400m, with a possible second, parallel, double- or triple-ditched boundary situated 80m to its west (Figure 6). The ditches of the main boundary are for the most part distinctively segmented and inturned, in a manner strongly reminiscent of some of the boundaries recorded in Yorkshire (Stoertz 1997, fig 45).

Although neither of the two sites mapped by the NMP represent a new discovery (a summary report on the Earsham example was published by Derek Edwards in 1978), they can now be recognised as forming part of a small but significant group of such sites, which hitherto appear to have received scant attention in Norfolk or the wider region. The seven sites known in Norfolk thus far are all evidenced as cropmarks. Only that at Scottow (Figure 7; NHER 36729) has been the subject of more intensive investigation, through small-scale excavation by the Norfolk Archaeological and Historical Research Group (NAHRG), which demonstrated that one of the five ditches making up the boundary pre-dated a Roman road (Sims 2006). An Iron Age (or Late Bronze Age to Iron Age) date for the others in the group can be postulated on the basis of their parallels elsewhere in the country. The most recent discovery, visible at Marsham on *Google Earth*, is also crossed by a Roman road (NHER 51694). Like the linear earthworks already described, distinctive topographic settings, particularly in relation to watercourses and watersheds, appear to have been favoured. It is of particular note that while all the known linear earthworks lie on or to the west of Norfolk's central watershed, the multiple-ditched boundaries are found almost exclusively to its east; a possible example at Lexham (NHER 17588) being the only exception. This may, to an extent, reflect the favourability of soils for cropmark formation, but the pattern is striking nonetheless.

How and why these boundaries developed remains a matter for debate. The establishment of a chronology for the Norfolk sites, and for their individual components, would be an essential first step in improving our understanding of them. As has been noted elsewhere (Boutwood 1998, 39, after Spratt 1987), many are likely to have been multi-phase and multi-functional, with symbolic and metaphorical meanings being of equal or greater significance than any practical function. The social context of Iron Age boundaries is particularly apparent for pit alignments, where any practical function remains enigmatic, and with which linear and multiple-ditched boundaries are often associated (Pollard 1996). Pit alignments are recorded only rarely in Norfolk, but the interrupted nature of the central 'ditch' belonging to the Earsham boundary, and the excavation of an Iron Age post-hole alignment c25m east of and parallel to the Launditch linear earthwork (Davies 1996, 76; NHER 15910), suggest they may have played an important role in boundary development (also see below).

Some consideration should also be given to the long-distance trackways of probable late prehistoric date mapped by the NMP in east Norfolk. These generally comprise sinuous alignments of tracks, defined by their flanking ditches and traceable across the landscape for several kilometres. Like the multiple-ditched boundary at Earsham, the distribution of existing barrows seems to have been of particular importance in their alignment. The most significant group was identified to the northwest of Hopton-on-Sea (NHER 43529; NHER 43544), dividing the former island or peninsula of Lothingland, and seemingly drawing on prior understandings of territory and ancestry associated with existing burial mounds (Albone *et al* 2007a, 66–8). A Late Bronze Age or earlier Iron Age date has been suggested, as the trackways compare well with examples known from Lincolnshire and East Yorkshire, where excavation has established a Late Bronze Age date for some examples (Stoertz 1997, 40; Boutwood 1998, 37–39). This suggested date is reinforced by the few sherds of Beaker and Iron Age pottery recovered during the excavation of a small section of one of the Hopton trackways (Trimble 1999, 9). Given that the trackways appear to have had similar meanings and associations as the linear boundaries, and perhaps functioned in a similar way, a related chronology might be suspected. The fact that parts of these trackways were defined by pit alignments and interrupted ditch segments, and that these may be earlier than the more continuous ditches (Albone *et al* 2007a, 66; NHER 43529), is further evidence for their complex and prolonged development, and of their relationship with other types of later prehistoric boundary feature.

Funerary Sites

Evidence for Iron Age funerary practices is extremely scarce across much of eastern England; so much so that mortuary rites have been interpreted as involving exposure or excarnation, leaving no clear trace in the archaeological record (Gurney 1998, 1–2; Hill 2007, 28). It is certainly the case that within Norfolk and north Suffolk there is a lack of evidence for a highly distinctive burial tradition comparable with the Late Iron Age Aylesford-Swarling-type cremations of Kent and southern Anglia (Hill 2007, 28), or the extensive, densely populated Arras barrow cemeteries of East Yorkshire, which date from the late 5th to 1st century BC (Stead 1979, 64; Dent 1995, 87). Nevertheless, excavations in Norfolk in recent decades have identified a number of sites where small, ditched enclosures, both square and circular, appear to have had a funerary or mortuary function. These numbers have been swelled considerably by the results of aerial reconnaissance and, specifically, the work of the NMP. Of the 35 sites within the county at which one or more of these enclosures is recorded, 74% have been mapped by the NMP, indicating a strong bias towards the areas the survey has covered. This is not to say that all of the NMP sites were first identified by the project, but several do represent new discoveries, while a considerable number represent new interpretations of previously known sites.

Within Norfolk, groups of square-ditched enclosures have been excavated at Caistor St Edmund and Trowse, to the south of Norwich (Ashwin and Bates 2000a), and at Longham, in the centre of the county (Ashwin *et al* 1999). The enclosures measured between 6.5m and 17m across. At all three sites, they shared an elevated location, polar alignment (aligned on or close to the cardinal points) and (in the majority of cases) probable inner banks. No evidence of central inhumations were identified at any of the sites. The Caistor St Edmund enclosures were thought likely to have contained shallow cremation deposits, the remains of which had not survived the plough. The Longham enclosure contained a central sub-circular pit, devoid of finds but perhaps representing some kind of interment. Although none of the enclosures was securely dated, a Late Iron Age or early Roman date has been postulated for the group (Ashwin and Bates 2000a).

The unexcavated examples, which share many of the characteristics described above, are known almost exclusively from cropmarks. As such they have contributed little to the question of whether the enclosures represent square barrows or an unmounded form of monument, embanked or otherwise. The apparent lack of evidence for a mound at any of the NMP sites does not necessarily confirm the original absence of such a feature. Only a fraction of the ring ditches known or suspected to be prehistoric round barrows have visible mounds, or even central grave pits, yet this is not generally taken to be an indicator of a non-funerary context.

The cropmark sites considerably enhance our knowledge of the number and distribution of square-ditched enclosures comparable with the excavated examples, and of their topographic and archaeological context. Like the excavated sites, those mapped by the NMP occur as small groups or isolated monuments. Most occupy elevated positions, often overlooking minor valleys and streams, although there are also examples from broad valley-floor locations. The sites are characterised by their square, sub-

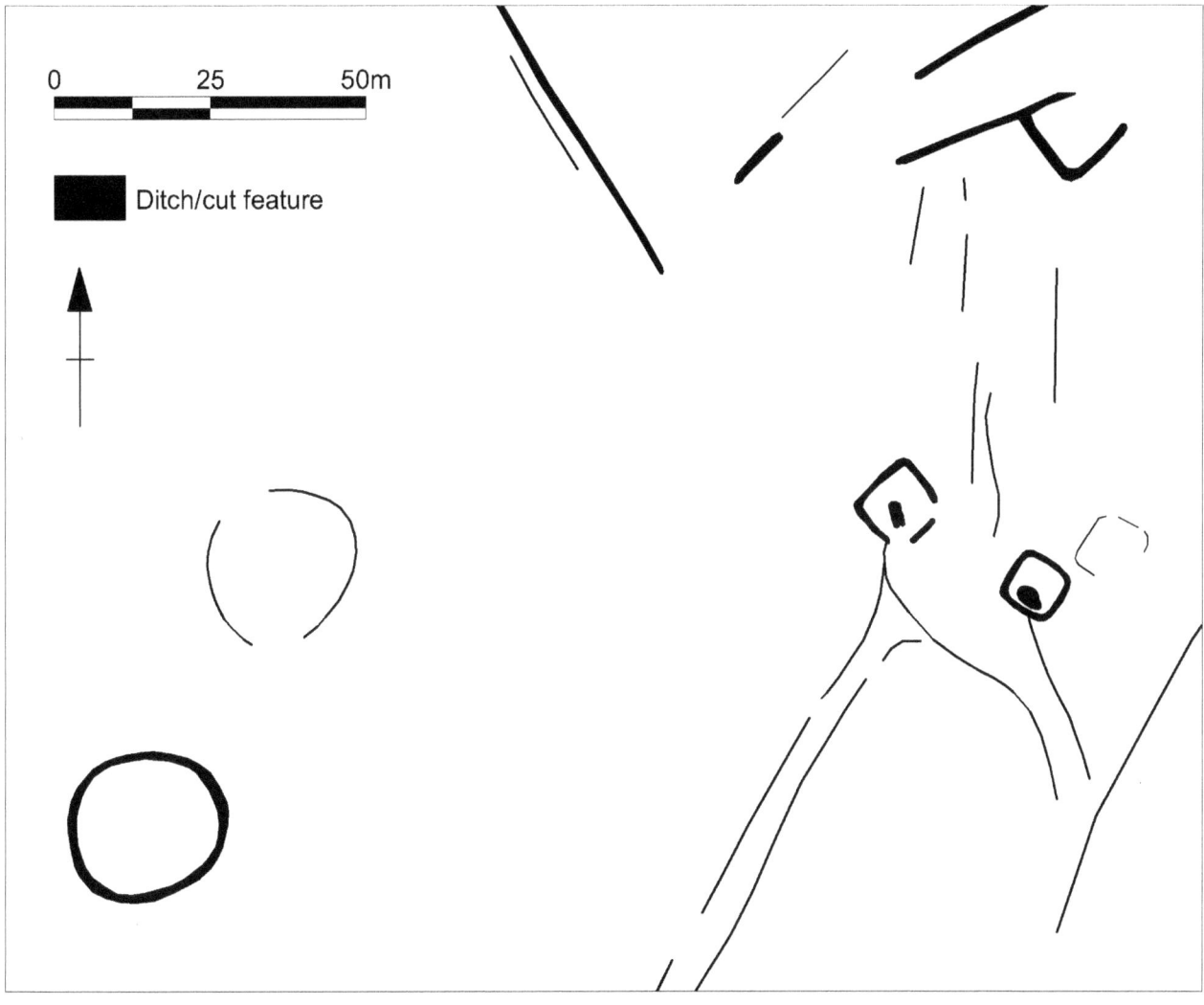

FIGURE 8. SQUARE-DITCHED ENCLOSURES AT ROUGHTON, WITH NEARBY RING DITCHES AND TRACKWAYS (COPYRIGHT ENGLISH HERITAGE/NORFOLK MUSEUMS & ARCHAEOLOGY SERVICE).

rectangular or (occasionally) trapezoidal plan, usually measuring between 7m and 16m across (Figure 8). In contrast to the majority of the excavated enclosures, it is not unusual for them to be accompanied by a central pit. Among those sites where more than one square-ditched enclosure is present, a greater variety in their layout is apparent than the linear alignments evident at Caistor St Edmund and Trowse. Similarly, only a proportion of the enclosures exhibit polar orientation, although this is evident at a considerable number of sites.

The NMP mapping has highlighted a number of clear spatial relationships, some of which have chronological and contextual implications. Many of the sites are located immediately next to, or within a group of, one or more ring ditches, while many others lie within 500m of the same (Figure 8). This relationship is mirrored both at Caistor St Edmund and at other sites in the region (Maxey, Cambridgeshire; see below). Some of the ring ditches almost certainly represent the remains of Bronze Age barrows, and the clustering of square-ditched enclosures within landscapes dominated by earlier prehistoric funerary and ceremonial monuments (as at Caistor St Edmund/ Trowse, Hanworth/Roughton, and Great Witchingham/ Morton on the Hill) is a notable trend, given the relative scarcity of such enclosures within Norfolk.

A significant proportion of the NMP sites appear to be positioned alongside trackways. These are generally sites not located directly adjacent to ring ditches or round barrows. Although the date of the trackways is not certain, a possible late prehistoric or Roman date is common. Whether the trackways and the square enclosures are contemporary is also uncertain, although at two sites in the neighbouring parishes of Hanworth and Roughton (NHER 13027 and NHER 38470; NHER 38476; Figure 8) the enclosures do appear to have been deliberately positioned alongside the trackways (or perhaps *vice versa*). The enclosure excavated at Longham lies adjacent to the Launditch, one of the linear earthworks now thought to be of Iron Age date (see above), which may have provided a similar setting. This association with earlier funerary monuments, trackways and major boundaries is reminiscent of some of the square barrows of East Yorkshire (Bevan 1999, 85).

There are a number of regional parallels for the Norfolk enclosures, known both from excavation and from aerial photography. Excavated examples include those located close to the Maxey henge, Cambridgeshire, two of which were cut by ditches dating to the later Middle Iron Age (Pryor and French 1985a, 237; 1985b, 260). Evidence for internal features such as graves was scant, although gravel mounds or internal banks may have been evident. Also in Cambridgeshire, a rectangular enclosure of Middle Iron Age date was excavated in the Ouse Valley (Jones 1997). Evidence for an internal grave or mound was again lacking. A square-ditched enclosure measuring 5m across was excavated at Brandon on the Norfolk/Suffolk border (Gibson 2004, 25, 58). This was tentatively dated to the Late Bronze Age due to its shared alignment with field boundaries of this date, although the ditches produced no dating evidence.

Aerial photographic evidence for square-ditched enclosures is more widespread. A few small rectangular or square enclosures have been recorded in Suffolk, but none has been excavated and two possible examples were reinterpreted by the NMP as being of probable medieval to post medieval in date (C. Hegarty, formerly Suffolk County Council, *pers comm*). Before any parallels were known from Norfolk, comparisons were drawn between the Caistor and Trowse enclosures and a group of square enclosures located in the East Midlands, Essex and the Welland Valley and known only from aerial photography (Whimster 1981, 121–3). In particular, the plan and linear arrangement of the enclosures at Caistor St Edmund mirrors that of groups of enclosures at Greatford, Lincolnshire, and Hemingford Grey, Cambridgeshire (Ashwin 2000, 138). Comparisons were also drawn with enclosure groups excavated at Mucking and Verulamium (St Albans), which comprised linear groups of small conjoined square enclosures containing a central cremation (Ashwin 2000, 138–9).

Subsequent aerial reconnaissance and air photo interpretation, combined with the work of the NMP, has now provided a number of possible parallels for the excavated sites within Norfolk. However, despite the significance of the group in a county (and wider region) where funerary evidence for the period is so rare, the unexcavated sites have received scant attention in previous overviews of Norfolk's Iron Age (Davies 1996; Davies and Williamson 1999). This is perhaps because they had not been clearly identified as such within the county's HER (formerly the Sites and Monuments Record), or because they were viewed as an extremely localised phenomenon of relatively late date. The NMP mapping has highlighted the widespread – albeit low density – distribution of such sites, and the variety in their orientation and layout. Its results suggest that while the burial tradition seemingly represented by the enclosures appears to have been widespread across the county, it was not intensively practiced, with the vast majority of the population receiving alternative rites, the nature of which remains an important area for further research.

The original form of the postulated funerary monuments is open to question, and thus potential chronological and functional distinctions remain hidden, although they are hinted at by the variety evident at the NMP sites. It is clear that the tradition differs significantly from the larger, densely populated Arras cemeteries with which it is inevitably compared, but the nature of the relationship between the two could be subtle, with shared characteristics and significant variances masked by a relatively superficial understanding of the form, date and use of the Norfolk sites. The absence of a prominent central grave shaft at the excavated Norfolk sites has been seen as a significant variation from the Arras barrow tradition (Ashwin and Bates 2000b, 138), but the presence of possible grave pits within several of the enclosures mapped by the NMP highlights the disadvantages of relying on the excavated evidence alone. At the same time, a substantial grave cut is often only a feature of the later, smaller East Yorkshire square barrows. The larger and earlier barrows tend not to have a deep central grave, the body having been placed on the former ground surface or in a very shallow cut. Similarly, rather than forming the extensive, densely-populated cemeteries seen as typical of the Arras tradition, the earlier East Yorkshire barrows occur as isolated examples or in small groups, often in elevated hilltop locations, harking back to the positioning and arrangement of Bronze Age cemeteries. These are features shared by many of the Norfolk sites, and given such similarities, the potential for some of them to pre-date the Late Iron Age should be considered.

The square-ditched sites are the most distinctive of Norfolk's postulated Iron Age funerary enclosures, but a number of circular sites also warrant consideration as part of this larger group. Small ring ditches of Iron Age date thought to represent funerary monuments or mortuary enclosures have been excavated at both Shropham and Watlington. At Watlington several circular mortuary enclosures, measuring between 8m and 13m in diameter and surrounding Late Iron Age unurned cremations, were excavated in advance of aggregate extraction (Town 2004, 11; NHER 39458). The cropmarks of at least three further ring ditches of similar size, two with central pits, were mapped by the NMP in the area immediately surrounding the excavations (NHER 50968–70). These features may be similar to approximately 60 later Iron Age to early Roman ring ditches, measuring 4.5m–10m in diameter, that surrounded grave-shaped pits at Fison Way, Thetford (Gregory 1992, 53–65; NHER 5853). Acidic conditions meant that little or no bone survived, but it was suggested that the elongated pits once contained inhumations (Gurney 1998, 2). Similar features, again containing grave-like pits, have also been excavated at West Stow, Suffolk (Martin 1999, 69, 71).

Given the relatively limited information that has come from excavations, and the difficulty of distinguishing such sites from the mass of other circular features with similar dimensions, the relationship between the square-ditched enclosures and the possible circular funerary enclosures is

FIGURE 9. A SQUARE-DITCHED ENCLOSURE AT MORTON ON THE HILL; ADJACENT TO IT (ABOVE AND RIGHT) THE CROPMARK OF A POSSIBLE CIRCULAR IRON AGE FUNERARY ENCLOSURE IS JUST VISIBLE (PHOTOGRAPH BY D. EDWARDS. NORFOLK AIR PHOTO LIBRARY REFERENCE NHER TG 1217A 19 JULY 1977. COPYRIGHT NORFOLK MUSEUMS & ARCHAEOLOGY SERVICE).

difficult to gauge. At a number of sites, the juxtaposition of circular and square enclosures provides some support to their interpretation as different forms or facets of broadly the same monument type. One of the circular mortuary enclosures at Watlington (NHER 50968) lies adjacent to a small square or trapezoidal enclosure. The positioning of the enclosure suggests that the two features were contemporary. A similar relationship is apparent at Morton on the Hill (Figure 9; NHER 17657 and NHER 50650). One of the ring ditches at Fison Way sat within a square enclosure measuring 9m across (Gregory 1992, 55–7). In Essex, aerial photography recorded a linear group of three small square cropmarks to the west of Great Dunmow. These measured c10m across and possessed central pits. A ring ditch of similar diameter lay immediately to the north (Lawson et al 1981, 30–1). Surface finds and nearby urned cremation burials of 1st to 3rd century date may indicate that they are of Roman rather than Iron Age date (Essex Historic Environment Record 1278).

Conclusions

It is intended that the overview given above, although brief, should serve to highlight the contribution of the NMP to Iron Age studies in Norfolk. That equally substantial contributions have been made by similar projects in other counties in the region (Essex and Suffolk, for example) is of little doubt, although space and resources have precluded a fuller integration of such data into the analysis above. Haselgrove and Moore, in their overview of recent work on the later Iron Age (2007, 3), have highlighted the research potential of developer-funded and metal-detected material, and the need for further integration with academic research. The same might equally be said, however, for much of the NMP data, both within Norfolk and nationally. The contribution made by the Norfolk NMP team to the revised Regional Research Frameworks (Medlycott and Brown, in prep) should go some way towards establishing at a regional level the higher profile that the results deserve.

The summary of the NMP results presented here has by necessity been limited to a discussion of a number of specific monument types. In broader terms, the Norfolk NMP is as yet unable to support or contradict Davies' model (1996; 1999) of settlement expansion in Norfolk during the Iron Age from a southwestern heartland onto the claylands. Only a small proportion of Norfolk's Boulder Clay Plateau has been mapped thus far, and much of those areas that have been covered is marginal and interspersed with lighter soils (along the Wensum Valley, for example). The inclusion of an additional 300 sq km of the Boulder Clay within the current Thetford-Norwich-A11 project area will hopefully provide the results — and the subsequent analysis — to corroborate or challenge such models. At the very least, it will go some way towards confirming or refuting the perceived 'poverty' of the Norfolk claylands from an aerial perspective, a perception that has been challenged recently by work in a number of other counties and regions (Mills and Palmer 2007).

Acknowledgements

This study has benefited from the work and advice of a number of individuals, not least former and current members of the Norfolk NMP team: Mark Brennand, Henrietta Clare, Nellie Bales and Alice Cattermole. Trevor Ashwin, Tom Williamson, Helen Winton, Andrew Rogerson and David Gurney have all provided invaluable information and advice over the last eight years, including comments on previous incarnations of this material. Any errors or omissions, however, are the authors' own.

Bibliography

Albone, J., Massey, S., and Tremlett, S. 2004. The National Mapping Programme in Norfolk, 2003–4. *Norfolk Archaeology* 44 (3), 549–555.

Albone, J., Massey, S., and Tremlett, S. 2007a. *The archaeology of Norfolk's Coastal Zone. Results of the National Mapping Programme.* English Heritage project no: 2913, Norfolk Landscape Archaeology unpublished report.

Albone, J., Massey, S., and Tremlett, S. 2007b. *The archaeology of Norfolk's Broads Zone. Results of the National Mapping Programme.* English Heritage project no: 2913, Norfolk Landscape Archaeology unpublished report.

Albone, J., Massey, S., with Tremlett, S. in prep. *The archaeology of Norfolk's aggregate landscape. Results of the National Mapping Programme.* English Heritage project no: 5241MAIN.

Ashwin, T. 1996. Excavation of an Iron Age site at Silfield, Wymondham, Norfolk, 1992–3. *Norfolk Archaeoogyl* 42 (3), 241–282.

Ashwin. T, 1999. Studying Iron Age settlement in Norfolk. In J. Davies and T. Williamson (eds), *Land of the Iceni: the Iron Age in northern East Anglia*, 100–24. Norwich, Centre of East Anglian Studies.

Ashwin, T. 2000. Excavations at Harford Farm, Caistor St Edmund (Site 9794), 1990, in T. Ashwin and S. Bates 2000a, 52–140.

Ashwin, T., and Bates, S. 2000a. *Norwich Southern Bypass, part I: excavations at Bixley, Caistor St Edmund, Trowse.* East Anglian Archaeology 91.

Ashwin, T., and Bates, S. 2000b. Excavations at Valley Belt, Trowse (Site 9589), 1990. In T. Ashwin and S. Bates 2000a, 141–91.

Ashwin, T. and Flitcroft, M., with Percival, S. 1999. The Launditch and its setting. Excavations at the Launditch, Beeston with Bittering, and Iron Age features and finds from its vicinity. *Norfolk Archaeologl* 43 (2), 217–56.

Bates, S., Hoggett, R. and Schwenninger, J. 2008. *An archaeological excavation at Devil's Ditch, Riddlesworth and Garboldisham.* NAU Archaeology unpublished report 1436.

Bates, S., in prep. *Bacton/Yarmouth pipeline, Norfolk.* East Anglian Archaeology.

Bevan, W. 1999. The landscape context of the Iron Age square barrow burials, East Yorkshire. In J. Downes and T. Pollard (eds), *The loved body's corruption*. Scottish Archaeological Forum, 69–93.

Boutwood, Y. 1998. Prehistoric linear boundaries in Lincolnshire and its fringes. In R. H. Bewley (ed), *Lincolnshire's archaeology from the air*, 29-46. Lincolnshire History and Archaeology Occasional Paper 11.

Bradley, R. 1993. Where is East Anglia? Themes in regional prehistory. In J. Gardiner (ed), *Flatlands and wetlands: Current themes in East Anglian archaeology.* East Anglian Archaeology 50, 5–13.

Brennand, M. 2004. Archaeological background and aerial photography. In A. Lyons, *Romano-British industrial activity at Snettisham, Norfolk,* 2–5. East Anglian Archaeology Occasional Paper 18.

Bryant, S. 1997. Iron Age. In J. Glazebrook (ed), *Research and archaeology: a framework for the eastern counties 1. Resource assessment*, 23–31. East Anglian Archaeology Occasional Paper 3.

Bryant, S. 2000. The Iron Age. In N. Brown and J. Glazebrook (eds), *Research and archaeology: a framework for the eastern counties 2. Research agenda and strategy,* 14–18. East Anglian Archaeology Occasional Paper 8.

Clark, J. G. D. and Fell, C. I. 1953. The Early Iron Age site at Micklemoor Hill, West Harling, Norfolk, and its pottery. *Proceedings of the Prehistoric Society* 19, 1–40.

Clarke, R. R. 1955. The Fossditch — a linear earthwork in south-west Norfolk. *Norfolk Archaeology* 31, 178–196.

Davies, J. A. 1996. Where eagles dare: the Iron Age of Norfolk. *Proceedings of the Prehistoric Society* 62, 63–92.

Davies, J. 1999. Patterns, power and political progress in Iron Age Norfolk. In J. Davies and T. Williamson, (eds) 1999, 14–43.

Davies, J. and Williamson, T. (eds), 1999. *Land of the Iceni: the Iron Age in northern East Anglia.* Norwich, Centre of East Anglian Studies.

Dent, J. 1995. *Aspects of Iron Age settlement in East Yorkshire*, unpublished thesis, University of Sheffield.

Edwards, D. 1978. The air photographs collection of the Norfolk Archaeological Unit: third report. In P. Wade-Martins (ed) *Norfolk.* East Anglian Archaeology 8, 87-105.

Gibson, C. 2004. *Lines in the sand: Middle to Late Bronze Age settlement at Game Farm, Brandon.* East Anglian Archaeology Occasional Paper 19.

Gregory, T. 1986. Enclosures of 'Thornham' type in Norfolk. In T. Gregory and D. Gurney, *Excavations at*

Thornham, Warham, Wighton and Caistor St Edmund, Norfolk. East Anglian Archaeology 30, 32–35.

Gregory, T. 1992. *Excavations in Thetford, 1980–1982, Fison Way, Volume 1*. East Anglian Archaeology 53.

Gurney, D. 1998. *Roman burials in Norfolk*. East Anglian Archaeology Occasional Paper 4.

Haselgrove, C. and Moore, T. 2007. New narratives of the later Iron Age. In C. Haselgrove and T. Moore (eds), *The later Iron Age in Britain and beyond*. Oxford, Oxbow, 1–15.

Hill, J. D. 1999. Settlement, landscape and regionality: Norfolk and Suffolk in the pre-Roman Iron Age of Britain and beyond. In J. Davies and T. Williamson (eds) 1999, 185–207.

Hill, J. D. 2007. The dynamics of social change in later Iron Age eastern and south-eastern England *c*. 300 BC–AD 43. In C. Haselgrove and T. Moore (eds), *The later Iron Age in Britain and beyond*. Oxford, Oxbow, 16-40.

Hinton, D. A. 1997. The 'Scole-Dickleburgh field system' examined. *Landscape History* 19, 5–12.

Horlock, S. with Albone, J. and Tremlett, S. 2008. The archaeology of Norfolk's aggregate landscape: results of the National Mapping Programme. *Norfolk Archaeology* 45, 337–48.

Hutcheson, N. and Ashwin, T. 2005. Iron Age Norfolk (*c* 700 BC – AD 43). In T. Ashwin and A. Davison (eds), *An historical atlas of Norfolk*, 3 edition. Chichester, Phillimore, 23-5.

Jones, A. 1997. An Iron Age square barrow at Diddington, Cambridgeshire. Third interim report of excavations at Little Paxton Quarry, 1996. *Proceedings of the Cambridge Antiquarian Society* 86, 5–12.

Jones, M. and Bond, D. 1980. Late Bronze Age settlement at Mucking, Essex. In J. Barrett and R. Bradley (eds), *Settlement and society in the British Late Bronze Age*, 471–82. British Archaeological Report 83.

Knight, D. Howard, A. J. and Leary, R. 2004. The Romano-British landscape. In D. Knight and A. J. Howard, *Trent Valley landscapes. The archaeology of 500,000 years of change*, 115–151. King's Lynn.

Lawson, A. J., Martin, E. A. and Priddy, D. with Taylor, A. 1981. *The barrows of East Anglia*. East Anglian Archaeology 12.

Martin, E. 1999. Suffolk in the Iron Age. In J. Davies and T. Williamson (eds) 1999, 45–99.

Massey, S., Brennand, M., and Clare, H. 2003. The National Mapping Programme in Norfolk, 2001–3. *Norfolk Archaeology* 44, 335–44.

Medlycott, M. and Brown, N. (eds), in prep. *Revision of the Regional Research Frameworks for the Eastern Region*.

Mills, J. and Palmer, R. 2007. *Populating clay landscapes*, Stroud.

Palmer, R. 2007. Seventy-five years *v* ninety minutes: implications of the 1996 Bedfordshire vertical aerial survey on our perceptions of clayland archaeology. In J. Mills and R. Palmer (eds), 88–103.

Pollard, J. 1996. Iron Age riverside pit alignments at St Ives, Cambridgeshire. *Proceedings of the Prehistoric Society* 62, 93–115.

Pryor, F. and French, C. 1985a. *The Fenland Project, number 1: the lower Welland Valley, volume 1*. East Anglian Archaeology 27.

Pryor, F. and French, C. 1985b. *The Fenland Project, number 1: the lower Welland Valley, volume 2*. East Anglian Archaeology 27.

Rickett, R. 1995. *The Anglo-Saxon cemetery at Spong Hill, North Elmham, part VII: the Iron Age, Roman and Early Saxon Settlement*. East Anglian Archaeology 73.

Riley, D. N. 1980. *Early landscape from the air*. Sheffield.

Sims, J. 2006. *Excavation at Scottow 2003 & 2005*. NAHRG (Norfolk Archaeological and Historical Research Group) unpublished report.

Spratt, D. A. 1987. *Linear earthworks of the tabular hills, northeast Yorkshire*. Sheffield.

Stead, I. 1979. *The Arras culture*. York.

Stoertz, C. 1997. *Ancient Landscapes of the Yorkshire Wolds*. Swindon.

Town, M. 2004. *Watlington Quarry, Norfolk: preliminary assessment of significance (Sixty Acre Field – mineral extraction phases 1, 1a and 2)*, Norfolk Archaeological Unit unpublished report 956.

Trimble, G. L. 1999. *Report on an archaeological evaluation at South Gorleston Development Area. Stage 2. Supplement to NAU Report 345 (December 1998)*, Norfolk Archaeological Unit unpublished report 374.

Wade, K. and Brown, N. 2000. Research strategy. In N. Brown and J. Glazebrook (eds), *Research and archaeology: a framework for the eastern counties 2. Research agenda and strategy*, 50–58. East Anglian Archaeology Occasional Paper 8.

Wade-Martins, P. 1974. The linear earthworks of west Norfolk. *Norfolk Archaeology* 36 (1), 23–38.

Wade-Martins, P. (ed) 1999. *Norfolk from the air. Volume 2*. Hunstanton, Norfolk Museums Service.

Watkins, P. J. 2008. *'The archaeology of Iron Age Norfolk'. An outline publication synopsis*. NAU Archaeology unpublished report 1716a.

Whimster, R. 1981. *Burial practices in Iron Age Britain. A discussion and gazetteer of the evidence* c *700 BC – AD 43. Part 1*. British Archaeological Report 90.

Williamson, T. 1987. Early co-axial field systems on the East Anglian boulder clays. *Proceedings of the Prehistoric Society* 53, 419–531.

Excavations at Snettisham, Norfolk, 2004: Re-investigating the past

Natasha Hutcheson

Introduction

The Iron Age site at Snettisham in north-west Norfolk has become synonymous with gold. As a result, this most enigmatic of later prehistoric sites has, in more recent years, also become synonymous with metal detecting. It was through this combination; this not unsurprising, but perhaps sometimes controversial marriage between metal detecting and archaeology, that the excavations undertaken at Snettisham in 2004 came about. In the spring of 2004 two metal-detectorists were 'digging' in the woods next to the 'gold-field' when they stumbled upon what appeared to be the remains of a wall. In response to this find, the author, at the behest of Norfolk County Council's Portable Antiquities Scheme officer, applied to two local funding bodies, the Scarfe Committee and the Council for British Archaeology East, to bring together some money to facilitate the excavation and analysis of archaeological material under controlled conditions in the location of the wall. This paper seeks to outline the results of that excavation and subsequent analyses of material recovered. However, as will become apparent, the story that unfolds from this excavation provides us with more detail regarding the recent history of the site rather than necessarily unravelling more on the distant past at Snettisham.

Snettisham: a brief history

The village of Snettisham is located on the eastern edge of the Wash in north-west Norfolk. The Iron Age site, which can be found on the promontory of Ken Hill just to the north of the modern village (Figure 1) first revealed its treasures in 1948 when a series of gold tubular torcs were uncovered during ploughing.

Following the discovery of two further collections of material, Rainbird Clarke, the then curator of Norwich Castle Museum, undertook an excavation at the site (Clarke 1954). In 1950 two further groups of material were recovered, including the 'Great torc' with its Gallo-Belgic coin hidden within its twisted golden ropes. Other single

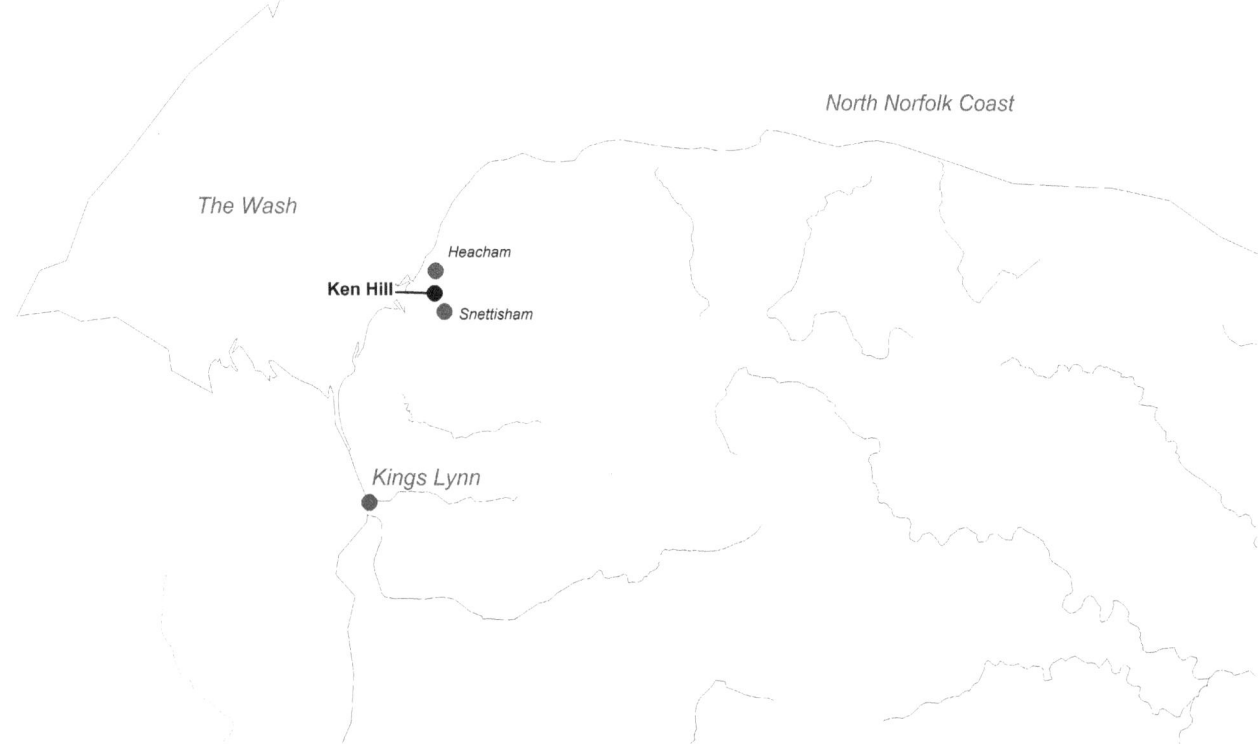

FIGURE 1. MAP SHOWING NORTH WEST NORFOLK AND LOCATION OF THE VILLAGE OF SNETTISHAM.

torc finds were made in 1964, 1968 and 1973. All of these finds were made accidentally and it was not until 1989 that more torc fragments were recovered, this time through metal-detecting. In 1989, the then landowner of Ken Hill, Sir Stephen Lycett Green, agreed to allow a local man to metal-detect the site; he found four fragments of torcs and an Iron Age gold coin. The following year, in 1990, the metal-detectorist went on to discover another hoard of material that included 70 ingot rings or bracelets, 9 coins, fragments from at least 50 torcs and two straight ingots (Stead 1991). Following the recovery of these finds the British Museum undertook a large open area excavation in 1990 under the direction of Dr. Ian Stead. During these excavations top soil was stripped from the 'gold-field' and a series of hoards were then located through the use of metal-detectors. Through this method a number of other pits containing caches of gold, silver, electrum and bronze torcs and other metal items were found (see Stead 1991 for further details on the excavations and finds made by the British Museum). During this period, another hoard is documented as having been recovered in the woods adjacent to the 'gold-field' by detectorist's working under cover of dark. Unfortunately this hoard has never emerged as a whole, but the few finds that have been recovered comprise silver coins of the Trinovante and Iceni tribes (Stead 1998, 149). In addition to the gold and other metals found at the site, the British Museum also plotted and excavated a portion of a ditch that appears to have circled Ken Hill. This ditch, which effectively encloses the gold-field, produced pottery from the Flavian period to the late 3rd century. The ditch, then, appears to be Roman.

In the years after the British Museum's excavations the site at Snettisham has been subject to investigations by metal-detectorist's, some with permission and many without. Those more recently detecting at the site have done so in liaison with the current landowner and local Portable Antiquities Scheme officer and as outlined above, it was material recovered during their explorations that prompted the excavations undertaken in 2004.

2004 Excavations

Method

The excavations undertaken in 2004 comprised a short, ten day field season. The area excavated was in the corner of the woodland adjacent to the gold field (Figure 2).

During an initial visit to the site it became clear that the major obstacle to exploring the partly uncovered wall was the number of trees in its immediate vicinity. Following discussions with the landowner and Estate Manager, it was agreed that as part of the management of the woodland, it would be possible to fell three trees close to the wall to facilitate opening a small area for excavation. Once the trees had been felled and moved, an area of approximately 8 x 8 metres was cleared. This was done in the first instance by using a mini-digger. The area was then cleaned by hand. Once the top layer of soil and woodland debris had been removed it was possible to see, in plan, the outline of a square structure approximately 6 x 6 metres (Figure 3).

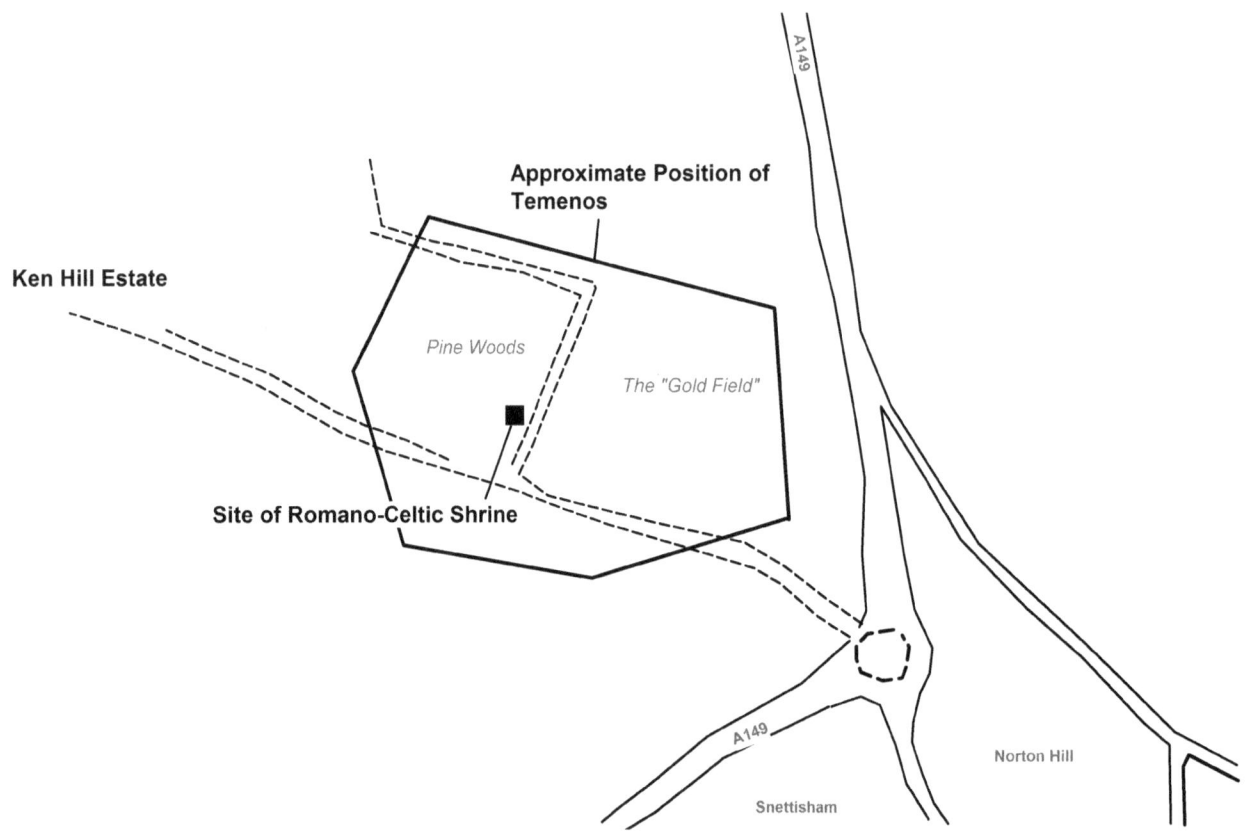

FIGURE 2. MAP SHOWING THE PINEWOODS AND SO-CALLED 'GOLDFIELD'.

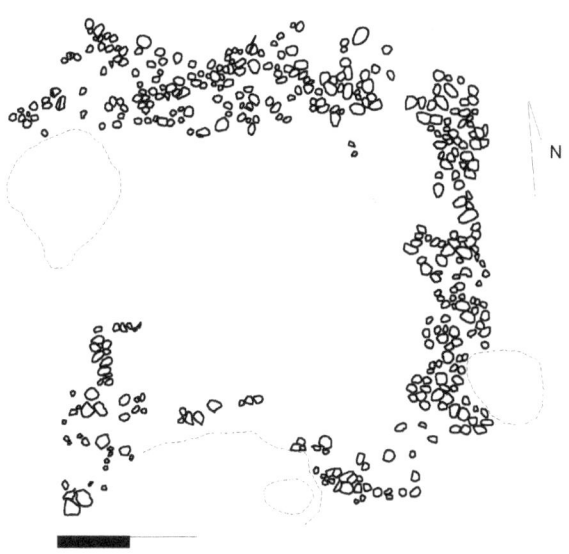

FIGURE 3. PLAN OF RECTILINEAR STRUCTURE – APPROXIMATELY 6 X 6 METRES.

Given the time constraints, it was decided the most efficient way to progress the excavations was through excavating a 1 x 1 metre test pit within the structure to assess the nature of the stratigraphy. What became apparent during the excavation of this test pit was that there was no obvious stratigraphy within the walled area. Therefore, to achieve a controlled record through the archaeological remains, a further five one metre square test pits were taken down in 5cm spits (Figure 4).

A number of trenches were opened to expose segments of the exterior of the structure. Two slots through the wall demonstrated the structure comprised a shallow carr stone foundation built onto the natural carr stone geology. It is probable that the superstructure of the building was wooden.

The Finds

Despite the small area that was excavated and the short amount time during which the excavations took place,

FIGURE 4. STRUCTURE AT KEN HILL SHOWING EXPOSED LOWER FOUNDATIONS OF NORTH AND EAST WALL AND TEST PITS UNDER EXCAVATION. THE LIGHTER PATCHES SHOWING THROUGH ON THE SOIL REPRESENT THE CARR STONE NATURAL BEDROCK.

a large number of finds were recovered. These included pottery, animal bones, *tesserae*, a few coins, two small 'blobs' of gold, a number of fragments of painted wall plaster, roof tiles and other fragments of ceramic building material, lumps of mortar and oyster shells. The *tesserae*, fragments of painted wall plaster (painted a dark purple colour) and ceramic building material along with the coinage point to the structure being Roman in date. Due to the confines of the funding available, it was only possible to employ finds specialists to look in more detail at a sample of the pottery and the bone. In addition, the Finds Liaison Officer at Norwich Castle Museum has identified the coinage.

Pottery

Approximately one third of the pottery (597 sherds weighing 5,275g) was scanned, spot dated, assigned broad fabric types and examined in terms of diagnostic vessel forms (the full report is lodged with the Norfolk Historic Environment Record). Pottery recovered largely spans the 3rd century BC through to the 3rd century AD; the Iron Age through to the Roman period. The pottery dating to both periods is fairly typical of a local assemblage, with few examples of imported or fine wares, although there were some shelly wares within the Iron Age component which may suggest trade or movement of materials across the Wash. With regard to the Roman wares, it is noted in the pottery report that late Roman fine wares (such as Oxfordshire red colour coat and Hadham red ware) associated with sites from the very end of the Roman period were not found at all.

A more detailed analyses of the pottery is not presented here, however, what is of import is the condition of the sherds. Both the specialist who looked at the Iron Age material (Sarah Percival) and the specialist that examined the Roman material (Alice Lyons) commented that the pottery assemblage was made up of small and abraded sherds; they were generally in poor condition often with their surfaces badly preserved. What this might tell us about the site will be returned to below.

Coins

In total, nine coins were recovered during the excavations. One, an Iceni silver unit (Pattern-horse), was in almost perfect condition when it emerged. Unfortunately, despite being recorded and bagged-up on site, this coin disappeared during the excavations. Adrian Marsden of Norwich Castle Museum identified the rest of the coins and like the pottery, they date from the Iron Age and Roman periods (see appendix a for coin list). Most pertinent to these excavations was a late Roman 'Falling Horseman' copy that was found lodged tightly underneath some tumble from the north wall of the rectilinear structure. This coin would have been in circulation in the 350s and 360s and as such, provides a useful *terminus post quem* for the destruction of the building.

Faunal Remains

Approximately 80% of the animal remains recovered during the 2004 excavations were examined (the full report by Alexander Wasse is held on the NHER). This 80% comprised a total of 1,973 fragments, weighing 12,640g. Of these, 583 fragments were identifiable, representing 29.5% of the total number. A range of animals were present within the assemblage including cattle, pig, caprine, horse (only two fragments), dog (one tooth) and small amounts red deer, roe deer and birds. Pig comprised the most common animal remains recovered, closely followed by cattle. Pig and cattle are both more prevalent than caprine, with the other animal types being far less common. A number of bones showed evidence of cutmarks consistent with skinning, disarticulation and defleshing and some showed some evidence of burning. A high proportion of pigs were killed as young animals, suggesting that they were being managed for consumption. In contrast, a majority of cattle appear to have survived into adulthood, suggesting that they may have been exploited as much for milk or traction as they were for meat. One of the two items of horse comprised a proximal metatarsal and top 4cm of the shaft which appears to have been cut off from the rest of the bone with a sharp knife or fine-toothed saw. As with the pottery assemblage, the range of animal bone seems to be consistent with what would be expected from an 'Iron Age through to Roman' site. Again, for the purposes of this report, one of the most notable comments that came out of the faunal remains study was that the majority of the assemblage, like the pottery, was fragmentary in nature. As with the pottery, this will be discussed in more detail below.

Interpreting the structure

Interpretation of the hoarding activities that took place at Ken Hill during the later Iron Age has been contentious. Clarke, in 1954, suggested the torc hoards represented the store of a metal-smith (1954, 70). Stead, following his excavations, has suggested that the material represented a tribal treasury (1991, 463). Other suggestions on why the hoards were buried include the possibility that they were disposed of in haste in the wake of Caesar's invasions in 55 and 54 BC (e.g. Rodwell 1976, 198 - 203; Cunliffe 1991, 120). The author, however, drawing on a range of evidence and recent studies on what the Iron Age record comprises has suggested the hoards are votive in nature and that Ken Hill was likely a place of religious or ritual importance during the later Iron Age (Hutcheson 2004, 92). It is probable that the some of the significance and richness of the site is related to its location. Although difficult to fully appreciate now due to woodland, Ken Hill is on a promontory overlooking the Wash. The Wash was undoubtedly an important place in terms of north-sea trade and movement of people.

Given the importance of this site during the later Iron Age, it seems likely that the remains of the rectilinear Roman building uncovered, which probably boasted a

Spit Number	Qty	Period	Pottery Spot Date
7 (base of test pit)	1	Later Iron Age	Later Iron Age
6	3	Iron Age	Mixed Iron Age
5	1	Later Iron Age	Later Iron Age
4	30	Roman	Mid/late C1 – C4
3	9	Roman	Late C1 – C4
3	2	Saxon	C7 – C9
3	2	Later Iron Age	Later Iron Age
2	1	Roman	Late C2 – C4
2	1	PMed	PMed
1 (top of test pit)	1	Roman	Late C2 – C4

FIGURE 5. POTTERY FROM TEST PIT 2.

mosaic floor, painted plaster walls and a tiled roof, was a Romano-Celtic temple. As would be expected, this temple was erected within an area enclosed by a ditch – a *temenos* ditch (see Figure 2).

It is not an entirely unexpected thing to discover a Romano-Celtic temple site within the vicinity of an Iron Age ritual/religious site. There are a number of famous examples such as the Temple of Sulis Minerva at Bath, where there are Iron Age antecedents, and the same is true at Hayling Island amongst other places (Downey, King & Soffey 1979; 1991). The relationship between 'special' Iron Age sites and Roman temple sites is also apparent elsewhere in north-west Norfolk. For example, at North Creake, in the vicinity of the place where a later Iron Age torc fragment was recovered, there is evidence of Roman temple site, and in the area of Fring where there are a range of Iron Age hoards of gold and silver coins, there is, in the valley overlooked by the hoarding sites, evidence for a Roman temple (Hutcheson 2004, 90 – 92).

Despite the 'tussles' over the interpretation of Ken Hill as a site of ritual significance the discovery of a Romano-Celtic temple, although exciting, is not ultimately unsurprising; there are, as mentioned, other sites that continue to be the focus of ritual activity from the Iron Age in the Roman period. What is of further interest about this particular temple site, however, is the apparent 'mess' that the archaeology was in. As discussed above, it became apparent early in the excavation that there was no obvious stratigraphy in and around the temple site and that to exert some control over the excavation process and create a record that could be analysed, it was necessary to excavate test pits in 5cm spits. Following analyses of pottery from the test pits, the lack of obvious stratigraphy was confirmed.

As can be seen from Figure 5, pottery is in places quite mixed. Roman and Post medieval sherds are found together in spit 2, above a mixture of Saxon and Iron Age pottery in spit 3. In addition, the later Iron Age pottery recovered from spit 3 lies above Roman pottery recovered in spit 4.

The mixture of material is not only visible when looking down through the site, but also when looking at a single context. Context 1009 was a broad spit that was excavated out of trench three, the trench opened to the east of the main excavation area. As can be seen in Figure 6, it contains quantities of Iron Age and Roman material, along with a few sherds of Saxon material.

Although not analysed due to the restraints of funding, within contexts such as 1009, Iron Age and Roman pottery was also mixed with Roman tile fragments and the occasional fragments of painted plaster, oyster shell and *tesserae*. The sample of pottery that was analysed did, however, illuminate further the impression made during the excavation that the site had been quite severely disturbed.

To explore when the temple site at Snettisham was disturbed it is necessary to look in more detail at reports on earlier excavations on Ken Hill and at other information held about the site on the NHER. For example, on examination of the plan in Rainbird Clarke's report of 1954, it can be seen that there is an area in the corner of the pine woods adjacent to the gold field that is labelled '59' (Figure 7).

Context	Qty	Pottery Spot Date	Context date	trench
10009	10	Later Iron Age	Mixed	3
10009	16	C1-C4	Mixed	3
10009	4	C7-C9	Mixed	3
10009	4	NCD	Mixed	3

FIGURE 6. POTTERY FROM CONTEXT 1009.

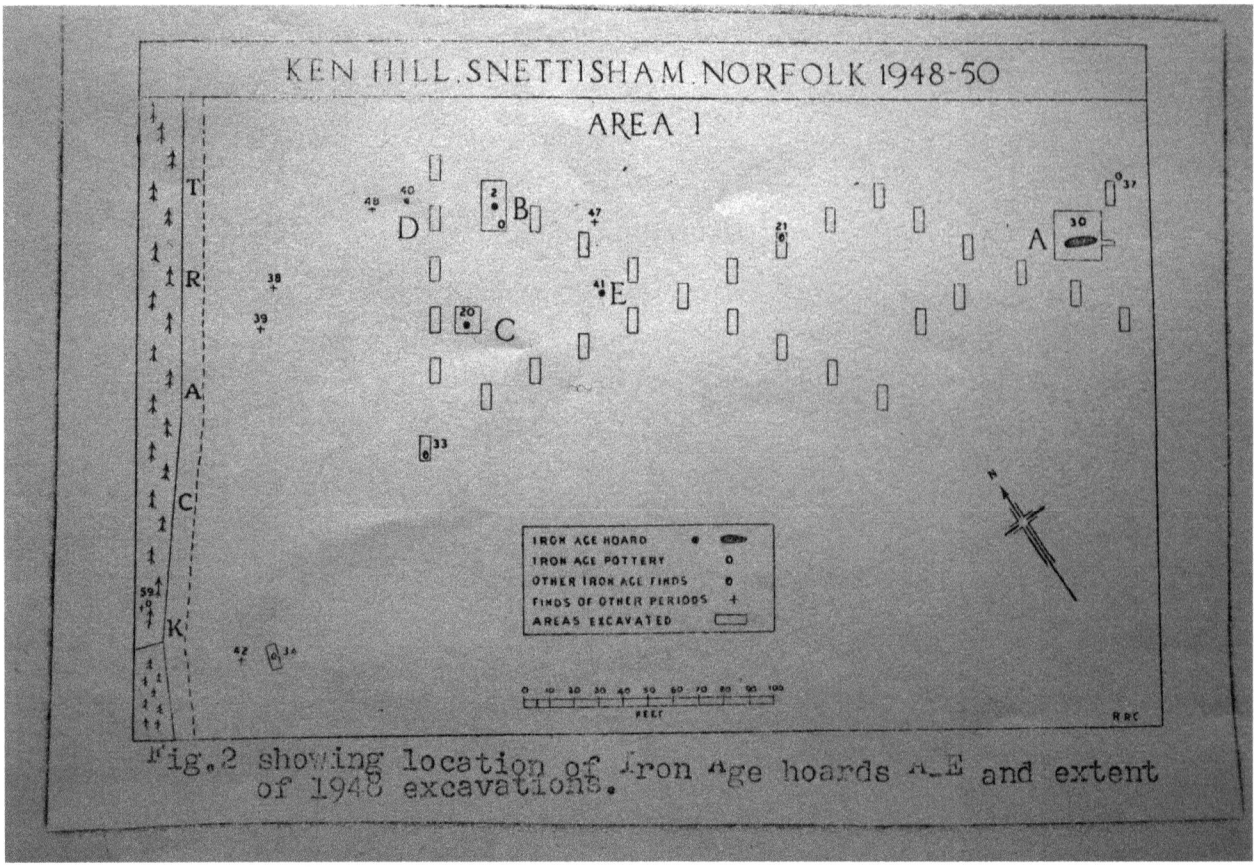

FIGURE 7. CLARKE'S PLAN OF KEN HILL IN HIS 1954 PUBLICATION. ABOVE AND THE LEFT OF THE LETTER K OF 'TRACK' IS THE NUMBER 59 – IN THE CORNER OF THE WOODS (FROM CLARKE 1954).

This appears to be the same location as the excavations under discussion in this report.

Upon further 'rummaging' in the Snettisham NHER file, a reference to 'RB sherds at 59' was discovered, along with evidence that in 1952 an amateur archaeologist had undertaken an excavation in this location. It is recorded on the NHER:

'In wood. Dump of mixed refuse. IA and RB pottery. Dug by CH Lewton-Braine. Oyster shells, wall plaster. Coarse red brick, *tesserae*, animal bones.'

It would seem then that the excavations of 2004 were undertaken in the same place as a previous excavation in 1952 and that a similar range of artefacts were recovered, although Lewton-Braine does not seem to have found/ recognised any wall foundations. It could be, therefore, that the mixed nature of the material recovered in 2004 was the direct result of previous work. Fortunately, Lewton-Braine did make some notes on what he had discovered. But, on reading his report, the plot regarding the disturbance at the site thickens. Lewton-Braine states that:

'shells, bones, sherds etc are not in layers, but scattered throughout the soil.'

It would seem that during Lewton-Braine's investigation of the site there were already signs that it had been disturbed. He notes that the cultural remains he discovered were very fragmentary, much like the pottery and animal remains recovered in 2004. The abraded and fragmentary nature of the material and the apparent mixing of material led Lewton-Braine to ask the same question as is being asked here – how had the site become so disturbed?

Having established that the earlier excavations did not cause the disturbance that was seen in 2004, the next obvious explanation is that the disturbance is related to the woodland within which the site is located. Following the same train of thought ,Lewton-Braine discovered that the adjacent pine wood, which was planted after the pine wood where the temple site stood, had been difficult to plant. He explains that the because the soil cover was so thin it had been necessary to dig the tree holes into the natural carr stone. Given the difficulties in planting the nearby pine wood, it is likely that in 1908, when the wood where the excavations took place was planted, similar difficulties were encountered. However, what was clear from the 2004 excavations is that there seem to be no pockets or residual signs of any stratigraphy between the trees. The site appears to have been well and truly disturbed across the entire area, not just where the trees were planted. There is no doubting that the planting of the pine woodland in 1908 and subsequent root growth would have had a great impact on the archaeology at the site. But, the complete destruction of the site can perhaps be explored from yet another angle.

As discussed above, it was noted by the specialists reporting on the Roman pottery that there was a complete absence of later Roman fine wares from the sample analysed. Given the nature of the general assemblage, this lack of later wares clearly struck the analyst as worth commenting on. Coupled with the lack of later Roman wares, there was, again as mentioned above, a coin dated to the 350s-360s wedged firmly beneath a section of north wall tumble – providing a good *terminus post quem* date for the destruction of the building. In addition, other than the odd sherd, there has been very little material recovered from the site that post-dates the Roman period. Current archaeological evidence does not point to Ken Hill as having continued to be a focus of attention in subsequent periods. Given that the soil appears to have been so thoroughly churned, that the walls of the structure were clearly destroyed and any mosaic floor had been broken up, could it be that this site was disturbed before the 20th century? Could it be that the evidence, unstructured though it is, is actually pointing to the very purposeful and thorough destruction of the temple site during the dying throes of Roman rule in Britain and the decades that followed?

Conclusions

Since the discovery of gold at Ken Hill, the site has been the focus of a great deal of archaeological and modern 'antiquarian' type interest. The quantities of gold that were recovered from the site and the subsequent 'treasure-trove' cases, along with the lack of full publication of excavations and 'nighthawking' has ensured that Snettisham has continued to remain enigmatic. These factors have also meant that amongst the archaeological and metal-detecting communities the site has become particularly sensitive. This has not helped in unravelling, protecting and presenting the history of the site. Despite these problems, the excavations undertaken in 2004 do provide a little more insight into the past life of Ken Hill. It can now be demonstrated that the 'special' nature of the location continued from the Iron Age into the Romano-British period with the implantation of a temple site in the area of earlier activity. That this should have happened is not unduly surprising. It is well known that the Romans sought to adapt indigenous places of import. In addition, the state of the archaeological remains of the temple may be providing some insight into the nature of its destruction, with that destruction perhaps being contemporary and purposeful; and marking a distinct end to the importance and presumably power that was associated with the site towards the end of the Roman period.

The detailed story of Ken Hill, both in terms of the past and more recent history, is one of enigma and intrigue, but it is hoped that the 10 days of excavation in 2004 have added a little more flesh on Snettisham bones, and potentially opened up new avenues of enquiry in terms of understanding the site.

Acknowledgements

Firstly thanks to Harry Buscall and John Austen, the landowner and Estate Manager, for agreeing to ten days of formal archaeological excavation taking place on Ken Hill. A great deal of thanks are owed to Andy Hutcheson who helped organise and run the excavations. Thanks are also due to the students at UEA who excavated with diligence and enthusiasm. The detectorists, Steve Brown and Keven Elfick, who had originally uncovered the wall, also assisted on site. Alex Wasse (faunal remains), Sarah Percival (Iron Age pottery) and Alice Lyons (Roman pottery) did an excellent job on a very tight budget to produce comprehensive reports. The full results of their work are all lodged in the NHER. Thanks are also due to Adrian Marsden who identified the coins.

None of the work could have taken place without the financial support of the Scarfe Committee and CBA East.

Bibliography

Clarke, R. R. 1954. The Early Iron Age Treasure from Snettisham, Norfolk. In *Proceedings of the Prehistoric Society* 20, 27-86.
Cunliffe, B. 1991. *Iron Age Communities in Britain.* London, Routledge, third edition.
Downey, R. King, A. and Soffe, G. 1978. *The Roman Temple on Hayling Island, Second Interim Report on Excavations 1977.* London.
Downey, R. King, A. and Soffe, G. 1979. *The Hayling Island Temple, Third Interim Report on the Excavations of the Iron Age and Roman Temple, 1976-78.* London.
Hutcheson, N. C. G. 2004. *Later Iron Age Society; landscape, metalwork and Society.* British Archaeological Report 361.
Rodwell, W. J. 1976, Coinage, Oppida and the rise of Belgic Power in South Eastern Britain, In B. Cunliffe and T. Rowley (eds) *Oppida: the beginnings of urbanism in Barbarian Europe* British Archaeological Report Supplementary Series 11, 181 – 367.
Stead, I. 1991. The Snettisham Treasure: Excavations in 1990. In *Antiquity* 65, 447-65.
Stead, I. 1998. *The Salisbury Hoard.* Gloucestershire: Tempus.

Appendix 1: The Coins

Context 10,038
Thurrock Type, late first century BC – Trinovantian.
Unidentified – possibly Greek – poor copy of an IA bronze unit.

Context 10,000
SF4 ?Roman Silver Denarius

Context 10,000
SF17 Unusual dished coin – British IA, 50BC/AD ?Corieltauvi.

Context 10,012
SF19 Silver Iceni Pattern-horse – missing from site.

Context 10,021
SF21 Falling Horseman copy – British – c. 355-364.

Context 10,000
SF22 Thurrock Type – late first century BC – Trinovantian.

Context 10,000
SF23 Falling Horseman copy – British – c. 355 -364.

North Wall tumble
SF26 Falling Horseman copy – British – c. 355 -364.

The Iron Age coins from Snettisham

Adrian Marsden

The site at Ken Hill, Snettisham, Norfolk Historic Environment Record site 1487 (hereafter abbreviated to NHER), has long been recognised as being of considerable significance. There are local tales that children were not allowed to play in Ken Hill woods because of the treasure believed to be buried there. Or perhaps this abandoned religious centre was still held to be the abode of sinister entities?

That the site was a religious centre is incontrovertible; over the years it has yielded many fabulous discoveries. The first torcs and hoards were found in 1948 and led to excavations which ran from that year until 1950. Further finds in 1964, 1968, 1973 and 1990 added considerably to the record. Over a hundred torcs of various types and materials were recovered together with Gallic and Gallo-Belgic staters and quarter staters and a large number of Linear type potins. One of the Gallo-Belgic quarter staters was actually retrieved from within a torc terminal, an enigmatic feature that is useful for dating evidence if nothing else.

Unfortunately, the site has been subjected to intensive illicit metal detecting over the years. Rumours persist of a further hoard of torcs being found in the late 1970s, not to mention the so-called Bowl hoard of several thousand Icenian coins which was illegally removed from the site in 1991 and probably smuggled out of the country. The loss of this information is to be deeply regretted but it seems unlikely that anything apart from second-hand or third-hand reports will ever surface to enhance the record.

Between 2003 and 2009 a metal detector survey accompanied by amateur excavation recovered a significant amount of material which, whilst it has not particularly altered our understanding of the site, has provided an assemblage that is of significant interest. This included Greek, Iron Age and Roman coins as well as quantities of scrap metal, generally gold, silver or electrum. Another excavation carried out at the site in 2004 is described in this volume by Natasha Hutcheson.

The large amount of precious metal fragments, comprising scraps of gold, silver and electrum, is interesting. These are clear evidence for metal working; some are plainly chopped from torcs and similar ornaments whilst others have been wholly or partially melted. It is possible, though unlikely, that they represent evidence for coining; a putative blank was recovered in the 1948 excavations (Clarke 1954, 58). However, the weight of this disc, 10.71g, does not correlate to any known weight standard for Iron Age stater issues and it is most probable that it is not connected with coining. It is an attractive proposition, given Snettisham's undoubted status in the late Iron Age, that minting was taking place there but the evidence so far recovered does not support such speculation.

This speculation is further undermined by two other objects which bear superficial resemblance to coin blanks (Rainbird Clarke 1954, 59). These discs of gold, on display in Norwich Castle Museum's 'Boudica Gallery', do not, however, convince the viewer as blanks. They are overly large and overly thin; they were probably hammered out from a Gallic stater and a quarter stater respectively (Sills 2003, 376). It is more likely that these coins were being hammered flat to provide gold sheet; certainly they would have been useless as coin blanks. Again, they are evidence for metal working but not coin production.

An object that is almost certainly an Iron Age blank was discovered by metal detectorist Vince Butler at Fransham in 2008 and acquired by Norwich Castle Museum under the terms of the Treasure Act (NCM Accession 2009.228, Figure 1). This weighs 6.06g, a weight very comparable to that of a Norfolk wolf type stater. The fairly pale colour of the gold is also perfectly consistent with this theory, considering the steady debasement of these issues. Two other blanks, one in gold and the other with gold surfaces over a base core were offered at auction in Suffolk in 2009; these lacked a provenance but were probably local finds and most likely also originated at a minting site (Lockdales Auction Catalogue Sunday, 25 January 2009, 31, no. 699). Coin moulds have been found at Saham Toney, Thetford and Needham, all in Central or South Norfolk (Davies 2009, 119). Their absence (thus far) from Snettisham argues further that the place was not a mint site.

The Roman coins from the site, presumably evidence for continued votive activity at Snettisham, need not really detain us here except to comment upon the relatively small numbers that have been unearthed. Indeed, the amount of Roman coinage is so small that, were it not for the small, possible Roman temple enclosure identified by Hutcheson, one would probably not even speculate that religious activity was taking place at Snettisham at this date. Other Roman temple sites, such as Great Walsingham (NHER

FIGURE 1. PALE GOLD DISC, ALMOST CERTAINLY A BLANK FOR A NORFOLK WOLF TYPE STATER, FROM FRANSHAM.

2024) and Hockwold (NHER 5587) have produced vast coin assemblages. That Snettisham tails off so much in the Roman period is interesting. Was this site regarded, after the Boudiccan revolt, as a focus for Icenian discontent and were the inhabitants of Roman Norfolk encouraged to carry out their religious activity at other sites? Certainly, given the finds from Snettisham, the site was a major religious centre in the late Iron Age and it would not perhaps be surprising to find this status left the new Roman masters of the former Icenian kingdom uncomfortable. Great Walsingham is some distance from Snettisham but not enormously far away; the relatively small amount of Iron Age material from that site compared to the enormous quantities of objects connected with Roman votive activity may be taken to imply that Walsingham took over from Snettisham as the principal religious site in this part of Norfolk.

One Roman coin is worthy of comment, a serrate *denarius* of Aulus Postumius Albinus (Crawford 1974, 389, no. 372/1) dating to 81 BC. The early date of this coin suggests it might well have been an Iron Age loss or votive deposit.

This paper is, however, concerned with the Iron Age coins recovered from these investigations and what they can tell us about the site in the late Iron Age. The assemblage comprises four groups of coins, handed over for investigation in 2003, 2005, 2007 and 2009, together with a few other coins discovered separately, either by excavation or metal detecting. The third group is of the greatest interest, made up as it is of much non-local material, including much plated, irregular coinage. This group is in the process of being acquired by Norwich Castle Museum under the terms of the 1996 Treasure Act although at the time this paper was written was in the keeping of the British Museum and the author has not been able to examine all of the material personally. All coins mentioned in this paper carry numbers given to them at the time of their discovery, either finder's reference numbers or small find numbers but, in the interests of brevity, these have been omitted in the catalogue below which lists all coins known to the author that have been discovered at the site since 2002. Some may have been missed but it is hoped that this catalogue is relatively complete.

The classification of the first group of these coins as Treasure rested on the premise that they formed part of at least two dispersed hoards, one of Icenian coins and the other of Trinovantian potins (Hill and Leins 2003, 43). It may be that some of these coins do constitute some of the components of dispersed hoards but the argument that all of them were connected is unsustainable. Most almost certainly represent casual loss at the site or accumulations due to votive activity. As will be seen, there are many other reasons against the Iron Age coins from Ken Hill being interpreted as the contents of a hoard; the mixture of denominations militates against this as does the fact that such a relatively high proportion of the coins are plated. The later groups have been rightly recognised as accumulated deposits that relate to votive activity; as such they also fall under the terms of the Treasure Act.

The Icenian material has a wide chronological spread and a mixture of denominations, ranging from Norfolk wolf type staters to late Pattern-horse silver units. Incidentally, this is further evidence that the Snettisham material does not represent a hoard.

A number of the Icenian coins are plated, a higher proportion than would be expected from such an assemblage. More have probably not been recognised as such. This raises interesting questions about the use or intended function of these coins which are discussed with reference to the plated foreign issues below. It seems likely that the preponderance of plated material reflects the particular usage of coins at this site and it is tempting to connect these examples to votive activity. If it was the symbolic act of giving a coin to the gods that was imbued

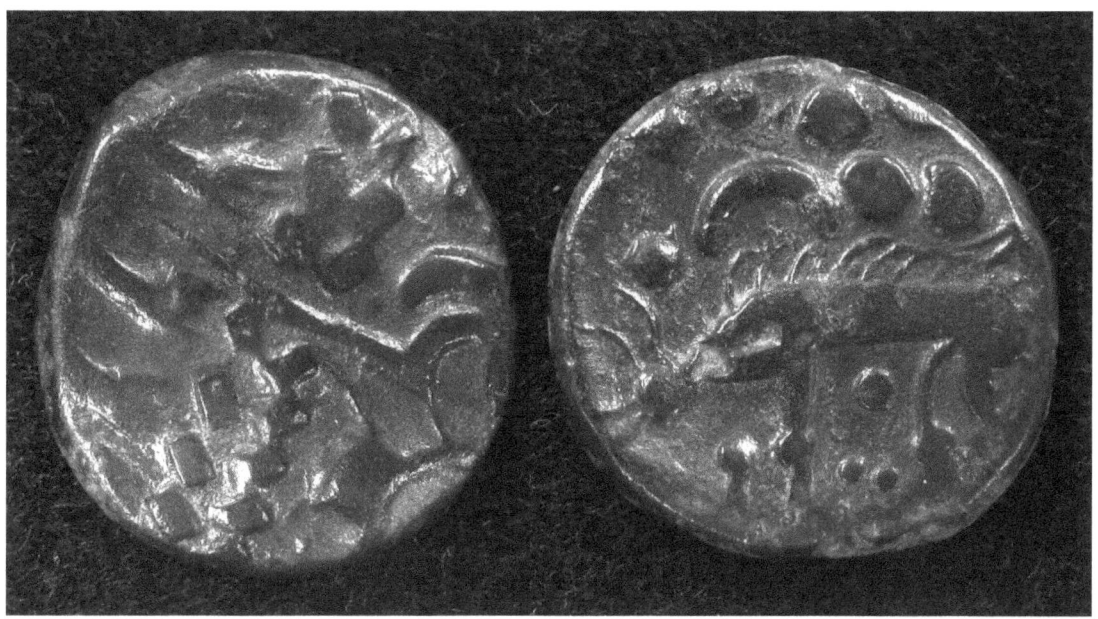

FIGURE 2. BASE NORFOLK WOLF JB TYPE STATER.

with meaning then it follows that the actual metallurgical makeup of that coin was less important than the act itself.

Some individual Icenian coins, although they do not tell us a great deal about coin use at Snettisham *per se*, are rarities and so should be mentioned in this paper.

Several boar-horse type silver half units were recovered. These are not particularly common finds. At least one is plated. Another, of good silver, has been fused through heat to another coin, perhaps a Bury type silver unit. This is interesting and suggests that some of these coins may have had a different fate intended for them than to have been offered up as votive gifts. They recall the chopped and partially melted fragments of gold and silver from the site and may be best placed within the same context, as the raw material for the working of precious metal.

Some of the subsets of Icenian coins are specific to north-west Norfolk, for example the ECEN symbol units, some die groups of Norfolk wolf staters with a left-facing wolf (also known as JB type staters: Figure 2, and the Bury D silver units (Figure 3). Snettisham, given its obvious importance, might be considered a logical site for the production of at least some of these issues. However, as mentioned above, no convincing evidence for this has so far been discovered. Given their distribution patterns in north-west Norfolk, however, they must have been struck somewhere relatively close to Ken Hill.

As mentioned, the Icenian material has a wide chronological spread; analysis of the groups by John Talbot found a surprising absence of his so-called phase six coinages and a low representation of his normally common phase seven coinages. This is puzzling and suggests a twenty or thirty year lack of coin usage at the site or at least at this part of the site.

The non-Icenian coins constitute a significant proportion of the assemblage. They range from Carthaginian and

FIGURE 3. ICENIAN BURY D TYPE SILVER UNIT.

FIGURE 4. BRONZE CARTHAGINIAN ISSUE, LATE 3RD CENTURY BC TO EARLY 2ND CENTURY BC.

Greek issues to plated staters and quarter staters, many from the Continent (or perhaps native copying of coins from the Continent), and further imply that the Snettisham coins do not represent a hoard.

There are several coins from the lands surrounding the Mediterranean. A bronze coin of Miletus and another of Massilia attest to the early appearance of coins at Ken Hill. It is uncertain whether these coins, together with an illegible Greek bronze, came to Snettisham as currency intended for trade or as votive gifts.

A hemistater of Carthage represents one of the oldest coins from the site, dating to the late 4th or early 3rd century BC whilst another Carthaginian coin, a bronze issue, is of comparable date (Figure 4). It shows a left-facing female head on the obverse and a horse standing in front of a palm tree on the reverse.

An identical issue was recently discovered at Heacham (Marsden 2010, 110) in 2009, perhaps suggesting some level of trade between Norfolk and the North African mainland in the later Iron Age. It is possible that the two coins found their way to Norfolk by other routes, through Spain for example, but it is most likely that they were brought over by Carthaginian merchants. Their presence in Norfolk, at a period so long before copper alloy coins had come into use, raises questions as to their significance.

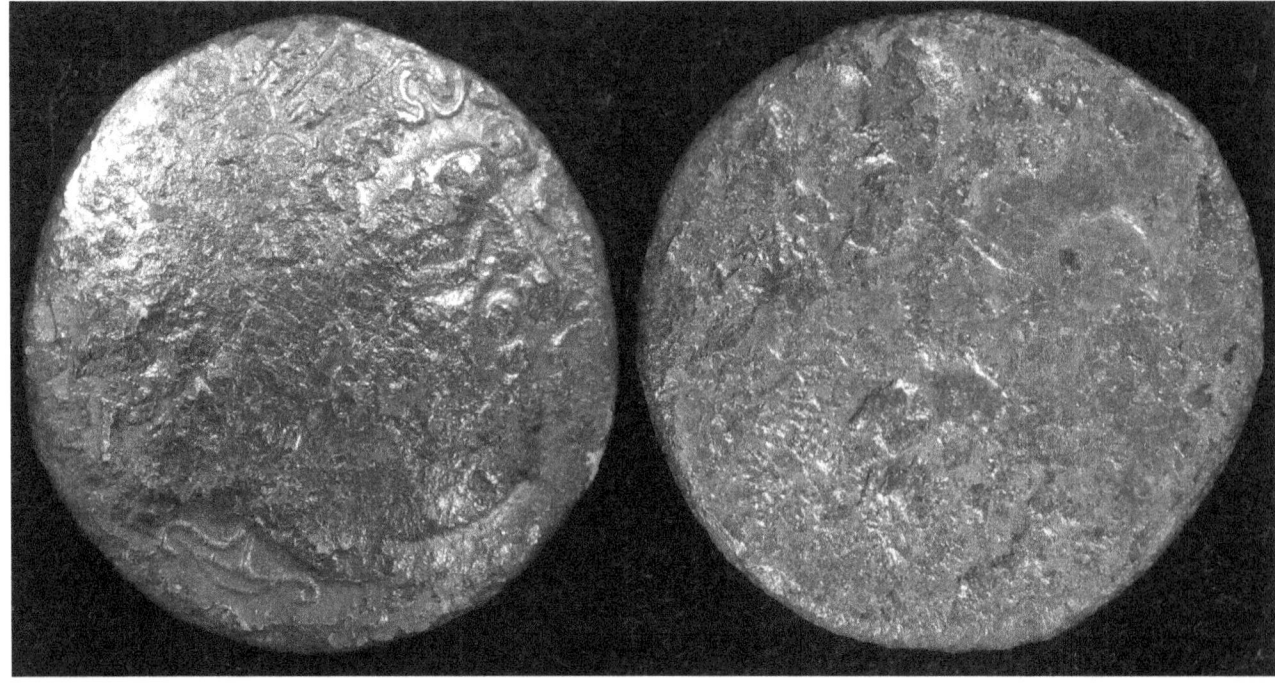

FIGURE 5. PLATED GALLIC STATER, 2ND CENTURY BC.

Indeed, these bronze discs, with appealing designs on both sides, may have been appreciated more as works of art than as currency and this may be why the example found at Snettisham, together with the other bronze coins, was chosen as a gift to the gods. It is probably also significant that this early use of foreign bronze coins did not translate into a native production of copper alloy units as happened in some of the neighbouring territories. The large number of later potins discussed below are also imports.

A large plated Gallic stater of the second century BC (Figure 5) is another coin that has travelled to Snettisham from the Continent. Although not quite as old as the Carthaginian bronze it still belongs, like the many Roman Republican *denarii* found in Norfolk, to a period before coin use had properly begun in Iron Age Britain. Of course, it could have come over the Channel much later (as was probably the case with many Republican *denarii*) or it could have arrived at Snettisham as bullion for metalworking, the discovery that it was a plated imitation leading to its being discarded. Nonetheless, it is most likely that this was one of the first coins to travel to Ken Hill.

The overwhelming number of the Snettisham coins belong to the first century BC, to a period when coin use in the Icenian kingdom was, if not established, at least beginning. The non-Icenian material is a mixture, composed in the main of Gallo-Belgic issues with a smattering of British coins from outside East Anglia and a large number of potins, most of them Trinovantian Thurrock types.

Ten Gallo-Belgic type DC quarter staters were recovered, two in the 2005 batch, seven in the 2007 batch and a further one in 2009, and constitute a strange group. Only three of these are clearly genuine, struck in a yellow gold of high purity (Figure 6). The rest have the appearance of plated copies, with a pale surface and black encrustations suggestive of a base core reacting with elements in the surrounding soil (Figure 7). They compare closely with the other plated coins from the Snettisham assemblage and raise further questions. Gallo-Belgic staters and quarter staters do turn up as stray finds in Norfolk although admittedly the staters in particular are normally found in hoards. Plated copies of these coins are not, however, encountered as a rule. Whilst plated Norfolk wolf type staters do occur as do plated copies of the later Freckenham type staters, the same is not true of the Gallo-Belgics. Why, then, these seven plated quarter staters? Do they represent local products? If they were produced at the site, were they forgeries intended to deceive or are they

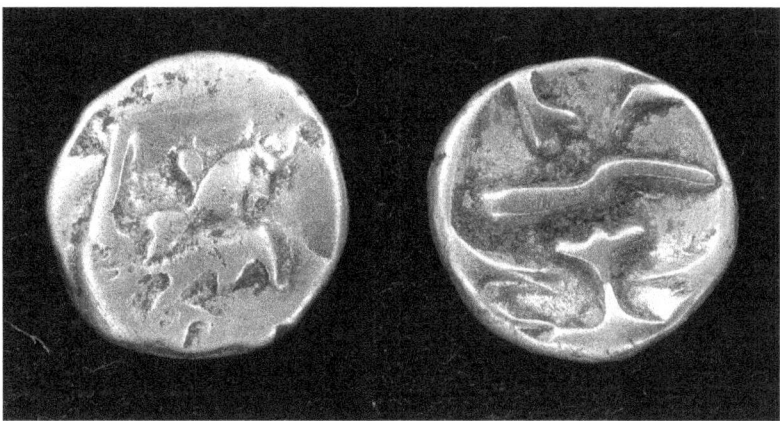

FIGURE 6. GALLIC TYPE DC QUARTER STATER, MID-FIRST CENTURY BC.

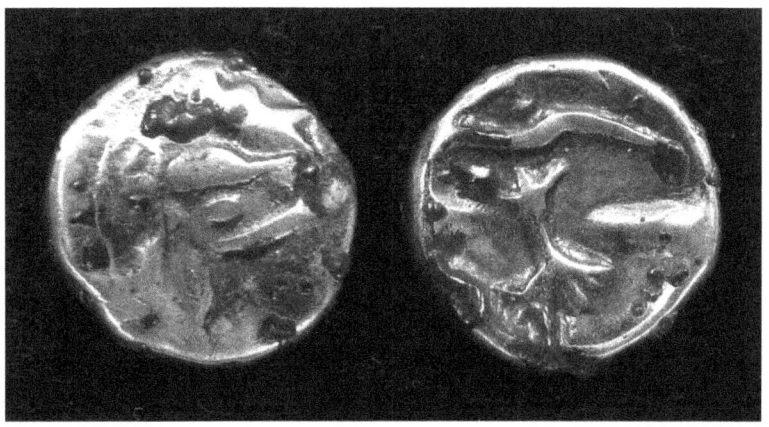

FIGURE 7. PLATED COPY OF A GALLIC TYPE DC QUARTER STATER, MID-FIRST CENTURY BC.

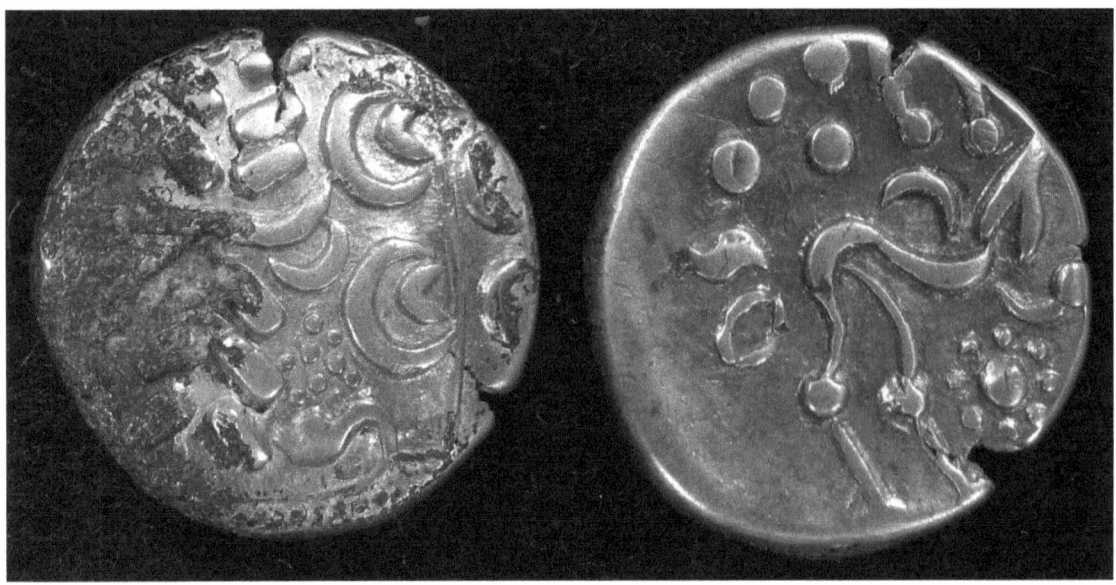

FIGURE 8. PLATED COPY OF AN UNINSCRIBED CORIELTAUVIAN HB TYPE STATER.

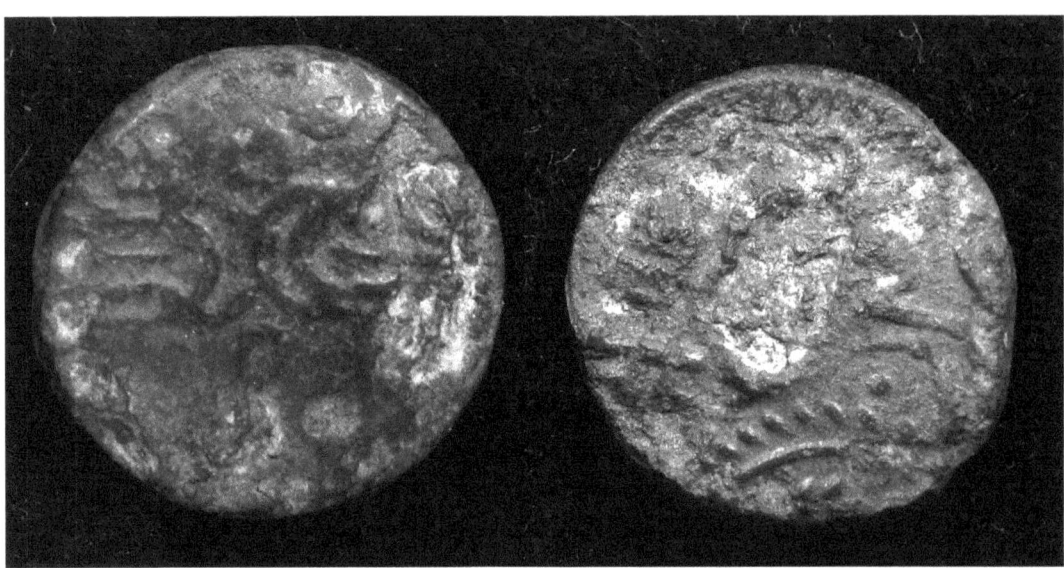

FIGURE 9. PLATED TRINOVANTIAN DVBNO TYPE STATER.

in some way connected with votive activity, representing some form of 'temple money'? At the moment these are not easy questions to answer.

Interestingly, much of the non-Icenian British material is also plated or appears to be so. This group includes a plated uninscribed Corieltauvian HB stater (Figure 8) and a Trinovantian Dubnovellaunus type stater (Figure 9). Both would have been high-value coins were they genuine.

This high proportion of plated material is strange. Whilst the plated Gallo-Belgic quarter staters mentioned above form a discrete group that may be connected to local production, the scatter of other plated coins from far away is less easy to explain. Were these coins being withdrawn from circulation at Snettisham because the Iceni did not want bad foreign coin circulating in their realm or were they deliberately selected as votive offerings because they were base? Given the high proportion of plated, local Icenian material, the latter explanation may be the correct one. Here we may have an anticipation of later Roman practice where so many coins offered up in a votive context were of irregular origin.

A Corieltauvian scyphate type quarter stater is a rare find (Figure 10), only two being listed in Hobbs' catalogue of the British Museum collection; both of these were from the original hoard found at Clacton in 1898 (Hobbs 1996, 54, nos. 180-1).

Another interesting group is provided by the five Trinovantian G type 'Clacton' quarter staters (Figure 11). This is an unusual group considering only about thirty of these coins are known in the first instance and that these

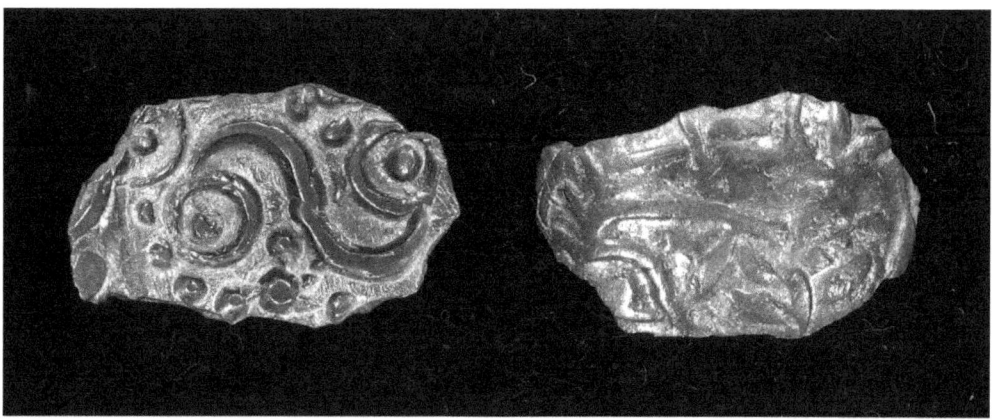

FIGURE 10. CORIELTAUVIAN SCYPHATE TYPE QUARTER STATER.

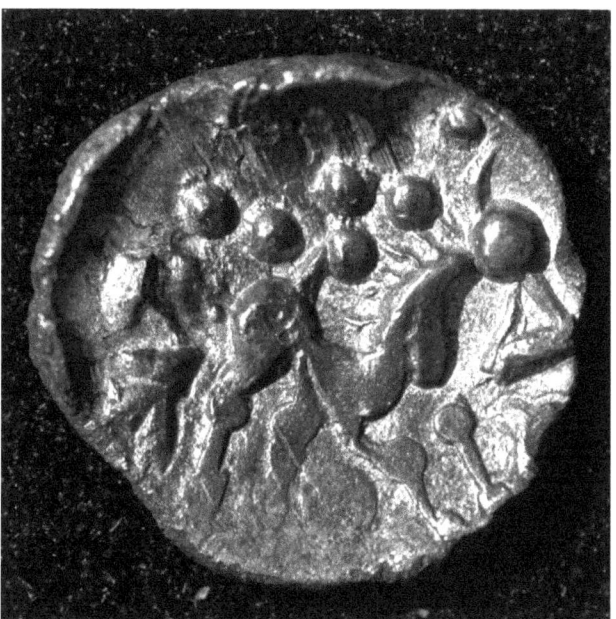 

FIGURE 11. TRINOVANTIAN G TYPE 'CLACTON' QUARTER STATER.

coins were furthermore produced outside Norfolk. This group probably does in fact represent a dispersed hoard. Unlike the group of Gallo-Belgic quarters, none are plated. What we might term a purse loss is the most likely explanation for the presence of these coins.

The 36 potins form a large and compact group, accounting for approximately 25% of the Iron Age coins recovered. They are almost all Trinovantian Thurrock types with an Apollo head on the obverse and a butting bull on the reverse. The dating of these issues is still a source of debate since no real evidence exists that can securely place them chronologically. It is accepted wisdom that they date to around 100 BC at the latest; however, this could easily be wishful thinking on the part of numismatists who wish to put back the appearance of a native British coinage to as early a date as possible. They are probably best placed in the first few decades of the first century BC.

Thurrock type potins are rare as stray finds in Norfolk; apart from Snettisham the only other location in the county that has yielded them in any numbers is a site in the Waveney valley. Given their proposed placement in the first half of the first century BC they may represent some of the earliest votive activity involving coins at Snettisham. Since, even putting their period of production forward to the first century BC, they would predate any native Icenian issues they may have furnished a useful source of votive offering to those unable or unwilling to give anything more splendid. Were these coins in fact being imported into the area to service a need for low-value gifts to the gods? It is strange that the Iceni did not, like a number of their neighbours, produce copper alloy units when they did strike their own currency. Perhaps the plated Icenian silver units were a more attractive alternative to bronze. Here, however, we enter into the realms of pure supposition when instead we might be wiser to see plated silver coins as simply an attempt to deceive the recipient and make a profit for the producer.

FIGURE 12. LINEAR TYPE KENTISH POTIN. FIRST CENTURY BC.

A large number of thinner potins of cruder appearance, the so-called Linear types, were discovered in the earlier excavations at the site in the late 1940s and many of these are on display in the Castle Museum, Norwich. One appeared in the later excavation and metal detector survey (Figure 12). These are Kentish products and their high tin content gives them a silvery appearance unlike the Thurrock types which are essentially of copper alloy albeit with a significant tin component.

Interestingly, there is an almost total absence of non-Icenian silver units, plated or otherwise, the foreign coins being almost always of gold (or plated copies of the same) or of copper alloy. Set against the large numbers of potins this is another strange anomaly. Were non-Icenian silver coins in some way not acceptable? Like so many of the questions raised by the Snettisham coin assemblage this riddle is not an easy one to solve.

It would come as no surprise that Snettisham, situated as it is on the north-western edge of Icenian territory, would have attracted visitors from beyond the tribal frontiers. The lands of the Corieltauvi lay north-west across the Wash whilst, to the south-west, beyond Peddar's way and the fen edge, the Catuvellauni were hardly distant. Indeed, it is fair to speculate, as has often been the case with religious sites across the ages, that Snettisham was not merely a religious centre but also a site where much trade between mortals took place. Even if the coins recovered at Ken Hill were all votive offerings many of these must have been brought there by visitors from beyond the Icenian realms. Many visitors to Snettisham may well have come a long way, their journeys being analogous to medieval pilgrimages where men and women travelled across Britain to worship at shrines such as Walsingham and Canterbury.

The Iron Age coins from Snettisham represent an interesting assemblage and the work carried out on them so far is still very much a work in progress. Many questions remain to be answered, the answering of which is not made any easier by the diverse and bewildering nature of the material.

Was the use of coins in a votive context a corollary to torc deposition? The finding of the Gallo-Belgic quarter stater in the terminal of one of the torcs is interesting here but does not really furnish any answers. Was the giving of coins connected to the chopping up of torcs and other items of gold and silver and the evidence for metalworking uncovered at the site? Were coins being melted down to make precious metal objects or was the reverse the case and objects were being dismembered to produce the metal needed for coining? Again, the answers are not easily forthcoming.

As argued above, it seems unlikely that coin production was taking place at Snettisham and the partially melted and fire-damaged coins imply that various forms of precious metal were going into the melting pot. The situation seems to have been a complex one with the most likely explanation being that recycling of gold and silver was carried out at the site and that this was probably connected in some way with votive activity. At the very least, however, the coins recovered from Ken Hill make it likely that this site was an important cult centre, a place of pilgrimage for men and women from areas well beyond the borders of the land of the Iceni.

Acknowledgements

Several people have been instrumental in the production of this paper. Thanks should go to Dr. John Davies for arranging the conference at which the first draft of this paper was delivered and to Dr. Andrew Rogerson for his initial sorting of the material when it came into Norfolk Landscape Archaeology's Identification and Recording Service. Steve Brown and Kevin Elfleet have been responsible for the recovery of the overwhelming majority of the latest parts of the Snettisham assemblage and their diligence is commendable. Above all, my thanks must go to John Talbot for his expert help in cataloguing many of the coins and his insightful comments on their significance. His illumination of what is still, to the author, very much a darkened landscape has been invaluable.

Catalogue

Greek coins

Hemistater of Carthage, c.310-270BC (2.26g)

Carthaginian bronze, late 4th/early 3rd century BC (2.32g)

Bronze unit of Massilia, 3rd century BC (5.43g)

Bronze unit of Miletus, magistrate Kleisippides, 3rd century BC (4.61g)

Bronze unit, further details illegible (4.82g)

Iron Age coins

Continental issues

Plated Gallic stater, 2nd century BC (5.09g)

3 Gallo-Belgic DC type quarter staters, Van Arsdell 69-1 (1.45g, 1.46g and 1.51g)

7 plated Gallo-Belgic DC type quarter staters (0.85g, 0.88g, 1.21g, 1.10g, 0.99g, 0.94g and 0.81g)

British, non-Icenian, gold and gold plated issues

Plated Corieltauvi HB type stater (3.55g)

Corieltauvi gold scyphate unit (0.59g: fragment)

5 Trinovantes G type gold quarter staters (1.31g, 0.96g, 1.10g, 1.05g and 0.76g:fragment)

Plated Trinovantes Dubnovellaunos stater, Van Arsdell 1650 (3.11g)

British, non-Icenian, silver issues

Corieltauvi, Boar-horse type silver unit (0.98g)

British potin issues

36 Thurrock type potins (4.25g, 3.07g, 3.41g, 3.15g:fragment, 3.57g, 4.84g, 4.22g, 4.02g, 5.48g, 5.55g, 6.17g, 3.58g, 4.10g, 3.14g, 2.53g, 3.44g, 3.65g, 3.47g, 2.05g, 3.90g, 2.80g, 4.26g, 3.79g, 4.01g, 3.38g, 3.51g, 3.93g, 2.81g, 3.92g, 3.28g, 1.31g, 2.72g, 2.88g, 2.78g, 2.80g and 2.18g:fragment)

Flat Linear I potin, Van Arsdell 129 (1.42g)

Icenian staters and quarter staters

2 Iceni JB type staters, Van Arsdell 610-2, (5.50g and 5.49g)

3 Base Iceni J type staters (3.33g, 3.40g and 3.17g)

Iceni, 'Irstead' type quarter stater (1.02g)

Plated Iceni, 'Irstead' type quarter stater (0.54g)

2 Iceni, 'Snettisham' type quarter staters (0.95g and 0.97g)

Icenian silver units and plated copies

2 Iceni silver units, early Boar-horse type (1.20g and 1.51g)

Iceni silver unit, Boar-horse type A, Van Arsdell 655 (1.15g)

5 Iceni silver units, Boar-horse type B, Van Arsdell 657 (1.06g, 1.10g, 0.98g, 1.18g and 0.65g)

Iceni silver unit, Boar-horse type C (0.57g)

Iceni silver unit, probably Boar-horse type (0.45g)

3 Iceni silver half units, Boar-horse type (0.50g, uncertain weight and 0.28g: fragment)

Plated Iceni silver half unit, Boar-horse type (0.38g)

5 Iceni silver units, Bury A types (1.20g, 1.21g, 1.18g, 0.84g and 0.88g)

5 Iceni silver units, Bury B types (1.36g, 1.23g, 1.17g, 1.00g and 0.49g:fragment)

Iceni silver unit, Bury type, further details uncertain (weight uncertain).

2 Iceni silver units, 'Snettisham' type (1.16g and 0.66g)

4 Iceni silver units, Face-horse Large Flan C types (1.28g, 0.92g, 0.92g and 0.60g: fragment)

Iceni silver unit, probably early Face-horse Large Flan type (0.67g)

Plated Iceni silver unit, Face-horse Large Flan C type (0.81g)

2 Iceni silver units, Face-horse 'Saham Toney' type (0.69g and 0.70g)

5 Iceni silver units, Face-horse type, Van Arsdell 794 (1.24g, 1.07g, 0.96g, 0.82g:fragment and 0.64g: fragment)

2 plated Iceni silver units, Face-horse type, Van Arsdell 794 (0.92g and 0.65g)

Iceni, Pattern-horse A type, Van Arsdell 679 (1.15g)

Plated Iceni, Pattern-horse A type (0.70g)

10 Iceni silver units, Pattern-horse ECEN type (0.99g, 1.14g, 1.13g, 1.08g, 1.13g, 0.77g, 0.82g, 1.02g, 0.84g and 1.11g)

9 Iceni silver units, Pattern-horse ANTED type (1.09g, 1.20g, 1.12g, 0.86g, 1.23g, 0.78g, 1.06g, 1.09g and 0.87g)

8 Iceni silver units, Pattern-horse, uncertain types (0.61g, 1.11g, 0.65g, 0.90g, 1.13g, 0.82g, 0.94g and 1.12g)

Plated Iceni silver unit, uncertain Pattern-horse type (0.60g:fragment)

Iceni silver half-unit, early Pattern-horse type (0.56g)

Iceni silver half-unit, ANTED type (0.37g)

Bibliography

Clarke, R. R. 1954. The Early Iron Age Treasure from Snettisham Norfolk. *Proceedings of the Prehistoric Society* XX, 27-86.

Crawford, M. H. 1974. *Roman Republican Coinage.* Cambridge, University Press.

Davies, J. A. 2009. *The Land of Boudica.* Oxbow, Oxford.

Hill, J. D. and Leins, I. 2003. North West Norfolk (1): Coins and objects of the middle and late Iron Age to the Roman period (2003 T169). *Treasure Annual Report 2003*, 43-4.

Hobbs, R. *British Iron Age coins in the British Museum.* London, British Museum Press.

Marsden, A. B. 2010. Summary Coin Finds from Norfolk, 2009. *Norfolk Archaeology* 46 (1), 110-14.

Sills, J. 2003. *Gaulish and early British Gold Coinage.* London, Spink.

Van Arsdell, R. D. 1989. *Celtic Coinage of Britain.* London, Spink.

Boars, Bulls and Norfolk's Celtic Menagerie

John Davies

Introduction

The recovery of objects through metal-detection in Norfolk has contributed significantly to the known corpus of Iron Age objects in the county over the last thirty years. This paper will focus on some discoveries related to the representation of animals within that material and will consider the extent to which the 'Celtic Zoo' played a role in representational art in this part of Britain. My main purpose here is to publish two very important finds, which are a boar figurine and a drinking horn terminal in the shape of a bull's head. However, the consideration of these separate objects also provides an opportunity to discuss the wider presence of animal-inspired art within the Icenian area.

The people of Iron Age Britain maintained a close association with their natural environment. Their dependence on the countryside and the natural world around them is frequently reflected in their art, which was predominantly expressed through the medium of metalwork. Bulls, boars and other animals played a prominent part in Celtic iconography (Megaw and Megaw 2001, 160). Miranda Green has noted how the Celtic bronzesmith and blacksmith 'revered the beauty and elegance of animals' and 'enhanced and promoted their aesthetic qualities' (Green 1992, 1). The inspiration for these objects was often through religion, ritual and myth. We know that animals were venerated and sacrificed in rituals. Parts of their carcases were regularly left unconsumed within settlements (Hill 1995). Some animals were even thought to possess magical powers.

Until now, there has been little written about the representation of animals in the craftsmanship of Iron Age Norfolk. However, there is now growing evidence for Norfolk's own iconographic menagerie, which will be reviewed in the context of these important new discoveries.

A boar figurine from east Norfolk. Figures 1-3

The discovery

This beautiful figurine was discovered in 1997 by metal-detection at Ashmanhaugh, some 20km north-east of Norwich. Despite repeated scrutiny at the site, nothing else of Iron Age or Roman date has been discovered in the vicinity.

The boar in Celtic society

Boars were a symbol of strength. They were considered as an appropriate symbol to adorn weaponry and armour. An example is the Witham Shield (Lincs), which depicts a stylised boar with elongated legs. More locally, boars feature prominently on the coinage of the Iceni, as well as on that of their western neighbours, the Corieltauvi.

Description

The Ashmanhaugh figurine is a stylised representation of a boar. It is three-dimensional and made of copper alloy. It carries little corrosion, although it is damaged in several places and details, such as tusks, upper section of the crest and front feet, are missing. It measures 87mm from the tip of the snout to the rear of the spinal crest. Its widest point is 23mm, measuring from ear to ear. The maximum height is 51mm.

This is an important addition to the known corpus of boar figurines from Britain. In 1977 Jennifer Foster compiled a corpus of twenty-two examples, with a further nineteen from continental Europe (Foster 1977). More recently, other examples have been found at Camerton (Jackson 1990) and Duncton, West Sussex (*Portable Antiquities Scheme Annual Report 2005/6*). None of the recorded English examples at that time came from Norfolk, Lincolnshire or the Fenland. This has been somewhat surprising as these are the areas of Britain which prominently featured representations of this creature on their coinage of the period. However, examples have now turned up and have been recorded in northern East Anglia. The first was discovered in 1990 at Cranwich, Norfolk (unpublished; basic description in Davies 2009, 112,117). This example will be considered further, below. The second came from Rothwell Top, Lincolnshire (Art Fund Review 2007/2008).

The British and continental examples all range in style between those realistically portrayed and others more stylised in their appearance. The Ashmanhaugh boar has an elongated snout with flattened muzzle, like figurines from the Gower peninsula (Foster 1977, Plate IVa) and Woodingdean, Sussex (Foster 1977, Plate V). It has a simple horizontal straight mouth. The tusks are broken away from either side and are missing.

FIGURE 1. THE BOAR FIGURINE FROM ASHMANHAUGH. COPYRIGHT NORFOLK MUSEUMS & ARCHAEOLOGY SERVICE.

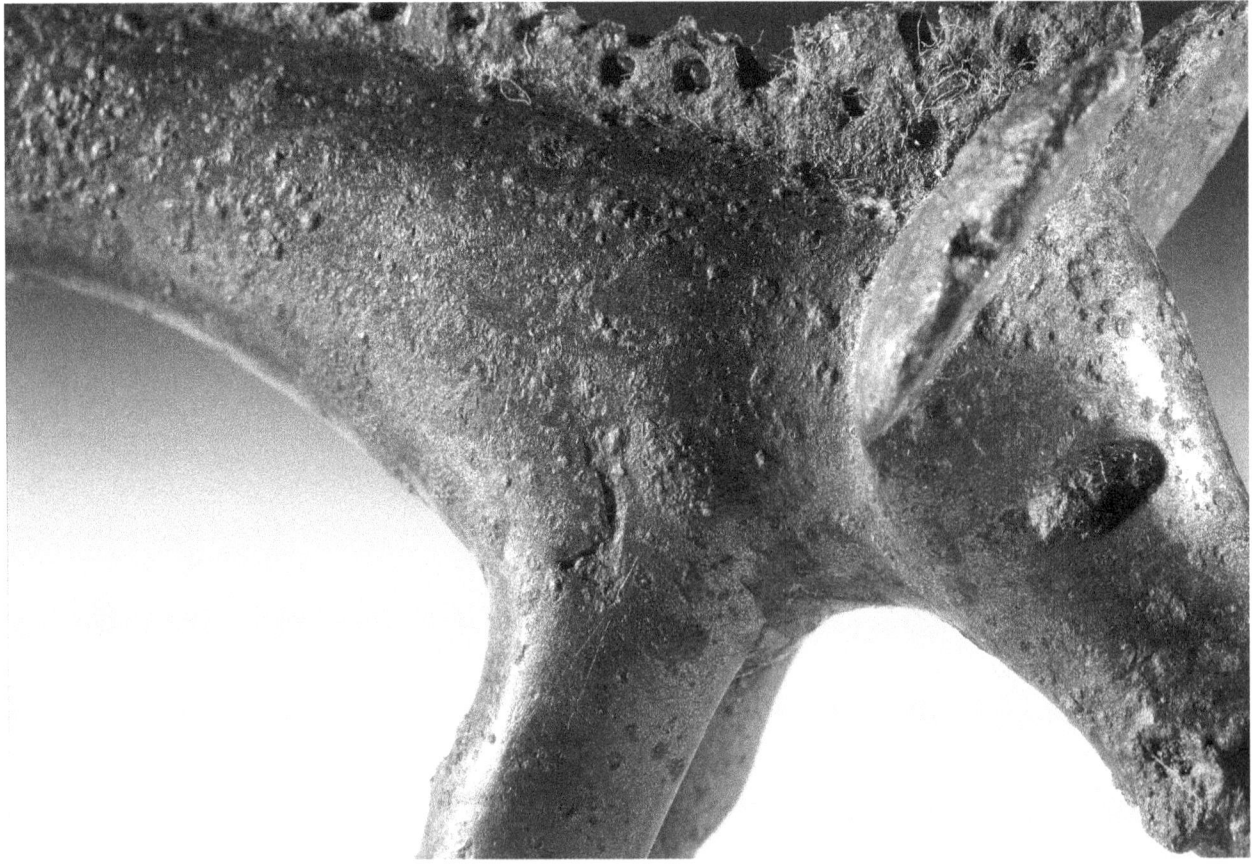

FIGURE 2. CLOSE-UP, SHOWING THE MARK ON THE RIGHT SHOULDER. COPYRIGHT NORFOLK MUSEUMS & ARCHAEOLOGY SERVICE.

FIGURE 3. CLOSE-UP, SHOWING THE MUZZLE, FACE AND RIGHT EAR. COPYRIGHT NORFOLK MUSEUMS & ARCHAEOLOGY SERVICE.

The first of two deliberate, unexplained, features in the casting is located on the right shoulder (Figure 2). This is a symbol in the shape of a 'tick' mark. It has no possible function and must have carried a meaning that was strong enough to warrant inclusion on the figurine in this way. I will return to the possible significance of this mark later in this paper.

The body of the boar narrows towards the waist. The feet are flattened and point forward - not cast in the shape of hooves. The front two have been broken off. Their form and angle to the ground suggests that the figurine originally stood on something curved.

A perforated crest runs the whole length of the back, from the top of the head. Prominent high crests are a feature of many boar figurines. However, this example has many tiny, closely-spaced, holes, which have caused a weakness and it has broken off along its entire length. Another perforated example is Hounslow C (Foster 1977, Plate IIIC), which had just six, much larger, perforations.

The boar's large ears point forward. Like Hounslow boar B (Foster 1977, Plate III B). The right ear of the Norfolk boar carries the second deliberate unexplained casting feature (Figure 3). This, again, has no possible function. It is a clear semi-circular notch, which must be symbolic. However, it does have a resonance with anther boar figurine from beyond Britain, which was discovered in France, at Soulac-sur-Mer, Dep. Gironde, just under 100km north of Bordeaux (Moreau, Boudet and Schaaf 1990). That example has a deliberately-placed patch of silver on its ear, which echoes the mark on the Norfolk example.

Discussion

It has been suggested that at least one of the Hounslow boars was used as a helmet crest (Green 1992, 152). It is known that other representations of boars could be used in this way, as depicted on a first century BC silver coin from Hungary (Green 1992, 158; Megaw and Megaw 2001, 161). The angle of the Ashmanhaugh boar's feet suggests that it was originally attached to a curved surface, which may have been a helmet. The figurine probably dates from the first century BC - AD.

A tantalising feature of the figurine is the hint of symbolic meaning present, as betrayed by the casting details outlined above. Their significance is apparent but their meaning remains obscure.

The prominence of the boar on the coinage in this part of Britain may signify that the creature had a particular significance in northern East Anglia. It is depicted on the coinage of the Iceni and that of their western neighbours, the Corieltauvi in some of the more prolific issues of silver coinage (Figure 4). The Icenian issue in question is a silver type, known as the boar-horse (Van Arsdell 1989, 655-1 to 663-1). The creature is stylised, with a body which widens towards the shoulder but with no neck or head developing from the body. A distinctive crest, characteristic of Celtic boars, runs the length of the back. This was the first really large series of silver coins produced under the Iceni. The silver issues produced by the Corieltauvi were similar in style, although they do exhibit a slightly wider variety of treatment (Van Arsdell 1989, 236-246).

FIGURE 5. THE BOAR FIGURINE FROM CRANWICH. COPYRIGHT NORFOLK MUSEUMS & ARCHAEOLOGY SERVICE.

The Cranwich boar. Figure 5

The bronze boar figurine discovered at Cranwich, on the Norfolk fen-edge, was briefly mentioned above. It was found by metal-detection in 1990 but has remained unpublished. It is now in private hands and the owner is unknown. A resin cast of the figurine was donated to Norwich Castle Museum by the finder in 2005.

This was a solid cast figurine and the boar has been portrayed in a lifelike way, contrasting in style with the Ashmanhaugh example. It sits on a 3-tiered rectangular plinth, with the outer edges measuring 51mm x 41mm. The whole figurine measures 47mm in height, from the bottom of the base to the top of the crest.

There has been careful attention to realistic detail. It is more in the tradition of the Lexden Tumulus figurine, from Essex (Foster 1977, Plate II) and the example from Colchester, Essex (Foster 1977, Plate XIe). It is depicted in a seated position, with folded rear legs, while the front legs are raised, very similarly to the Colchester example. The head is bent towards the right. A crest runs from between the out-turned ears, down the back, to the tail. Hair on the face and upper body has been textured realistically but is more stylised with flowing lines on the haunches and on the crest.

The Lexden figurine was dated to the late pre-Roman Iron Age (Foster 1977, 7-10) and that from Colchester to the Roman period (Foster 1977, 21). The Cranwich example may be considered to date from the first century AD.

FIGURE 4. THE IMAGE OF A BOAR, DEPICTED ON THE ICENIAN COIN, KNOWN AS THE BOAR-HORSE TYPE. COPYRIGHT NORFOLK MUSEUMS & ARCHAEOLOGY SERVICE.

FIGURE 6. THE BOVINE DRINKING HORN TERMINAL FROM NEEDHAM. COPYRIGHT NORFOLK MUSEUMS & ARCHAEOLOGY SERVICE.

A bovine drinking horn terminal from Needham. Figure 6

Discovery

This striking object was discovered at Needham, south Norfolk, in 2008, once again by metal-detection. The location was immediately south-west of the location of a known Romano-British settlement, which was partially excavated by Professor Sheppard Frere (Frere, 1941). Clay moulds for making Iron Age silver coins were also discovered there, suggesting that this may have originally been an Icenian settlement of some status. No other evidence of that date has been discovered, although this may have been removed by extensive gravel working across the area.

The bull in Celtic society

Cattle were important in everyday life to the farming Celts. They were used for draught work, especially ploughing, as well as being important for milk and leather. The possession of cattle was a measure of wealth, as reflected in the early Ulster chronicle, the '*Tain Bo Cuailnge*', or 'cattle raid of Cooley' (Kinsella 1969). Bulls were equated with possessing strength and they were also considered to have great powers.

Description

The extraordinary object from Needham is a cast copper alloy drinking horn terminal. It is broadly conical in shape, with the shaft and tip curving round and forming a bull's head. The shaft is hollow. The condition is good, with a fine green patina, although patches of green corrosion are present along the shaft, as well as on the head and horns. The head can be described as Celtic in style. The complete object measures 78mm in length. The maximum diameter of the open terminal is 19mm, narrowing to 15mm. The shaft narrows towards the terminal and reduces to 9mm at its narrowest point, at the bull's neck.

Part of the open socket is broken, with a fragment missing from its side. A moulded ring, with narrower ring either side, is located approximately two-thirds along the shaft, in line with, and joined to, the bull's chin. The head, which forms the tip, is solid cast. It curves round and looks back towards the open socket. It has large and prominent lentoid eyes. The face is short and there are longitudinal grooves at the nose, which has a hole through the nostrils.

Two horns project upwards and outwards. The left horn terminates in a round knob, while that from the right horn is missing and the broken horn has been rounded off smoothly. Its condition indicates an ancient break. A doe-headed knife handle from Birdlip (Glos) has similar spheres on the tips of the horns. The Norfolk bull's expression is dramatised by brows which over-hang the eyes, formed by the horns. The brows become less pronounced towards the centre but then form a central lump between the eyes.

A very close parallel for this item is another metal-detector find which also appears to have been discovered in Norfolk (*The Searcher*, February 2009). This similar find is slightly smaller, described as 60mm in length, and similarly hollow-cast. The open end has holes either side for attachment. The narrow end curves round and forms the neck of an animal head, in a very similar way to that of the Needham bull. Again, this example has lentoid eyes and a long muzzle, which narrows towards large flaring nostrils. A difference is that it once had ears, one of which stands proud from one side of the head but the other has broken off. Although this is a parallel for the Needham example in its style and key features, it differs in the type of creature being portrayed. It may be more accurate to describe this as *dragonesque*, although its closeness to the Needham terminal might suggest that it was just possibly intended to portray another bull.

Two other cast copper alloy terminals were discovered at Snettisham in 1989. Although their precise function has not been agreed, it is possible that these too were from the tips of drinking horns. They are not fully published but one has been illustrated (Gurney 1990). They were both subsequently acquired by the British Museum. The sockets were much shorter than the Needham example. The illustrated terminal is just 50mm in length and its socket is wider than those described above, measuring 30mm. The overall similarity in style and form is, however, unmistakable. The illustrated example appears to represent a bird, possibly a swan, head. The beak has a very close shape to the snout of the unprovenanced dragon/bull terminal described above.

A more distant parallel must also be considered here. A pair of gold drinking horns was discovered within the Klein Aspergle grave-group, within a princely tomb at Hochdorf, Switzerland (Harding 2007, 39-40). There, within an earlier late Halstatt context, both drinking horn terminals were decorated in the form of rams' heads.

Bulls' heads were used regularly to adorn large metalwork items in Britain. Bovine bucket handle escutcheons are known from Felmersham (Beds), Thealby (Lincs), Welshpool (Montgomeryshire), Lydney (Glos) and Holyhead Island (Anglesey). They are also known to adorn the ends of iron fire dogs, with known examples coming from Capel Garmon (Denbigh), Mount Bures (Essex), Barton (Cambs), Welwyn (Herts), Baldock (Herts) and Stanfordbury (Beds). They were also used on more delicate items, such as a mirror handle from Ingleton (Yorks).

Discussion

Drinking horns are not common finds within Iron Age contexts in Britain but elaborate examples are well known from Europe. A burial at Eigenbilzen in Belgium contained part of a gold ornamental mount from a drinking horn (Harding 2007, 42). The princely tomb at Hochdorf, mentioned above, contained a total of nine drinking horns. The Schwarzenbach, Saarland, princely burial of the 5th century BC contained gold discs, from drinking horn caps (Frey 1971).

Within Britain, other examples of drinking-related objects are known from the territory of the Iceni. Tankard handles have come from Billingford and West Rudham in Norfolk, both examples of which are held at Norwich Castle Museum. The Needham drinking horn may be dated to the first century BC - AD.

The significance of food and drink preparation and consumption in prehistoric societies sometimes had an importance beyond that of the merely functional. What we might see as domestic activities could overlap with specialised rituals (Bradley 2005,106). The association of a drinking horn with elaborate Celtic style animal-inspired art is consistent with this view.

The Crownthorpe drinking cups. Figure 7

Discovery

In 1982 the Norfolk Archaeological Unit undertook a survey of an important Roman site at Crownthorpe, to the west of Wymondham in central Norfolk. The detector user working with the team discovered a large bowl-like vessel, which contained a further six smaller vessels, which had been deliberately buried (Davies 2009, 9-10). The group of vessels formed a drinking set of the type used within a Roman household. There was a strainer bowl, a patera bowl, two shallow bowls, a deep saucepan and two drinking cups. The cups form a matching pair, each carrying handles decorated with Celtic style swimming ducks, unparalleled outside this hoard.

Ducks/birds in Celtic art

Birds were a recurring presence in Celtic mythology and regular motif in their art. Examples of their use include the bronze flesh-fork from Dunaverney, Co. Antrim, which depicts a procession of swans, cygnets and ravens along its shaft, and a small bird mount from a vessel rim from St Catherine's Hill, Winchester (Hants), which appears to depict a duck. There is also a bronze duck figurine, with a flat bottom, from Milber (Devon). A beautiful bronze bowl from Keshcarrigan (Co Leitrim) has a complete handle formed in the shape of a curved duck or swan's neck and beak.

FIGURE 7. A DRINKING CUP WITH DUCK SHAPED HANDLES, FROM THE CROWNTHORPE HOARD. COPYRIGHT NORFOLK MUSEUMS & ARCHAEOLOGY SERVICE.

Description

The bronze cups from Crownthorpe are a closely matching pair. Each has an ovoid body on a small pedestal foot, with two projecting handles. The bases and handles were cast, using the *cire perdue* method, while the bowls were raised and beaten into shape. No hammer marks are visible but they were removed by later working and polishing.

The top surface of the rim and the upper and lower mouldings of the pedestal base are ornamented with a zig-zag line in relief. The small semi-circular handles are round-sectioned and their lower attachment is a round, buffer-like, terminal. There is an upper horizontal element with fluted mouldings on the extensions that curve round the rim. A slightly flared base supports the figure of a swimming duck. The ducks' bodies have a grooved pattern which suggest wings and feathers. They had been cast with hollows for the eyes, which were inlaid with champleve enamel, which has retained its red colour. The pedestal bases and handles are attached to the vessels with brass rivets.

These vessels emulate Roman silver examples, such as those from Hockwold-cum-Wilton (Johns 1986) and Welwyn Garden City (Stead 1967). They were probably locally produced, based on the Roman silver imports, but with local additions. The ducks are certainly not in the classical tradition and are typical of the Celtic Zoo. There are close parallels for these ducks on the lids of wine-strainers from Santon Downham, Norfolk, and Brandon, Suffolk. This deposit has been dated to approximately 60AD.

Norfolk's wolf. Figure 8

Another creature represented within the iconography of the Iceni is the wolf. It appears on their coinage, on an early uninscribed gold type known as the *Norfolk Wolf* (British JA and JB; Van Arsdell 1989, types 610-1 to 610-5).

Wolves were native to Britain during the Iron Age. As the natural woodland was cleared, they would have retreated to higher ground and parts of northern Britain. They were exterminated fairly early from lowland Britain (Yalden 1999, 132) and would not have been present in large numbers, if at all, in northern East Anglia at that time. So, it is perhaps strange that this creature should have been chosen for prominent depiction on their coinage.

The wolf is less commonly depicted than other creatures considered in this paper. There is little evidence to suggest that they were exploited or hunted. Their bones occur within site assemblages in very small numbers. They were a wild, undomesticated, creature, with a fierce reputation.

The Iron Age in Northern East Anglia: New Work in the Land of the Iceni

FIGURE 8. THE WOLF DEPICTED ON TWO GOLD COINS OF THE ICENI (NORFOLK WOLF TYPE STATER AND QUARTER STATER). COPYRIGHT NORFOLK MUSEUMS & ARCHAEOLOGY SERVICE.

FIGURE 9. A HORSE DEPICTED ON A SILVER COIN OF THE ICENI (BURY A TYPE SILVER UNIT). COPYRIGHT NORFOLK MUSEUMS & ARCHAEOLOGY SERVICE.

The *Norfolk Wolf* coin was one of the first issues of the Iceni. It is a gold stater, thought to have been produced between 65-45BC. The wolf is depicted as a fierce-looking long-legged creature, with arched shoulders and wide open jaws, with large teeth. Varieties face both left (British JB; Van Arsdell 610-2,3,5) and right (British JA; Van Arsdell 610-1). In recent years two smaller examples, or quarter staters, of the Norfolk Wolf have been discovered in Norfolk (JA Quarter). Both have been acquired by Norwich Castle Museum.

The wolf is not represented on other tribal coinages. Neither was it represented in the form of figurines or other forms of decoration, like the bull or ram. It appears to have been an icon peculiar to the Iceni.

The horse. Figure 9

When considering representations of animals within the Icenian area, mention must be made of the horse. This creature was of great importance to this tribe, as reflected in the very high proportion of horse-related items, such as terret rings, linch pins and bridle bits, found within their metalwork. It can be surmised that this was an important horse rearing area. More generally, horses enjoyed a high status within Celtic society and many divinities were closely associated with them (Green 1992, 72).

Despite its importance in everyday life the horse was not represented in the form of figurines like other creatures, such as the bull and boar. Its image was restricted to coins. Within the coinage of the Iceni, horses were represented on all but one of their issues - in which the *Norfolk Wolf* was used to replace it.

The engravings of horses on Icenian coins varied considerably. Gold staters within Talbot's *Early Boar Horse* series and BHB / BHC types (Talbot, this volume) carry a distinctive stocky and powerful beast, in strong relief. The most beautiful rendering is seen on the early *Bury type* silver units, which again shows the horse in a rounded high relief, in a prancing attitude.

Closing thoughts

The important discoveries of Iron Age objects considered here show that representations of animals were indeed a regular feature within Iron Age Norfolk. This diverse range of animal representations has been identified largely through the contribution of finds made by metal-detection. Within Norfolk's own Celtic menagerie, we have evidence for the boar, bull, duck, swan and possibly dragon to accompany the wolf and horse, which were previously known from Icenian coinage.

This material provides a significant contribution to the study and re-assessment of Celtic art in Britain, which is in itself undergoing a revival (Garrow, Gosden and Hill, 2008). Objects designed to represent animals can be seen to have permeated different aspects of everyday life and

FIGURE 10. THE ICENIAN BOAR-HORSE SILVER UNIT. THIS VARIANT SHOWS A PELLET MARKING THE RIGHT SHOULDER.

the examples from Norfolk represent activities which included fighting, feasting and drinking.

The Ashmanhaugh boar figurine also adds an intriguing and mysterious element to this group of objects, with the fascinating mark on its right shoulder. There is evidence elsewhere which appears to corroborate a significance associated with pig shoulders; in particular on the right side. At Llanmaes in south Wales, in an Early Iron Age context, an abundance of pig bones at the site shows this to have been valued as a feasting meat (Current Archaeology 233, August 2009, 32). However, it was noted there that there is a very strong pattern of only the right fore-quarters of the pig being incorporated into the site's midden, indicating a specific selection and separation of that specific portion. This observation echoes the recognition of the marking on the Norfolk figurine. A further example comes from Hallaton in Leicestershire, where excavations at this Iron Age ritual site recovered a large animal bone assemblage, of which 97% were pig bones slaughtered before they were 18 months old (Score and Clay 2011). It was noted that while all anatomical elements were present, there was a clear absence of right forelimbs among them. Yet another addition to this growing list comes in the form of the Boar-horse coin type of the Iceni, (previously mentioned above). Specific sub-types of this issue (Van Arsdell type 655-1, 657-3, 659-3) depict a pellet prominently featured on the right shoulder of the animal; a feature to which no significance has previously been attributed (Figure 10). We are not yet in a position to explain the importance of the right shoulders of boars at that time but this expanding corpus of examples, which draws attention to that part of the animal in terms of both faunal remains and in representations of the creature, shows how they clearly possessed significance in some respect. These observations will be pursued elsewhere (Davies *in prep*).

Attention has also been drawn elsewhere to a whole range of symbols used by the Iceni in their objects and coins, (Davies 2009, 110-11). Although it is not yet possible to more than guess at their meaning, it is clear that these symbols were not mere decorative space-filling devices and that they had meaning and significance. The casting details recognised on the Ashmanhaugh boar figurine make a significant addition to this intriguing list of examples. In particular, the marking of the right ear suggests a mysterious connection, with a significance spanning spanning a thousand miles across north-west Europe.

Acknowledgements

I would like to thank Andrew Fitzpatrick, of Wessex Archaeology, and Tim Pestell, of Norwich Castle Museum, for providing helpful information during my research for this paper. Figures 1-9 were taken by Neil Jinkerson and 10 was by John Talbot.

Bibliography

Art Fund Review 2007/2008.

Bradley R., 2005. *Ritual and Domestic Life in Prehistoric Europe*. London, Routledge.

Current Archaeology 233 August 2009. The champion's portion? Prehistoric feasting at Llanmaes, 29-35.

Davies, J. 2009. *The Land of Boudica: Prehistoric and Roman Norfolk*. Oxford, Heritage/Oxbow.

Davies, J. *in prep*. The Wild Boar in late British Prehistory.

Frere, S. 1941. A Claudian site at Needham, Norfolk. *Antiquaries Journal* 21, 40-55.

Frey, O-H. 1971. Die Goldschale von Schwarzenbach. *Hamburger Beitrage zur Archaologie* 1(2), 85-100.

Garrow, D., Gosden, C. and Hill, J.D. (eds) 2008. *Rethinking Celtic Art*. Oxford, Oxbow.

Foster, J. 1977. *Bronze Boar Figurines in Iron Age and Roman Britain*. British Archaeological Report 39.

Green, M. 1989. *Symbol and Image in Celtic Religious Art*. London, Routledge.

Green, M. 1992. *Animals in Celtic Life and Myth*. London, Routledge.

Gurney, D. (ed) 1990. Archaeological finds in Norfolk 1989. *Norfolk Archaeology* 41(1), 101.

Harding, D. W. 2007. *The Archaeology of Celtic Art*. London, Routledge.

Hill, J. D. 1995. *Ritual and rubbish in the Iron Age of Wessex*. British Archaeological Report 242.

Jackson, R. 1990. *Camerton: The Late Iron Age and Early Roman Metalwork*. London, British Museum Press.

Johns, C. 1986. The Roman silver cups from Hockwold, Norfolk. *Archaeologia* 108, 1-13.

Jope, E. M. 2000. *Celtic Art in the British Isles*. Oxford, University Press.

Kinsella, T. (trans) 1969. *The Tain*. Oxford, University Press.

Megaw, R. and V. 2001. *Celtic Art*. London, Thames and Hudson.

Moreau, J., Boudet R. and Schaaf, U. 1990. Un sanglier-enseigne a Soulac-sur-Mer, Dep. Gironde. *Archaeologisches Korrespondenzblatt* 20, 439-442.

Portable Antiquities Scheme Annual Report 2005/6. A first-century BC to first-century AD figurine of a boar from Duncton, West Sussex. 37.

Score, V. and Clay P. 2011. Rituals, hoards and helmets. *The Archaeologist* 80, 24-25.

The Searcher 282, February 2009.

Stead, I. M. 1967. A La Tene burial at Welwyn Garden City. *Archaeologia* 101, 1-62.

Van Arsdell, R. D. 1989. *Celtic Coinage of Britain*. London, Spink.

Yalden, D. 1999. *The History of British Mammals*. London, T&AD Poyser.

Icenian coin production

John Talbot

Introduction

During the Late Iron Age the inhabitants of East Anglia used alloys of silver and of gold to produce a sophisticated and beautiful coinage. A number of problems confront any attempt to produce a classification and chronology of the coinage, not the least of which is that most issues are un-inscribed. With the encouragement of Dr Philip de Jersey, lately of the Celtic Coin Index in Oxford, I have endeavoured to develop some new insights into the coinage by completing a die study of all recorded examples of this coinage.

As my study of the coinage proceeded I became increasingly aware both of its complexity and of the underlying organisation of the people that produced it. In accordance with common usage I shall refer to these people as the Iceni. One objective of this paper is to convey a sense of the sophistication of the coinage as well as to provide a few interesting conclusions and findings from my study.

The die study itself took some nine years to complete and was based on a coin by coin examination of the photographic records of over 9,500 coins as well as a physical examination of the coins present in major public and private collections. This is believed to be the first time, since the dramatic increase in the availability of material as a result of metal detecting, that an entire British Iron Age tribal coinage has been the subject of such a study. The die study was completed a year or so ago, since when I using the results as a basis for further analysis of the coinage and these are some early results of that work.

The method of coin production and the die study

Icenian coins were produced by striking a metal pellet, sitting on a concave anvil die, with a convex hammer die. The striking surface of each die carried a cut design, a mirror image of which was produced on the relevant side of each struck coin. Each die was produced manually and although many dies were very similar none were identical. A key element in the die study was to build a corpus of known dies by carefully examining each recorded coin to identify the dies which were used to strike it.

Fortunately the hammer and anvil dies were not physically connected and it was common for each hammer die to be used with several different anvil dies and vice versa. Thus the die study has often revealed lengthy sequences of dies which are linked to each other through recorded coins. Dies wear with use, and because new dies were gradually introduced into a 'mint' it is possible to produce a definitive chronological sequence within a linked group of dies without relying upon guesswork. Such sequences facilitate the identification of the latest coins included in a hoard and can produce relative chronologies when hoards contain significant volumes of material from more than one mint.

An example of a chronological sequence for the Ecen silver unit is shown in Figure 1 to illustrate the use of dies to establish chronology. This table shows the obverses and reverses of specific coins together with the identification number of the coin from the Celtic Coin Index (e.g. 96 3598) and my own die reference; always alphabetical for obverse dies and numerical for reverse dies. Strikes from a worn die often look quite different to strikes made when the die was new. For instance it is not immediately clear that die J on coin 68 1265 is the same die which was later used on coin 95 1775, but to facilitate the die study records have been maintained of changes in dies as they deteriorate. As an example of this process, an illustration of an "intermediate state" of die J (coin 95 1789) has been inserted into the sequence in Figure 1.

I refer to dies that can be linked into a single interconnected chain as being a "die group". The die study has revealed a number of examples where what was thought to be a single Icenian issue is actually composed of distinct die groups which have differing distributions and which appear to have been produced separately but at the same time follow strict design parameters. The identification of die groups which were originally produced separately from other similar groups is not straightforward. A high survival rate of coins relative to the number of dies helps to establish whether one is dealing with separate groups of dies that have never been linked or with gaps in a continuous die chain that will eventually be filled as more coins come to light.

Counts of the number of dies found in particular coinages can indicate production volumes and the original relative importance of different issues. When the number of dies used to strike an issue is given in this paper this is always

FIGURE 1. A CHRONOLOGICAL DIE-LINKED SEQUENCE OF ECEN SILVER UNITS.

the combined total of both obverse and reverse dies, unless otherwise stated.

A feature of British Iron Age coinages is that the dies were almost invariably much larger than the struck coins and therefore each coin will only contain a part of the design on the actual die. This complicates die identification and as an aid to the study I have developed a technique for producing composite photographic images of dies using two or more coins. These are used in a number of the figures in this paper which accounts for the irregularity in the shape of certain illustrations. The obverses of the JB staters shown in Figure 3 are examples of composite images. A description of the technique by Ian Leins is included in an article in the Numismatic Journal (Talbot and Leins 2010).

Ordering the Coinage

As part of the study I have developed a hypothesis for the organisation and chronology of the coinage. This now includes the division of coinage production into four main periods:

- Early local coinage – this was the first period of production and issues were sub-regional in terms of minting and distribution and without any apparent stylistic links between the gold and the silver coinages.

- First denominational coinages – the next series of issues reveal clear denominational groupings sometimes incorporating all of the known denominations; fractional units, silver units, quarter staters and staters.

- Middle denominational coinage – the denominational groupings can now be allocated to three main streams of coinage. In earlier work this and the preceding period were classed as a single middle phase of production (see Talbot and Leins 2010).

- Late denominational coinage - the final period saw the introduction of inscriptions into the denominational coinage and a marked reduction in the use of gold. The coinage continued to be produced in three main streams.

These periods are intended to give a general indication of the development of the coinage and I have given indicative dates to these periods later in this paper. I suspect that the transition from one of the periods to another would have been a gradual process, particularly when there were separate streams of coinage. The separate periods probably reflect change which can only be identified with the benefit of hindsight!

In assessing the relative chronologies of various issues of coinage I have relied heavily upon the data from coin

Saenv dies A:2   Saenv die A paired with Ece B reverse die 22

FIGURE 2. AN ECE B UNIT AND A SAENV UNIT SHARING AN OBVERSE DIE.

hoards used in conjunction with the die study. If for instance the final few dies from type A are present in a hoard, yet only the first few dies from type B, then there is obviously a strong indication that B postdates A.

The hoards dating to the Boudiccan revolt have proved to be exceptionally valuable in providing relative dating evidence. (Talbot forthcoming). These hoards have been found to contain "older" issues in reasonably consistent proportions and I have developed relative chronologies for the later issues by comparing hoard content with casual losses. A detailed discussion of the methodology is beyond the scope of this paper but it has generated a number of unexpected conclusions, an example of which relates to the Aesv and Saenv coinages. These coinages were thought to postdate the Ece coinages and to be one of the final Icenian coinages (see Hobbs, 1996, p 30 and Van Arsdell, 1989, p 211- 212) but the analysis of the revolt hoards suggested that they pre-dated the Ece B coinage. This conclusion was later given strong support when I recorded the obverse die, which had been used to strike all known Aesv and Saenv units, being used in a worn state in conjunction with a fresh Ece B reverse die. This is illustrated in Figure 2. The new ordering is not absolutely definitive as the Ece B reverse die used with the Saenv obverse has so far not been linked to a known Ece B obverse die and thus cannot be put into a proven chronological sequence. It is therefore conceivable, but unlikely, that the Ece B reverse die used with Saenv reverse was an old die or style of die suddenly brought back into use, intentionally or otherwise.

There is no generally accepted nomenclature for the various issues of British Iron Age coinage and most Icenian types are commonly and validly identified by a number of different names or references. Unfortunately some of the rarer types have no accepted name. Other types have misleading names or a name given to what was thought to be a single type but which I or others have separated into two or more distinct types.

It has sometimes been necessary to create a number of new names for Icenian types in order to reflect the underlying logical structure of the coinage. Most of the new names relate to the denominational groupings of coins as it makes

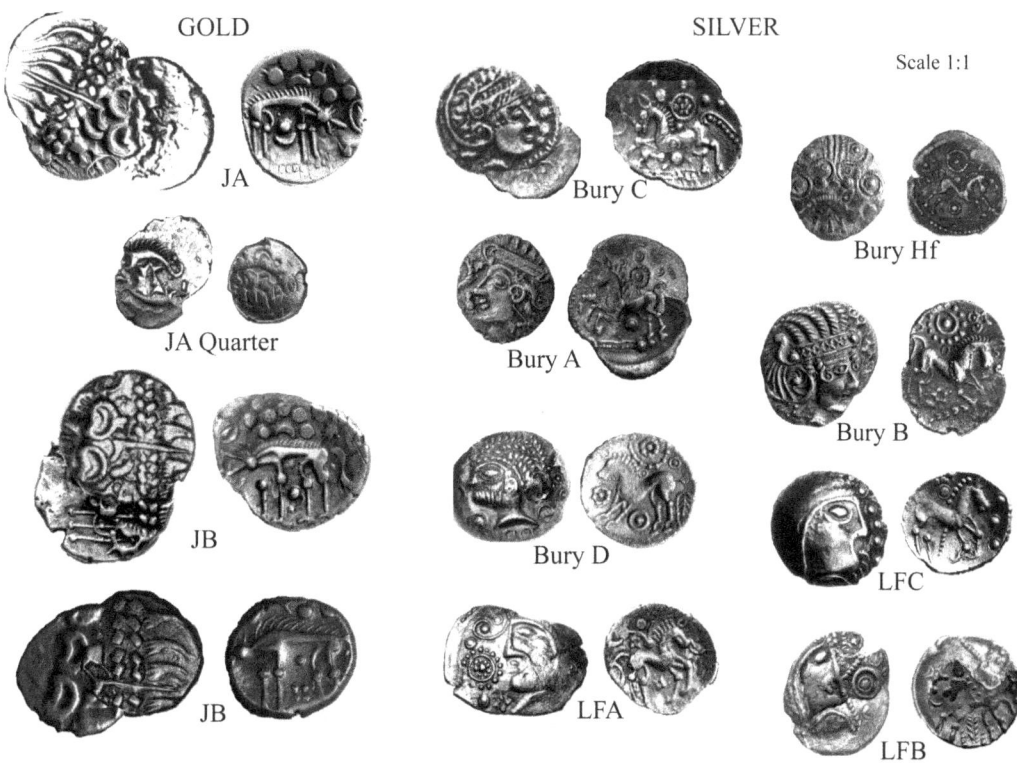

FIGURE 3. EARLY LOCAL COINAGE.

sense to have a single name for such a group which can be used in conjunction with the denomination (for example, Irstead unit and Irstead stater). In almost all cases a name has been used for a group that was already well accepted for one of the component denominations. A concordance for the main Icenian types referred to in this paper is set out as appendix 1.

The main periods of production are discussed in more detail below.

Early local coinage. Figure 3

The main silver coinage of this period is made up of silver units, the earliest of which weighed up to 1.5 grams and had a very high silver content. The obverse of these 'early face horse' units carried a left or right facing head and the reverse a horse, both with considerable extra ornamentation. The early results of the die study into the early face horse coinage, including photographs of all dies known at the time, have been published (Talbot 2006) and examples of many of these types are shown in Figure 3. This coinage also contains fractional units which appear to have been issued at half the weight of the closely related units, which are from issues known as Bury A and C. The fractional units are rare, and only 14 are known, but those were struck from a total of 18 dies, suggesting that the original issue was of reasonable size and dies are yet to be found. An example is included in Figure 3 showing the complex obverse and the clearly Bury related reverse.

The silver units of this period appear to have local distributions, although examples of all types are found at the major centres of Icenian activity such as Saham Toney or Snettisham. Figure 4 illustrates the sub-regional distribution, excluding major Icenian centres, of two similar types, Large Flan A ("LFA") and Large Flan C ("LFC"). It can be seen that the former has a strong focus south of Norwich in the Waveney Valley whereas the latter is strongly biased around Thetford in Breckland. It is probably not a coincidence that both areas contain sites from which pellet mould debris has been recovered.

The main gold coinages of this period are the Norfolk Wolf staters (British JA or JB). The right facing JA is the earliest and is both the heaviest and generally the purest in gold content. The left facing wolf JB was produced in much greater volume and is a more complex issue than JA. Work on the JB issue is still underway but there appear to be a number of different die groups with distinctive distributions suggesting sub-regional production. Two die groups with markedly differing distributions are illustrated in Figure 5.

There are only three known examples of a very rare quarter stater from this period which is related to the JA stater. These three examples are struck from five different dies suggesting a reasonably significant level of production.

There appears to be no stylistic link between the early gold and the early silver coinages and the design of the early silver coinages is particularly complex; I suspect that much will be learned from further study of these and from a comparison with other regional coinages when these have been subjected to a comprehensive die study. It is likely that many design elements which may at first sight appear purely decorative, originally had other significance. I have seen a possible example of this within the LFA coinage where a chronological sequencing of dies reveals that early dies each carried several engravings of a diamond-like symbol which was abruptly replaced by a hollow star which was engraved several times on all subsequent dies.

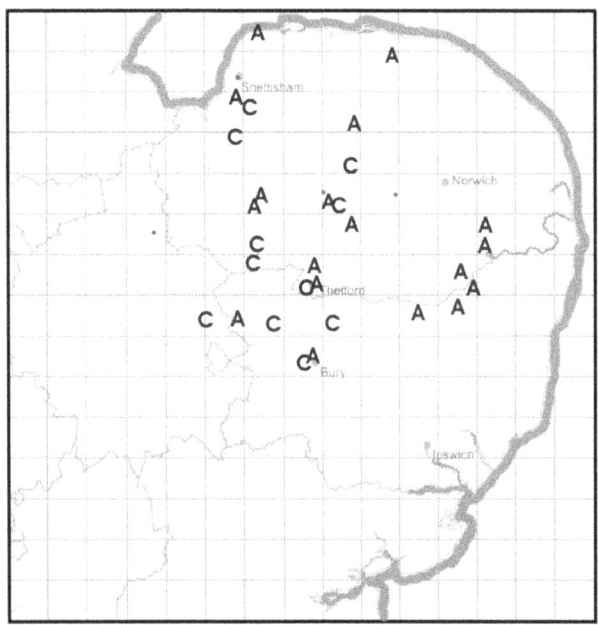

FIGURE 4. THE DISTRIBUTION OF CASUAL LOSSES OF LFA AND LFC.

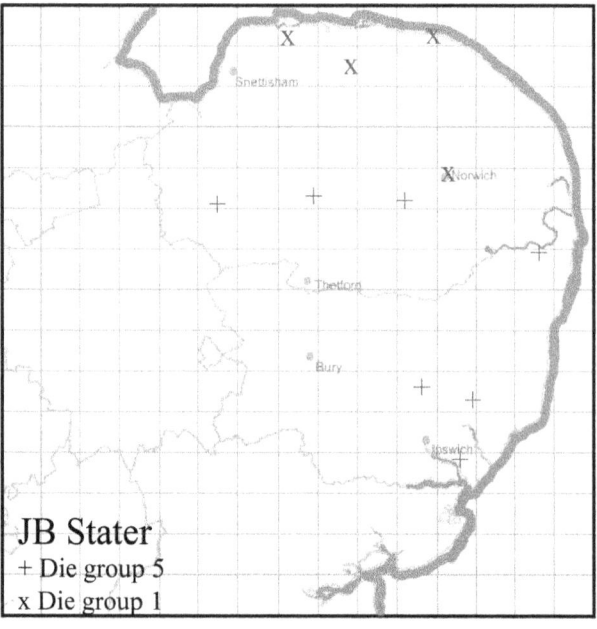

FIGURE 5. THE DISTRIBUTION OF CASUAL LOSSES FOR TWO DIE GROUPS OF JB STATERS.

FIGURE 6. BURY C DIE 8 SHOWING DIE BEFORE AND AFTER RECUTTING.

One or other of these symbols occurs on many early local silver unit coinages, but never together on a single die. This particular symbol change has been helpful, alongside other evidence, in establishing the relative chronology of these early coinages.

Further evidence of the importance of some of the symbols is provided by the changes illustrated in Figure 6. This illustration shows the considerable effort expended in changing a pellet below a horse to a ring by re-cutting a Bury C die. Careful examination of the recut die reveals that the change necessitated re-cutting one of the horse's rear legs to accommodate the new symbol.

Unfortunately it is not always readily apparent which symbols play a similar role to that subsequently played by script and which had other contributions to make. A Canadian numismatist Geraldine Chimirri-Russell (Chimirri-Russell, 2003) has provided valuable assistance here by showing that certain continental issues of the period used elements of design to convert the profile of a head on a coin to a three quarter view of the head when the coin is viewed at an angle. I have found similar effects used on a number of early Icenian issues, examples of which are shown on Figure 7.

FIGURE 7. ICENIAN BURY SERIES COINS SHOWING THE 'CHIMIRRI-RUSSELL' EFFECT.

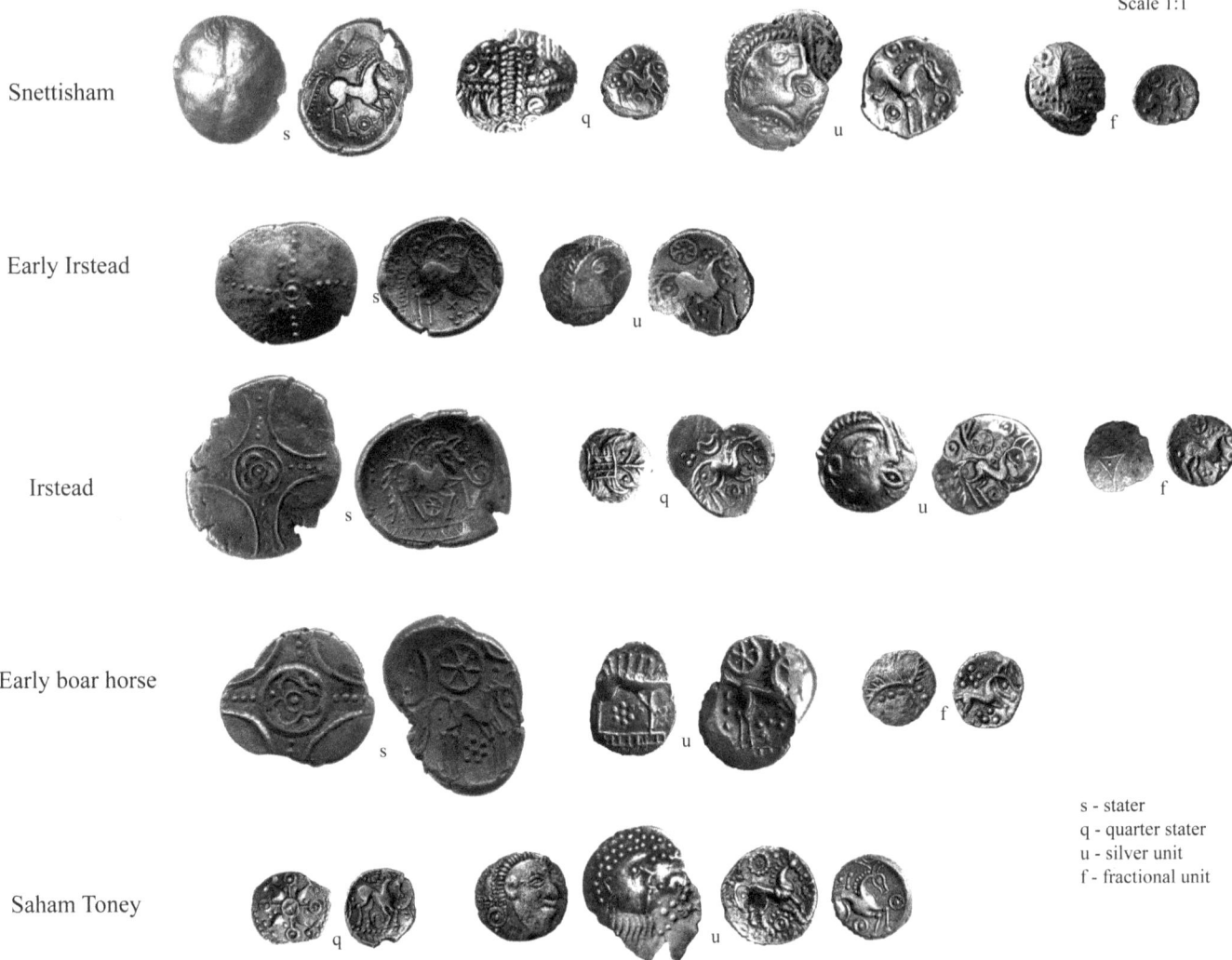

FIGURE 8. THE FIRST DENOMINATIONAL COINAGES OF THE ICENI.

In these examples scrolls in front of the face provide a second eye when the coin is rotated to show frontal view and the nose and chin are cut into the die at differing depths so that they are aligned as the coin is rotated. The illustrations reveal that other design elements such as lines from the mouth and the beard also appear to play a part in enhancing the three-dimensional imagery.

First denominational coinages. Figure 8

The next period saw the emergence of coinages which seem to have been issued in linked denominational groupings. The relationships are apparent from the reverse dies whereas the obverse design elements are typically denomination specific, often showing a degree of continuity through succeeding issues. These coinages generally had a wider area of distribution than the issues of the first period. The die study has revealed an unusually direct relationship within one of the denominational groupings when an Irstead silver unit was found to have been struck from a gold quarter stater reverse die. This is the first recorded example of a single die being used for different denominations in the British Iron Age coinage and is illustrated in Figure 9.

Examples from the five main coinages are shown in Figure 8 together with examples of the denominations making up each coinage. Where possible the main coinages have been given a name which was previously in common usage for at least one of its component denominations.

The Snettisham issue was the earliest of these coinages and was substantial. I have so far recorded 47 dies for the gold coinage and 45 for the silver; more dies are likely to be found as there are relatively few known coins for each recorded die. The intermediate Early Irstead coinage has a low survival rate and has been separated from the ensuing Irstead coinage as most staters and all silver units can be readily identified as being distinct from their Irstead counterparts. The final stater dies became identical in style to the first Irstead staters and this coinage may eventually prove to be die-linked to, and form a continuum with, Irstead.

FIGURE 9. IRSTEAD GOLD QUARTER STATER AND SILVER UNIT SHARING A REVERSE DIE.

The Irstead coinage was predominantly struck in gold, with a particularly large issue of quarter staters. Neither the previous Early Irstead nor the subsequent Early Boar Horse ("EBH") coinages included quarter staters. It may be that the Irstead quarter staters had a longer period of issue than the other Irstead denominations and also formed part of one or both of the other two coinages.

The EBH coinage is very distinctive, with exceptionally deeply cut dies. This coinage is unique amongst major Icenian issues in having almost as many recorded fractional unit dies as there are for full units (twelve compared to thirteen). It appears clear that EBH followed Irstead but it is uncertain whether or not there was an overlap in production between the last few dies of Irstead and the first few of EBH.

The Saham Toney coinage was mainly issued in silver, with the only known related gold coinage being a small number of quarter staters. The Saham Toney group is unusual in having a range of stylistically different units in the group, all of which are die-linked.

Work is still underway on the distribution and other features of the separate die groups which make up many of the types in these denominational groupings and also in comparing the respective distributions of different denominations within each issue.

The end of this period and the beginning of the next may have marked a period of some instability in East Anglia as at least three hoards of staters are dated to the end of production of Early Boar Horse or shortly thereafter (Talbot and Leins, 2010, 10-14).

Middle and Late Denominational Coinages. Figure 10

The final periods of coin production saw a number of changes from earlier periods including a rapid reduction in the use of gold and much larger silver issues than hitherto. Another change was the emergence of at least three streams of coinage which appear to have been produced simultaneously. I refer to each stream as the production of a "mint group" rather than an individual mint as the evidence suggests that in the cases of mint groups A and B there was more than one site producing coinage although under some form of central direction. This period also saw the introduction of inscribed coinage, although this was produced in parallel with the un-inscribed late face horse ('LFH') series.

The larger issues of late silver units are summarised in Figure 11 below, ranked by the total number of known dies used in their manufacture.

Figure 11 is an attempt to indicate the original relative importance of the major issues of late silver units based upon the number of dies from which they were struck. The table shows that the issues which are now the most common, such as Anted and Ecen, were originally very much less important than BHC and also probably much less important than EPH(A) where survival levels are low and new dies are still regularly encountered.

The three streams of coinage are easily separated on stylistic grounds as illustrated in Figure 10. The form of the horse, and in particular its head, is diagnostic; see for example the reverses of BHC, Anted and Ecen from the first group and similarly EPH(A) and LFH from the second group. The relative chronology of these coinages is based upon analysis of the Boudiccan Revolt hoards and is logical and well supported by the evidence. Nonetheless, elements of the ordering are not in line with some previous thinking including the relative timing of LFH which is discussed below. A new element to the chronology is the placing of Saenv prior to Ece B, as discussed above.

The largest group of coinage includes BHB and BHC as well as the Anted and Ecen series and is referred to as mint group A. This mint group appears to represent the continuation of the major mint or mints operating in period 2, as can be seen by comparing the form of horse used on, say, BHC with that used in the previous period on the EBH issue. Mint group A issued gold staters in a denominational grouping with each of its main silver units although production of gold declined over the course of the period. The final issues were Anted and Ecen and there are only seven dies known to have been used to strike the related gold staters. It has been suggested that a sub-group of three of these stater dies relate to the Ece units and thus mint group C as their reverses seem to be inscribed Ece but this is unlikely as there are no other stylistic links between the

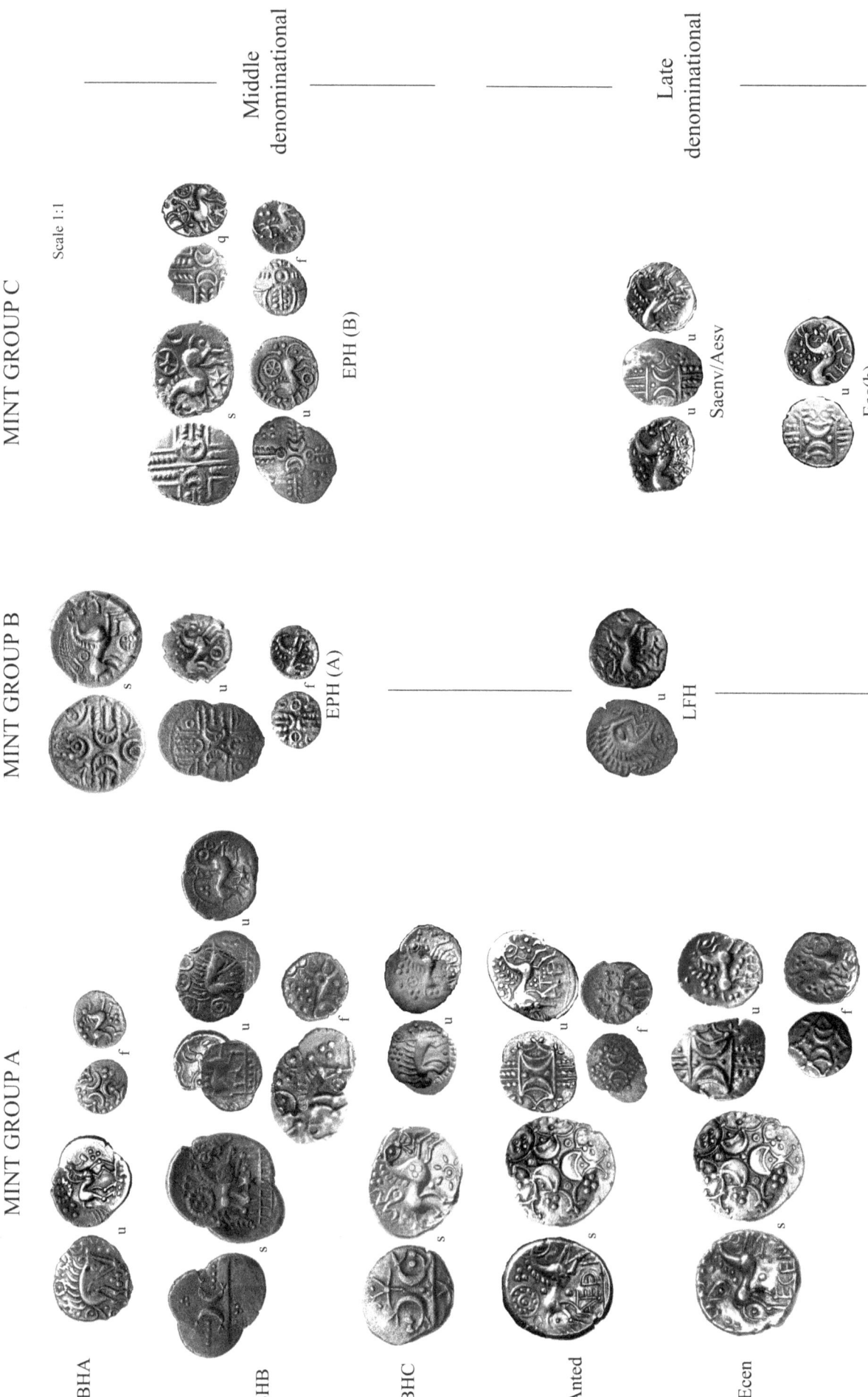

FIGURE 10. THE MIDDLE AND LATE DENOMINATIONAL COINAGES.

Type of unit	Number of dies	Surviving coins
LFH	204	1374
BHC	144	435
EPH(A)	89	132
Ecen (including Symbol)	73	1577
Anted	72	1161
BHB	47	264
EPH(B)	30	129

FIGURE 11. THE RANKING OF LATE SILVER UNITS BY THE NUMBER OF DIES USED IN PRODUCTION.

sub-group of staters and the other coinage of mint group C. All silver units had corresponding fractional units but so far only one type of quarter stater has been tentatively linked to a stater from mint group A (not illustrated).

The second largest mint group is B, which has no obvious predecessor mints, yet which produced silver coinage in great volume during this final period of coin production. As shown in Figure 11 the LFH series was the biggest single silver issue of the Iceni and involved the use of at least 200 dies. EPH(A) was also a very large issue, but as it was earlier than LFH it is not well represented in the Boudiccan hoards and so is relatively rare today. The survival rate per die for EPH(A) is one of the lowest for a significant issue of silver units in the whole Icenian series and it is possible that much of the issue was recalled for re-minting as LFH.

The two issues of mint group B are still being studied but already display a number of very interesting features:

- Both issues appear to have been produced in a large number of separate die groups and certain die groups appear to have distinctive regional distributions for non-hoard coins. This suggests there were separate mint sites which produced coins following centrally controlled design criteria. The dies themselves do not appear to have been prepared centrally as many of the die groups have distinctive dies which, although cut to follow standard designs, are readily separable on an artistic basis.

- There has been much speculation about whether LFH predated the inscribed silver issues such as Anted. The hoard analysis suggests that LFH was issued over a longer period than contemporary issues and continued until the final stages of Icenian coin production. Indeed in respect of one die group of LFH, coins with a known provenance are at present only recorded from Boudiccan revolt hoards, the absence of provenanced casual losses suggesting that it this may be one of final issues of the Iceni.

- Despite the large size of the silver unit issue LFH, there are no other known related denominations in either silver or gold. The earlier EPH(A) was issued with a fractional unit which, whilst rare, is already known from seventeen dies. There was also a debased gold stater issued in conjunction with EPH(A) although this was apparently a small issue emanating from a single pair of dies.

Mint group C is the smallest of the three main streams of coinage and its reverse dies are readily recognisable as they bear an image of a horse with a distinctive Y shaped head. This group appears to have its stylistic origins in the Saham Toney unit of the previous period, (see the Y headed horse illustrated on the Saham Toney unit in Fig 8).

Preliminary work on the distribution of casual losses suggests that mint group C had a more restricted central Norfolk distribution than the other two mint groups. This group seems more likely than the others to have produced coinage on an intermittent basis probably from a single site.

Later local types. Figure 12

In addition to the major issues of coinage already covered in this paper there were also a series of smaller issues often appearing to be quite local in distribution and many of which have close stylistic links to the Late Iron Age coinage of the regions immediately to the south of East Anglia ('North Thames'). These include the Esv Prasto coinage which has frequently been mis-described as the final Icenian issue. An early reading of the inscription caused the coins to be attributed to Prasutagus, the husband of Boudicca, until clearer examples appeared and the corrected reading of the obverse die, 'svb esvprasto', was given by Jonathon Williams (Williams, 2000). Because of the general interest in this issue I include below some observations arising from the present study:

- The seventeen known Esv Prasto coins were struck from three obverse and five reverse dies giving a die count which is low in comparison with most other issues of Icenian silver units.

- The heaviest Esv Prasto unit only weighs 1.05g. This makes the issue underweight when compared to the late Icenian silver units which typically weigh between 1.2 and 1.3 grams when in good condition.

- The Esv Prasto coins are not found in the Boudiccan Revolt hoards. They are very rare

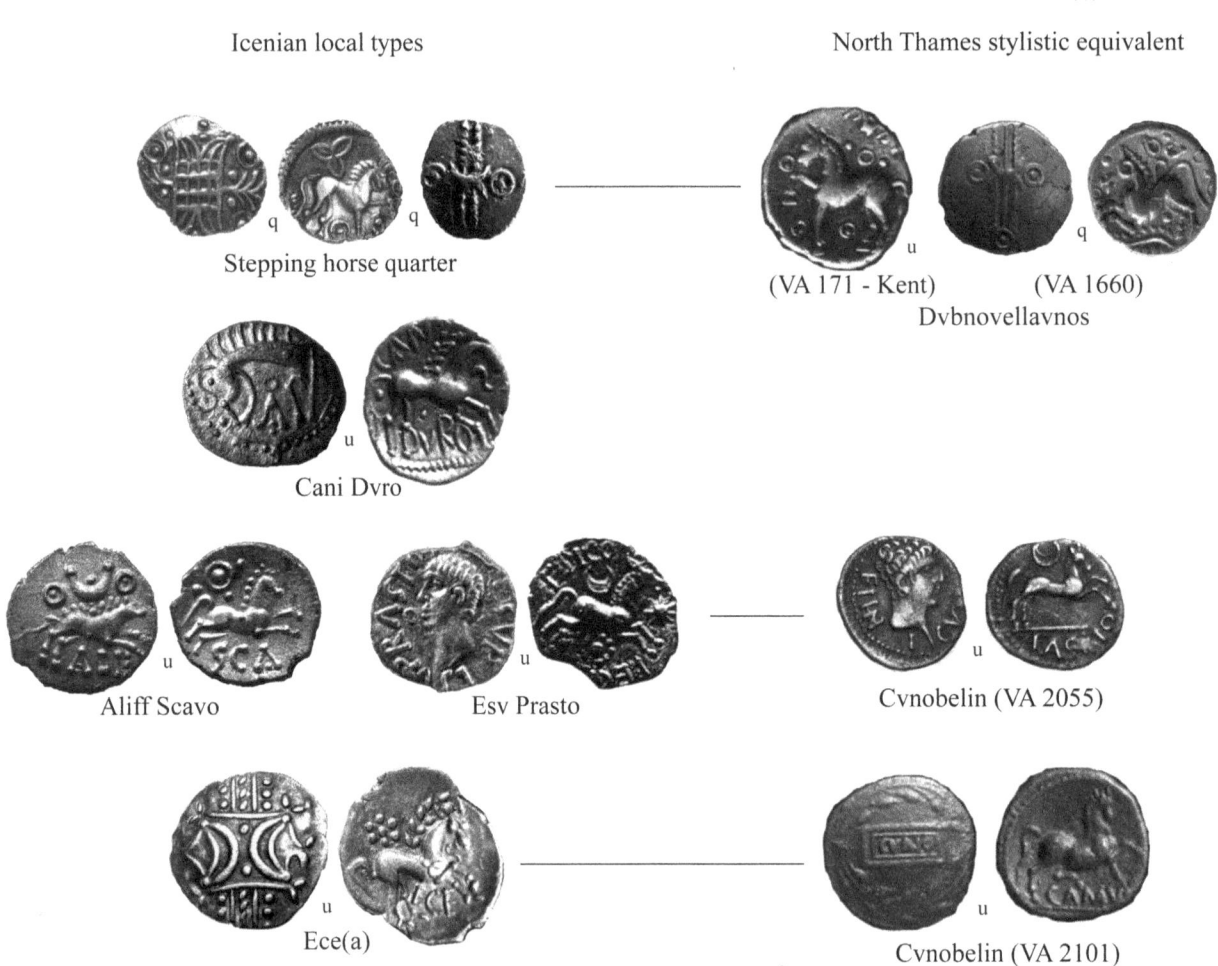

FIGURE 12. LATER LOCAL COINAGES.

and have only been found at Joist Fen, Fincham and another location in western Norfolk. The Fincham assemblage is not believed to be a hoard and although the group of coins recovered from Joist Fen has sometimes been regarded as a late hoard, this is not borne out by the account of their discovery. The Joist Fen coins appear to consist of more than one hoard and to include casual losses. It was originally described to the local coroner as being 'a collection of strays'. (Briscoe, 1964)

- The absence of these coins from the Boudiccan Revolt hoards is not in itself definitive as the hoards generally exclude lighter issues such as fractional units.
- The obverse inscription is similar to that on the Esvprasv coinage of the Corieltavi, known to be late in that series, and to the relatively late Icenian Aesv/Saenv coinage, discussed above.

The only evidence to support speculation that the Esv Prasto coins postdate the other issues considered in this paper is the lengthy Latin inscription and what is perceived to be a Roman style of design. I believe that this issue fits well into a group of smaller Icenian issues that are stylistically linked to North Thames coinage. The designs of both the obverse and the reverse of the Esv Prasto unit are very close to a slightly less ornate pre-conquest silver unit of Cunobelin (VA 2055), an example of which is shown in Figure 12. The Cunobelin unit was discussed by Dr Philip de Jersey as his type D4 (De Jersey, 2001, 12-13). De Jersey demonstrates that this is one of a small number of Cunobelin's silver issues that were struck in, or for use in, Catuvellaunian territory.

It is an intriguing thought that the legend on the Esv Prasto coin, which has produced so much excitement to those fascinated by Boudicca and her husband Prasutagus may eventually prove to have its greatest value in assisting future studies into the relationship between the Iceni and their neighbours. My own conclusion is that the Esv Prasto unit is a local West Norfolk issue probably issued in the last decade or so prior to the conquest.

Three other Icenian issues which appear to have close links to North Thames coinage are shown in Figure 12 together with examples of the Trinovantian coinage that most closely resembles them. The importance of symbols on the Icenian coinage has already been touched upon and it is interesting that the Icenian 'Stepping Horse' quarter stater not only shares an identical obverse with VA1660, but that the reverse shares a trefoil device above the horse which occurs nowhere else in Icenian coinage.

Period	Number of coins			Number of dies		
	Gold	Silver	Total	Gold	Silver	Total
Early local	465	593	1058	150	219	369
First denominational	1012	299	1311	138	135	273
Middle denominational	499	1205	1704	61	396	457
Late denominational	24	4994	5018	7	429	436
Total	2000	7091	9091	356	1179	1535
Others	12	457	469	11	51	62
Total	2012	7548	9560	367	1230	1597

FIGURE 13. SUMMARY OF RECORDED COINS AND DIE NUMBERS.

Over-view of the Icenian Series

Figure 13 provides an overview of the entire Icenian series based upon my die study and using the periodization referred to in this paper. The allocation of the issues into the two final periods is based upon my work on the late hoards and is beyond the scope of this paper but in summary, the middle denominational period includes the boar horse coinages (BHA, BHB and BHC) and the early pattern horse coinages (EPH(A) and EPH(B)) and the late period includes the inscribed issues and the LFH coinage.

The overview in Figure 13 enables a number of important observations to be made about the Iron Age coinage of East Anglia. These include the following:

- So far I have recorded 1,597 separate dies used in producing 'official' Icenian coinage. For many of the issues of coinage the average number of coins known for each die is high in comparison to those generated from other studies of ancient coinages and it is now unusual to find a new die. EPH(A) is one of the few issues where new dies are regularly found and for many other issues I believe that the vast majority of dies are now recorded. This conclusion was supported by the recent Wickham Market hoard of 835 Icenian staters; these coins were found to be struck from a total of 85 dies of which only 14 were previously unknown. This was despite the hoard increasing the number of known coins of the five types in the hoard from 395 to 1,230.

- The comparison between the total of known coins and of die numbers for each period shows the disproportionate survival rate of the late coinage as a result of recoveries from the Boudiccan revolt hoards. After including the late local coinage of Ece(A), some 58% of all known Icenian coins, but only 29% of known dies, are from the final phase of the last period of coinage.

- The table of die numbers starkly illustrates the decline in the use of gold in the final periods of Icenian coinage production and a corresponding increase in the use of silver.

Figure 14 includes plated coins in a summary of total recorded coins and known dies and also includes hypothetical indicative dates for the various periods covered in this paper. Alongside the die study I have been developing a working hypothesis for the dating of the major coinages and this work is ongoing. There are few firm dates but, as referred to above, a number of Icenian issues are clearly closely related to those of Cunobelin and earlier leaders of groups immediately to the south of the area dominated by Icenian coinage. These clues have helped to provide some parameters, as have the Gallic Wars, the Roman conquest of AD 43 and the Boudiccan revolt of AD 60/1.

The coinage is assumed to start in the middle of the first century BC. It appears clear from hoard evidence that the first local coinages covered in this paper supersede Gallo-Belgic E. A number of writers who have studied Gallo-Belgic coinage attribute Gallo-Belgic E to the Gallic Wars

Period	Official issues		Plated coins		Hypothetical dating
	Coins	Dies	Coins	Forged dies	
Early local	**1058**	369	**118**	62	50BC–15BC
First denominational	**1311**	273	**11**	20	15BC–5AD
Middle denominational	**1704**	457	**88**	116	AD5–AD25
Late denominational	**5018**	436	**147**	169	AD25–AD43
Total	**9091**	1535	**364**	367	
Others	**469**	62	**3**	6	
Total	**9560**	1597	**367**	373	

FIGURE 14. SUMMARY OF OFFICIAL AND PLATED COINS WITH HYPOTHETICAL PERIODS OF ISSUE.

which ended in 51BC (see for example Sills, 2003, 2 -3) Whilst their arguments appear logical, and I have adopted them in my hypothesis, they are not beyond doubt (see for example Haselgrove, 1987, 80-81).

In the suggested chronology the terminus of the coinage has been taken as the conquest in 43AD. The assumption that Icenian coinage ceased after the conquest is based upon analysis of the available evidence, including in particular the late hoards, (Talbot forthcoming), but unfortunately, as with the starting date for the coinage, the evidence is not definitive and production may have continued for a few years post conquest. Fortunately the relative dating of major coinages during the period of Icenian minting is much more straightforward and is largely based upon hoard evidence although the dates for the various periods of production shown in Figure 14 are only indicative.

An ongoing area of work on the Icenian coinage is to assess whether there was a fixed relationship between the various denominations of coinage within a given issue. I have found some tentative evidence for a fixed relationship between gold and silver coinage based on metal content; applying this to die usage and the chronology in Figure 14 suggests a similar average annual value of coinage production for each of the first two periods. The annual value then declined with the increasing silver output not compensating for the reduction in gold. These are tentative conclusions, based upon rather too many assumptions, but potential explanations could include reducing economic activity, which is reflected in the decline in the use of gold as well as the possibility that the latter two periods were rather shorter than my hypothesis presently suggests.

In this paper I have referred to the various mints groups in operation in East Anglia prior to the Roman conquest, particularly during the final phases of Icenian coin production. The evidence does not suggest that the major mint groups represented the production facilities of sub-tribal political groupings with distinctive geographic territories within East Anglia. There were distinctive elements of design for each mint group but whilst there are sometimes geographic areas of partial dominance, and certainly areas of concentration for die groups within a type, the coinage was mixed in most places and issued to common weight standards. The closest modern analogy seems to be with competing commercial interests in a single geographic area (such as Royal Bank of Scotland, Clydesdale Bank and Bank of Scotland all issuing banknotes in Scotland) but with regions where one or other of the interests have dominance. I realise that these final comments are moving well into the realm of speculation and the banking analogy may suggest to some an offensive level of sophistication in the Iron Age; perhaps it betrays my own financial rather than archaeological background. In my defence I can only say that I have found the coinage of this tribal region to be highly organised and tightly controlled in weight and design from the earliest days of its production and that I suspect this level of sophistication is a reflection of the society that produced it.

Bibliography

Briscoe G. 1964. Icenian coin finds in Lakenheath, Suffolk. *Proceedings of the Cambridge Antiquarian Society*, 56-7, 123-124

Chimirri-Russell, G. 2003. Changing artistic perspectives on Celtic coins. In Edited Alfaro C. (ed), 13th Congreso internacional de numismatica. Madrid, 441-445.

De Jersey, P. 2001. Cunobelin's silver. *Britannia* 32, 1-44.

Gregory, T. 1992. Snettisham and Bury: some new light on the earliest Icenian coinage. In M. Mays (ed), *Celtic Coinage: Britain and Beyond*. British Archaeological Report 222, 47-68

Haselgrove, C. C. 1987. *Iron Age coinage in south-east England: the archaeological context*. British Archaeological Report 174.

Hobbs, R. 1996. *British Iron Age coins in the British Museum*. London, British Museum Press.

Sills, J. 2003. *Gaulish and Early British Gold Coinage*. (London, Spink.

Talbot, J. 2006. The Iceni early face/horse series. In P. de Jersey (ed), *Celtic Coinage: New Discoveries, New Discussion*. British Archaeological report International Series 1532, 213-41.

Talbot, J. forthcoming. *Iron Age coinage in East Anglia*.

Talbot, J. and Leins, I. 2010. Before Boudicca: the Wickham Market hoard and the middle phase gold coinage of East Anglia. British Numismatic Journal 80, 1-23.

Van Arsdell, R. D. 1989. *Celtic Coinage of Britain*. London, Spink.

Williams, J. H C. 2000. The Silver Coins from East Anglia attributed to King Prasutagus of the Iceni – a new reading of the obverse Inscription. *Numismatic Chronicle* 160, 276-81.

Appendix 1 Concordance of types

Talbot	Allan	VA	BMC
EARLY LOCAL COINAGE			
Norfolk Wolf gold			
JA stater	British JA	610	212 - 216
JB stater	British JB	610-3 & 610-3	217 - 278
JA quarter	-	-	-
Face horse silver (see Talbot 2006)			
Bury A unit*	Lx10	80.1	3524 - 3527
Bury C unit*	-	-	3528 - 3532
Bury B unit*	-	-	3533 - 3535
Bury D unit	-	-	-
Bury E unit	-	-	-
Bury fractional	-	-	-
LFA unit*	-	-	3548 - 3549
LFB unit	-	-	-
LFC unit*	-	-	3550 - 3551
FIRST DENOMINATIONAL COINAGES			
Snettisham			
Stater	Within British Lb	1505	3353 - 3383
Quarter	-	-	3420 - 3434
Unit	-	665.7 & 665.9	3541 - 3545
Fractional	-	-	-
Early Irstead			
Stater	British Nc	624	3390 – 3395 (& 3399)
Unit	-	-	3539 & 3546
Irstead			
Stater	British Nc	626-1	3396 – 3404 minus 3399!!
Quarter	British Nd	-	3437 - 3439
Unit	-	665.3	3538
Fractional	-	-	3789
Irstead B unit	-	665-1	3536, 3537 & 3547
Early boar horse			
Stater	British Nb	626-4,7,9 & 12	3405 - 3419
Unit	-	-	3440 - 3444
Fractional	-	-	3787 -3788
Saham Toney			
Quarter	-	-	-
Unit	-	665-5	3540, 3552 - 3555
LATE DENOMINATIONAL COINAGES			
Mint group A			
BHA			
Unit	Boar Horse A	655	3445 - 3454
Fractional	-	681	3777 - 8
BHB			
Stater	British Nc	620-1,7 & 9	3384, 3386 - 3389
Unit	Boar Horse B	657	3455 - 3472
Fractional	-	-	3513 - 3516
BHC			
Stater	British Nc	620-4 & 5	3385
Unit	Boar Horse C	659	3473 - 3511
Fractional	-	661	3517 - 3520
Anted			
Stater	-	705	3790
Unit	Type V	710, 711 & 715	3791 - 4027
Fractional	-	720	4028 - 4031
Ecen			
Stater	-	-	4032
Unit	Type VI	730, 732, 734, 740, 750, 752, 754 & 756	4033 – 4215 & 4219 - 4344
Fractional	-	736, 738 & 744	4216 -4218
Mint group B			
EPH (A)			
Stater	-	-	-
Unit	Early pattern horse A	679	3763 - 3766
Fractional	-	-	3779 - 3780

	LFH		
Unit	Normal face horse A-C	790, 792 & 794	3556 - 3762
Mint group C			
EPH (B)			
Stater	-	-	-
Quarter	-	-	369
Unit	Early pattern horse B	675	3767 - 3774
Fractional	-	-	3256 - 3257
Saenv/Aesv			
Unit	Type IX	770 & 775	4540 - 4572
Ece (B)			
Unit	Type VIII	762, 764 & 766	4431 - 4538
Fractional	-	-	-
LATER LOCAL ISSUES			
Stepping horse quarter			
Quarter	-	628	3436
Ece (A)			
Unit	Early pattern horse A	760	4348 - 4430
Cani Dvro			
Unit	Boar horse D	663	3521 - 3523
ALE SCA			
Unit	-	996	4576
Esv Prasto			
Unit	Type X	780	4577 - 4580

* These names are either those or are based upon those given to a number of early silver units by the late Tony Gregory (Gregory 1992)

The language of inscriptions on Icenian coinage

Daphne Nash Briggs

1 Introduction

The earliest surviving inscriptions in any medium incontrovertibly written in Britain are on coins issued before the Claudian conquest. Striking gold and silver coinage was an extremely expensive and risky thing to do with community treasure, and above all with treasure already consecrated to a god (Haselgrove and Wigg-Wolf 2005). Their types were composed with scrupulous care, almost certainly by, or in consultation with, priests (Creighton 2000). At a time when the use of writing was largely confined to religious specialists for record-keeping, magic and divination, when inscriptions were added to coin dies by engravers literate in the Roman alphabet they must be taken as scrupulous efforts to reproduce the sounds of the words they represent. Hence, coin inscriptions in their pristine state are valuable linguistic fossils. Accurate representation of non-Latin speech would only ever have been of concern to a small minority of literate native speakers, most actively in the century preceding Claudius' conquest and from the 5th century AD onwards. Inscriptional evidence for vernaculars of any kind is extremely rare during the period of Roman rule: this is why pre-Roman coin inscriptions are potentially such a valuable, if frustrating, source of linguistic information.

Ancient British gold and silver coins can only ever have been issued episodically, primarily to fund military undertakings, to reward successful soldiers, and to pay fines and indemnities (Sills 2000; Sills 2003c, 2–4, 87–124; Sills 2005). Norfolk's Iron-Age inhabitants seem to have formed a loosely confederated cluster of territorially discrete clans, cantons or *pagi*, each with its own rulers and polyfocal centre. There were long-term cultural and historical differences between the western and eastern sections of the county (Davies 1996; Davies 2009) and coinages were struck in three to five different districts during the 1st centuries BC and AD, sometimes simultaneously (Chadburn 2006, 137; Rudd 2008). Inscribed Icenian coinage falls within the period *c* AD 10–45/50.

As it will raise some awkward linguistic questions this paper will focus on coin inscriptions, leaving Norfolk names and place-names transmitted only through Latin and Greek manuscript sources for review on a separate occasion. At least when we have a good reading from a head-of-series coin die we can be confident that we have a given word spelt as it was intended to be read in its own place and day. It is generally assumed that the language represented on all ancient British coins must be Celtic. The purpose of this paper is to present grounds for thinking that most of the names or titles of office on the Iron-Age coinage of Norfolk are in fact based on something else that may have been either philologically West Germanic or is at least suggestive of West Germanic speech habits.

2 Coin inscriptions in Iron-Age Norfolk

These will be discussed in approximate chronological order. The first coins in Norfolk to bear inscriptions (names 1–5; Figures 1–8) form a set that shares an identical Pattern–Horse format but were struck in a complex, overlapping sequence. There were vast quantities of silver units throughout the series but gold staters only at its beginning, inscribed ANTEÐ, ECEN and ECE. Minting gold may have stopped abruptly around AD 25–30 (Rudd 2008) whilst silver continued until around the time of Claudius' invasion. Pellet moulds suited to making coin blanks found stratified in phase II of the monumental ritual site at Fison Way, Thetford, and associated with other material tentatively dated to the late AD 40s or early 50s (Gregory 1991, 193–6), suggest that the last Icenian silver coins, whichever they were, may have been made after the Claudian conquest and possibly even after the AD 47 revolt.

The inscribed Pattern–Horse series was initiated during a period of relentless political expansion by the Catuvellauni that was already under way in the mid 1st century BC and intensified under Cunobelinus (*c* AD 10–40/42), who put pressure on all his neighbours and seems to have taken outright control of the Trinovantes. Icenian Pattern–Horse coins have duly come to light in greatest numbers in areas of Norfolk close to their borders with his dominions. Their shared design, overlapping distributions and, perhaps, the content of their inscriptions, together with a number of distinctive features of Norfolk settlement archaeology that contrast with the cultural scene amongst the Catuvellauni and Trinovantes (Davies 1996; Davies 1999; Davies 2009), all suggest that in this generation the Iceni were actively and successfully taking political steps to define and safeguard their own way of life in very challenging times, partly by coming together to forge a confederate identity. The Pattern–Horse series was, however, not the only one in 1st-century Norfolk, which can never have

Pattern–Horse gold staters: ANTEÐI, ECEN, ECE

fig 1　　　　　fig 2　　　　　fig 3

Pattern–Horse silver units: ANTEÐ, ECEN, ECE, SAENV, AESV

fig 4　　　fig 5　　　fig 6　　　fig 7　　　fig 8

fig 7a

Pattern–Horse silver fraction: ANTEÐIO / …SIA…

fig 9

Boar–Horse silver unit: CANI DVRO

fig 10　　　　　fig 11

been fully unified, and other inscribed silver coinages, in Boar–Horse and Face–Horse formats, were also struck, as described below (names 6–10). Two of these were probably struck around or after the time of Cunobelinus' death, which occurred between c AD 40 and 42 (names 7–10).

Pattern–Horse series coins c AD 10–40 (Figures 1–9)

The first inscribed Icenian coins bear the single words ANTEÐ[I(O)], ECEN, ECE, SAENV and AESV. Some gold staters inscribed ANTEÐI, ECEN and ECE share obverse dies (Chadburn 2006, 279), but differences in geographical distribution amongst the various silver issues indicate that they were probably issued and eventually buried or lost in different administrative districts or *pagi*. It is possible that the Iceni had between three and five such districts (Chadburn 2006; Rudd 2008), and if the core of the confederation was tripartite, we may see it symbolised on coinage in a variety of tripled motifs including the centre of the obverse design of uninscribed Freckenham 2–3 gold staters (AC 80–85; VA 626; c 30-10 BC), inscribed Pattern–Horse gold staters (Figures 1–3), the symbols into which the ECEN inscription on silver units morphed when literate engravers became unavailable (Chadburn 2006, 314), and the three symbols united by the emblematic item above the portrait on Esuprastus/Esico silver units (Figure 15).

ANTEÐ[I(O)] heads the first series, SAENV and AESV start later than ECEN and ECE, and the last of the ECEN series may be the latest of all. ECEN is a large series and the superbly engraved early dies, whose inscription can safely be regarded as accurately spelt, wore out and got replaced in the silver series by copies made by competent but sometimes illiterate engravers who produced confused pseudo-legends (e.g. ED, EDN) until the attempt to use an alphabet was abandoned and lettering was replaced by a triangle or tribrach emblem (AC 345).

ANTEÐI and ANTEÐIO / ...SIA...

ANTEÐI or ANTEÐ is the first reverse inscription on the Pattern–Horse series in both gold and silver (c AD 10–40; Figures 1, 4) and may belong to the eastern canton of the federal territory (Chadburn 2006, 484), closest to the Trinovantes–Caturellauni and with a political focus in the Norwich–Caistor St Edmund area. ANTEÐI seems not only to be linguistically Celtic but also to be lacking a convincing Germanic parallel. It also occurs on an issue of tiny fractional Icenian silver coins (Figure 9; AC 410) that may in fact lie very early in the series, as the obverse design is modelled on coins of Tasciovanus and early Cunobelinus (Rudd 2004). These have a Roman-style obverse bearing simply the inscription ANTEÐI or ANTEÐIO on a tablet within a circular border, and on the reverse a horse with the partially legible inscription ...SIA... (perhaps ...SLA...). Until a more complete reading of this reverse inscription comes to light it is pointless to investigate it further. In format the inscriptions on the silver fractions, taken together, seem to match AL FE / SCAVO and SVB ESVPRASTO / ESICO FECIT (below), in which case they probably likewise name two levels of authority for the coinage – one immediate (...SIA...) and the other ultimate (ANTEÐIO). If this is so, the form ANTEÐIO, so far attested only on one die, probably represents a Latinised version of a full word in an oblique grammatical case (cf SCAVO and SVB ESVPRASTO below), meaning 'under' or 'for *Anteðius*'.

A third instance of the same name occurs on 1st-century Dobunnic coinage in the forms ANTEΘ RICOV and ANTEÐ RICV (Sills 2003b). There is no way at present of telling whether there is any connection between the similarly inscribed Dobunnic and Icenian coinages and it is safest to regard the two or several individuals represented by the same name as unconnected. If ANTEÐI[O] is indeed a title of office and not the personal name of an individual, there is no reason why it should not have been used at different times in different places.

Understanding this word turns upon interpretation of the letter Ð (Evans 1967, 410–20; Lambert 1994, 91; Russell 1995, 207), for an outline of which see coda 1 below. Given the most probable sound-value for Ð in pre-conquest Britain, ANTEÐIO would have sounded somewhat like /Antedsio/ in the Brittonic of the day. ANTEÐIO contains two elements, as follows.

ANT-

In an important discussion, Evans (1967, 136–41) related the first element of this uniquely British compound name to a common prefix *ande-* in the Celtic languages. He listed 86 Gaulish and British personal names with complete versions of the *ande-* prefix, almost invariably spelt with *-d-* before the *-e-*: the very few exceptions include all the instances of British ANTEÐ[IO], Gaulish *Anteremius*, and the alternative spelling of Gaulish *Andebrinnaco* as *Antebrin(n)ac(o)* (Evans 1967, 137–8). *Ande-*, *ante-* and *anti-* are common Indo-European [IE] prepositional prefixes connoting motion to or from, intensity, and increase, and Evans related the *ant-* of ANTEÐ[IO] to Irish *and-* and *ind-*, Welsh *an(n)-*, meaning 'habitual', and Gaulish *ande-* / *anda-* / and *ando-*. The prefix is however not confined to any one language family and occurs in Italic, Celtic and Germanic alike (*IEW*, 48–9). Evans, for instance, mentioned Germanic *and-* and Greek *anti-* (1967, 137). *Anta-*, 'opposite, facing' (*IEW*, 49), which can also mean 'without', gives additional Germanic prefixes in *and-*, *ent-* and *ant-*, including OE *and-*, *ant-*, which is a common intensifying prefix that often denotes opposition, as in *and-saca* 'an adversary'.

EÐ-

1. Evans understood ANTEÐ[IO] as a contraction of **ande-teðði-* (1967, 139 n 19), with which Delamarre (2003, 293–4) concurred. Delamarre derives **teðði-* from IE **tep-*, 'heat' (*IEW*, 1069–70), whence Old Irish *te*.

Ande-teðði[os] would then mean something like 'The Very Hot One', perhaps evoking the power of the Sun and the inner fire with which a hero in a battle-frenzy could overheat (Puhvel 1987, 185–6; 193). With this sense it would form a continuum with ECEN, ECE, SAENV and AESV (see below). Teðði- names, with this element in full, are rare and occur mainly in northern Gaul and the Germanies (Delamarre 2003, 293; Whatmough 1970, 829; 1147; 1307).

2. Another possible approach might be to relate -EÐ- to IE *sed-*, 'sit' or 'seat' (*IEW*, 884). *Sed-* gave rise to a lot of vocabulary in many different Indo-European languages (*IEW*, 885–6). As *sedos* it gave the Gaulish word for a war chariot, Latinised as *essedum* (cf. Gaulish *sedlon, sessa*, 'seat': Delamarre 2003, 268; cf Germanic *sessaz*, 'seat': *HGE*, 325): written as *Aθθεδο-* or *Aððedo-* it is analysed as *Ad-sedilos* (Delamarre 2003, 33–4). In the Germanic languages cognate words retained a distinctly sounded initial /s/. In Brittonic the *sed-* element cannot have had such a clearly articulated /s/, or that is how it would have been spelt. Instead, it was a subtler, more lisping sound that could even become /h/ (eg Welsh *hedd*, 'peace': Jackson 1953, 516–17; 520). Hence, when the prepositional prefix *Ad-* was compounded with *-sed-* it was heard in Brittonic as containing *tau gallicum*, represented on coins as Ð, ÐÐ, Θ or ΘΘ (see coda 1). If ANTEÐI[O] were built with the prefix *ande-* compounded with *-sed-,* following elision of the -e- a weak /s/ could have caused the /d/ of *ande-* to harden into /t/ whilst the /d/ of *sed-* before the ending *io* was heard as *tau gallicum*, in which case ANTEÐI[O] could be translated as 'one who sits in front (presides)' – a title of office that would be a close counterpart of Latin *praeses*, meaning protector or governor, the relevance of which will become apparent when ESVPRASTO is discussed (no. 9 and section 3), or of *antistes*, meaning overseer or president, especially the priest or priestess in charge of a cult and its temple (*LSL* sv), and as such attested for instance at the shrine of Mars Lenus at Trier (Green 1997, 115). One might also compare Welsh *annedd*, plural *anheddau*, 'home, stay, abode' (F. White, pers comm).

3. ANTEÐI[O] may not make any independent sense in Germanic. There are, for instance, no readily comparable names in the compendious listings in *ADN*. Its prefix, ANT[E]-, is perfectly valid in Germanic (see above), as is its ending; *-jo* or *-i-o* forms a common Germanic masculine nominal suffix meaning 'one who...' (Carr 1939, 164). Either would Latinise readily as *-ius*, and for reasons already given, the silver fraction inscribed ANTEÐIO was probably intended to be read in Latin. EÐ-, pronounced either as /eds/ or /ed-h/, is more problematical. Germanic had no *tau gallicum* and if ANTEÐI[O] were pronounced with a Germanic accent it would have sounded something like /Anted-hio/, /Antethio/ or /Antezio/. If any of these was understood at all in terms of Germanic vocabulary, the name might have been heard as a heat- or fire- epithet derived from IE *ai-dh, i-dh*, 'to burn, give light' (*IEW*, 11), which gave Germanic *aiðaz* (*HGE*, 6), O.Sax *êd* 'firebrand' and OE *âd* 'funeral pyre'; or as an oath-word from IE *ai-, *oi-*, 'solemn utterance' (*IEW*, 11), giving Gothic *aiþs*, Old Icelandic *eiðr*, OE *âð* and OSax *êð*. Curiously, either of these roots would correspond semantically, but not linguistically, to the primary Brittonic senses of the word.

Result: Linguistically Celtic and either a name evoking the heat and power of the Sun that could equally apply to a god, priest, champion warrior, ruler or tribal sub-unit, or a title of office for a high priest, governor or military leader. Clumsy secondary sense might be made of the word in Germanic, but it is difficult to parallel in an early Germanic context.

ECEN

ECEN (Figures 2, 5), probably from the central canton of the federal territory, centred on the Thetford–Ashill area of the Breckland (Chadburn 2006, 484), has long been regarded as a version of the tribal name, better known to us from Classical sources as Iceni, for further discussion of which see coda 2. Attempts to understand either word in Celtic have had equivocal results (Rivet and Smith 1979, 373–5; cf Sims-Williams 2006, 80). ECEN is unlikely for instance to be derived from IE *ek^w* 'horse', which gave Latin *equus*: IE /k^w/ ought not to produce the simple hard /k/ of ECE(N) and *Iceni*. Instead, it should alter either to the /p/ of Gaulish and Brittonic *Epona* and *Eppillus* or the /ch/ of Old Irish *ech*, 'horse' (*IEW*, 301) cf, in Germanic, OE *eoh*, ON *iôr* 'horse'.

Something more promising emerges if ECEN is considered as potentially Germanic and is based on IE *aig-* 'oak' (*IEW*, 13). In the older Germanic languages this root produced OSax *êk*, OFris *êk*, ON *eik*, OE *âc, æc*, OHG *eih*, 'oak', whereas in Celtic words for oak derived from a different IE root, *deru-* or *dru-*, 'tree', especially oak (*IEW*, 214–5; Delamarre 2003, 149). In the Germanic languages *dru-* and *dreu-* also gave rise to plenty of vocabulary, including words for 'tree', 'stag', 'strong' and 'true' (*IEW*, 215–6), but not to the name of the oak. ECEN can be further divided into *ec-* 'oak' plus suffix *-en*. The latter can

(1) denote 'made of' (Nielsen 1998, 139), as in OFris. *êzen, êtzen*, OHG *eichen*, OE *æcen*, 'oaken'. If ECEN is an adjective it is either the first element in a compound name or a potentially complete word that qualifies a tacitly understood noun as 'oaken one' (god? priest? leader? people? place?). By-names and kennings for gods and heroes abound in traditional literatures (West 2007, 129; cf discussion of AESV below: Cassell's *Dictionary of Norse Myth and Legend* lists 156 titles and epithets just for Odin).

(2) be abbreviated from *-no(s)* after a glide vowel *-e-* to ease pronunciation (something known to occur in early Germanic: Nielsen 1989, 139). For discussion of *-no(s)* see SAENV below. In this case, ECEN would mean 'lord of oaks', just as Roman Silvanus was 'lord of the

wildwood', and could be understood as the name or epithet of an Icenian tutelary deity, named on coins in the singular in exactly the same way in which the Romans portrayed and named (Dea) Roma on Republican denarii.

Taken in either sense, it is therefore at least possible that ECEN might represent a totemic theonym. A sacred tree – often oak or ash – linked earth with sky in many European religious traditions. The striking Bronze-Age monument at Holme-next-the-Sea with its upturned oak tree and tightly crafted oak palisade (Pryor 2001; Davies 2009, 67–8) and the serried ranks of massive posts and fences constructed like a symbolic grove to surround the last incarnation of the ceremonial site at Fison Way, Thetford, in the late 50s AD (Gregory 1991; Robinson and Gregory 1987, 44–7; Bradley 2005, 184–7; Davies 2009, 130–2), do lend credence to the conjecture that one of the tribal deities honoured in late prehistoric Norfolk was connected with oak trees in public cult practice (Nash Briggs 2009c).

Result: Doubtful etymology in Celtic but intelligible in Germanic as the first element either of a priestly title or a theonym.

ECE

On purely numismatic grounds this extensive coinage, perhaps from the wealthy western canton of the federal territory (Chadburn 2006, 484), with its polyfocal centre in the Snettisham–Fring–Sedgeford–Ringstead area (Hutcheson 2004, 91) represents a separate mint-series from ECEN (Chadburn 2006, 323), and for the illiterate this was signalled by the arrangement of the inscription which, unlike ECEN and indeed the other inscriptions of the Pattern–Horse set, is not normally tied in with the horse's hind leg (Figures 3, 6). This does not of course mean that it necessarily signifies a different word, and if ECE is merely an abbreviated version of ECEN, then all the observations above apply to it too, and the different inscriptional forms might have been used simply to differentiate between issues struck for different purposes or from two separate tribal subdivisions.

Alternatively ECE might conceivably represent an (abbreviated?) adjective derived from IE *aiu- 'vital energy' (*IEW*, 17) plus suffix -g /-c/, cf OHG *ewa*, *ewig* and OE *ece* 'eternal'. If applied to a ruler, its significance would then have been honorific, somewhat like the Roman title *Augustus*. If applied to a clan or god it would resemble, as an epithet, the late Roman *Sol Invictus* – the Unconquered Sun.

Result: Of doubtful Celtic etymology but intelligible in Germanic, either as an abbreviated oak-word or as an honorific epithet meaning 'vigorous' or 'everlasting'.

SAENV

If we consider the care with which all British coin dies were composed and their inscriptions were written we have to note the way in which SAENV and AESV (below) are spelt (Figures 7–8). Both may belong to the ancient and wealthy western North-Sea-facing canton of the federal territory (Chadburn 2006, 484). The -ae- both of SAENV and of AESV can be understood as representing the double sound /ah-eh/, with stress upon the /a/. SAENV cannot be regarded as a simple variant or mistake for the Gaulish and Brittonic adjective *seno-* meaning 'old', which is a well-attested element in Gaulish and British nomenclature and is never spelt with a diphthong, especially one that accents the component /a/. *Seno-* has cognate forms in some Germanic languages, including Gothic *sineigs* 'old age' (*IEW*, 908), likewise with a slender vowel. SAENV must, instead, be taken as a different word in its own right and can be split for discussion into the components SAE- plus suffix -NV.

SAE-

The root here may well be geographical, signifying dangerous terrain, from IE *sai- 'pain, illness, to injure', via *sai-uo* (cf Latin *saevus*, 'savage': *IEW*, 877). It lies behind the name *Saevo*, described by Pliny the Elder in the 1st century AD as an enormous massif, *mons ingens*, 'as big as [the mountains] of the Ripaean range', which marked the northern limit of lands inhabited by the Ingvaeones (North-Sea Germans) and formed a vast island-studded bay (the Belt) that he said reached to the Cimbrian peninsula (Denmark: Pliny *NH* 4.13.96; Reichert 1987, 582). A Gothic name SAIVS is attested (*ADN*, 1312), and Gothic *saiws*, 'sea, lake, marshland' (*HGE*, 314) also preserves the /w/ that would be expected in the word on philological grounds (Paul Kavanagh pers comm). In fact, a very similar name *Saeviu, 'the Savage' or 'he of the sea/lake/marsh', may prove to be the correct reading of this Icenian coin inscription, if what appears to be a clumsily reversed letter N on some well-preserved examples of an otherwise carefully engraved die in this scarce series (Figure 7a, eg C Rudd *List* 70 no. 44) is read not as a blundered SAENV but as SAEVIV, 'the savage one'. This is entirely possible, but awaits confirmation from clear readings of other dies.

IE *sai- gave rise to some peculiarly Germanic vocabulary for a lake, large water, or the cruel sea, as in Gothic *saiws*, OE *sæ*, OIcel *saer*, 'the sea', cf. OE *sænig* 'of the sea, maritime'. Campbell (1959, 400; 406) traced the phonetic history of OE *sæ* back through *sæi to *sâi- to *saeui-. Gothic preserved an archaic /w/ into historical times, and in the 1st century AD, when Goths were still resident in central–northern Europe, the Germanic language family is thought to have been in an early phase of internal differentiation (Tac. *Ger.* 44.1; Nielsen 1989, 37–45). Whether or not /w/ is conserved in this Icenian coin inscription, which is in any case not inscribed in Gothic, it would be unsurprising if it contained a *sai- word from the same lexical continuum (cf Campbell's *sâi-).

-NV

If SAENV proves to be the correct reading of this inscription, -NV may represent *-nos, a widespread and very ancient IE suffix that, when applied to deities or rulers, signified 'master/mistress of' the preceding element in the word (West 2007, 137). It occurs in Latin, Celtic and Germanic religious vocabularies, as for instance in Latin Neptu-nus and Volca-nus, Gaulish Epo-na, 'mistress of horses', and the -neihiae and -henae suffixes of the Matres inscriptions concentrated in Lower Germany. It also occurs in the name of the Continental Morini, who were wetland-dwellers on the opposite shore from Kent, where the Channel meets the North Sea. Morini can be understood equally well as a Celtic and as a Germanic ethnonym, from IE more, 'sea' (also 'standing water' in Germanic: *IEW*, 748). It gives mare in Latin, mor in Gaulish, Welsh, Cornish, and Breton, muir in Old Irish, mor in OE, meer in German and eventually various words for marshes in the Germanic languages, including English mere (Nielsen 1989, 21). SAENV could then be interpreted, like ECEN, as meaning 'Lord of the lake' (perhaps a particular sacred water into which offerings were put) or 'Lord of the high sea' and form all or part of the by-name of a tribal deity or title of a priest or official.

Result: An implausible spelling mistake in Celtic but, if built on a Germanic root, intelligible as (part of?) a theonym or title of office. SAEVIV or SAENV also appears, like ECEN, to be a deliberate choice of Germanic vocabulary.

5 AESV

AESV, like SAENV, may belong to the western canton of the federal territory (Chadburn 2006, 484). AESV, probably abbreviated from a longer word, comes from a widely distributed and very ancient European religious idiom, probably of Bronze-Age descent and long propagated in shared oral religious traditions in Italy, Gaul, Britain and Germany. In linguistically Celtic and Gallo-Roman usage and in contexts influenced by either Celtic or Latin, ESV- and EISV represent what seems to have been its customary pronunciation (Jackson 1953, 324): in Britain, EISV appears on Dobunnic coinage, where it is sometimes paired with RICOV or RICV (Sills 2003b). As the first element in a compound name ESV- is attested in Britain in the Latinised Icenian title ESVPRASTO and on Corieltavian coinage as ESVPRASV: see section 3 for further discussion and Breeze (2002a) for the spelling of Corieltavi. In Germanic and many Italic contexts the word was normally spelt with an opening A- (see below).

For the etymology of this epithet see Evans (1967, 200–2) and West (*IEPM*, 120–1). Versions are found in Celtic, Germanic, Italic (*aisos, aisis*) and Etruscan (*aesar*), always meaning 'gods'. All these words are built on the same root, perhaps but not certainly IE *esu-s* (from *su-*) meaning 'good' or 'excellent' (*IEW*, 342), whence it furnished a solemn euphemistic epithet or placatory title meaning something like 'The Good One' when applied to a deity too dangerous to name more plainly: a parallel would be the by-name *Eumenides*, 'Kindly Ones', given by the Athenians to deadly avenging Furies. It would mean 'Divine Lord' or 'Holy One' when applied to human rulers (Chadburn 2006, 325). Names of gods and heroes are easier to transfer relatively intact between traditions than almost any other aspect of language, and the honorific Esus/Aesu- epithet for a dangerous deity is a strong candidate for membership of the oldest epic tradition in north-western Europe.

Explicitly spelt as AESV, the Icenian inscription raises exactly the same phonological issues as SAENV (above), with its emphasis upon a stressed and audible /a/ in the opening syllable. So far, in Britain, the spelling AESV seems only to be attested in Norfolk at this early historical period, where it occurs again in the name of a 2nd-century potter working in Brampton who stamped his work with AESVMINVS (Robinson and Gregory 1987, 59). As it happens, the second element in this Latinised name would make sense both in Celtic and in Germanic, and may represent a compromise formation typical of a multilingual environment (Nielsen 1989, 122–31). Gaulish *minio-, meno-* 'gentle', reflected in names like Adminius and Uiminus (Delamarre 2003, 226) would give a meaning 'Gentle one of Aesu', whilst in Germanic *minniz* or *minnaz*, 'less' or 'small' (*HGE*, 271) would give a name *Aesumin[n]iz* meaning 'Lesser one of Aesu', apt perhaps for a younger son, and have been constructed like ESVPRASTO (name 9) and Runic *Asugasdiz* (below). For the alternatives *Aesica/Esica* see ESICO (name 10).

AESV has very close parallels in the root word's known Germanic reflections, which always sound an /a/, as in ON *ás*, pl *æsir* (*ass, anses*, the sky- and power-gods who protect warriors and travellers). Common (prehistoric) Germanic, before separation into distinct eastern and western branches, is thought to have sounded /n/ in positions between vowels where the second one was followed by an /s/ (here, the *esu-* part of AESV) and is seen in the archaic spelling *ansuz* in an Icelandic Runic poem (Elliott 1959, 55) and in the name of a goddess, *Vihansa* (*Wih-ansa*, War Goddess), to whom a centurion of Legio III dedicated a spear and shield at Tongern, Belgium (Simek 1993, 361; Kaufmann 1968, 35–6). Gothic (East Germanic) retained many features of early Common Germanic until the mid 6th century and beyond and we are told that *anseis*, meaning *semidei*, 'demigods', was an honorific title that the Goths applied to victorious kings (Jordanes [*Getica*] 13.78; West 2007, 120–1). However, by the 5th century AD the nasal component of *a-n-ses*, 'gods', was being lost from West Germanic (Campbell 1959, 47 para 121; Nielsen 1989, 10; 77; 99), leaving just the initial stressed /a/, as seen in a Runic inscription of c AD 400 from Denmark naming *Asugasdiz*, (probably gen. sg. from *Asugas*: Reichert 1987, 55). Also relevant in this connection is a bronze finger ring excavated from the Butt Road cemetery at Colchester (late 3rd or 4th century AD). Its bezel was inscribed, in two lines of punched lettering within and separated by three scored guide lines, with the words ASV and ASVS (*Britannia* xii 1981, 384 no. 35).

In 1st- and 2nd- century Norfolk, as well as in some later Romano-British documents and a few inscriptions in Gaul (Evans 1967, 200 n 2), I think we may see a step in this phonological development that is intermediate between primitive Germanic *anses and Runic *Asugasdiz*. Of especial interest in the current discussion are two 3rd–4th-century vernacular Romano-British names, *Aessicunia* and *Aesibuas*, from lead curse-tablets at Bath (Tomlin 1988, 74; 129; 156; 233). *Aessicunia* might be a Brittonic formation (cf. Delamarre 2003, 131 sv *cuno*- 'hound'), but its spelling with Ae- and -ss-, remarked upon by Tomlin as possible hypercorrections (1988, 74; 234), might be better accounted for if it simply meant 'Of the race or clan of Aesus', precisely like Celtic *Esugenus* (Evans 1967, 200), cf OSax *manno cunni*, OE *manna cyn(n)* (mankind) and OE *eotena cyn, giganta cyn* (of the race of giants: West 2007, 126), compounding a normal Germanic genitive of the god-name, *Aes-as (cf. Campbell 1959, 223), spelt and sounded in mid-word as *Aes-si-*, with *-kunja*, representing the masculine noun *kunjan (cf Gothic *kuni*, O Sax *kunni*) meaning 'clan, tribe, race, generation' (*HGE*, 224). Similarly, *Aesibuas* (=*Aesi-buwaz, comparable in form and meaning with Runic *Asu-gasdiz*, 'guest of Aesu', *c* 400 AD) compounds *Aesi-* with a noun *bûwaz, 'dweller' (*HGE*, 65), from **bôw(w)anan* 'to dwell, inhabit', as in OFris *buwa*, OSax *buan* 'to dwell' (*HGE*, 52). Both names represent the very widespread European practice of associating the bearer of a name in friendship or kinship with a god (West 2007, 130). Such names may well have been common in aristocratic British clans in which priesthoods and magistracies traditionally ran.

In all these British examples AESV retains both vowels of the primitive Germanic form of the divine title, perhaps with a faintly nasal ring to the /a/, on which the word-stress will have fallen. For the characteristic development of accent on the first syllable in Germanic see Campbell (1959, 30) and Nielsen (1998, 49); in the Celtic languages, Goidelic also accented the first syllable (Russell 1995, 29–31), whilst Brittonic developed a penultimate accent (Russell 1995, 119–21), perhaps before the first century AD.

Result: An ancient religious epithet that could be applied alone or as the first element in a compound name or title to a deity, person, official, or group. The word that lay behind it gave rise to many theophoric names both in Celtic and Germanic and was specific to no one language or cultural environment. However, the spelling and pronunciation AESV would be an error in Celtic, which would have used ESV- or EISV (see discussion of -PRASTO), whilst AESV has strong parallels in Germanic, including one peculiarly West Germanic feature.

All the remaining coin legends of Iron Age Norfolk are influenced by the Latin inscriptional conventions that were coming into use elsewhere on British coinage in the generation before Claudius' invasion. It is generally and probably correctly assumed that the explicit display of Romanised imagery and the Latin language reflects official ties of friendship or alliance with Rome.

Boar–Horse format silver coins (Figures 10–11)

6 CANI DVRO

This inscription (AC 230) is contemporary with ANTEÐ[I] and mid-series ECEN and a little later than ECE, so was probably struck in the late 20s or 30s AD. Like ANTEÐI it may belong to the eastern canton of the federal territory, and its geographical distribution overlaps with the inscribed Pattern–Horse series. Both parts of the inscription appear on the reverse of the coin, CANI above and DVRO below the horse, where the D is tied in to the horse's hind leg.

It is uncertain exactly how CANI and DVRO should be read: all three plausible permutations of the pair of names can be defended but each runs into particular difficulties. They could be two separate personal names or titles, though this is an arrangement otherwise unattested on the same side of an Icenian coin; or a personal name CANI[...] together with a place-name DVRO[...] at which *Cani- ruled or where the coinage was struck. This is not an implausible conjecture but it would be an unusual format: Tasciovanus and Cunobelinus, whose coin designs were influential in Norfolk (Rudd 2008), always placed their personal names and their seats of power on opposite sides of their coins. Alternatively the names could be taken together to form a single compound place-name *CANIDVRO (Rudd 2007, 2–7), Latinised and with a Latin locative ending as seen on coins of Tasciovanus (VERLAMIO: VA 1808–1) and Cunobelinus (CAMVLODUNO: VA 1977–1). The problem with this is that the coin's layout does appear to separate the two elements visually and it would be unique to have a place-name without an equally explicit mention of the ruler whose place and coinage it was (unless this is hidden in the obverse symbol under the boar: Figure 10). It is also unusual to find *-durum* as the second element in a British place-name. Here, therefore, I will simply review the two elements separately without expressing a strong preference for one particular reading.

CANI

1. Possibly a loan-word derived from a very ancient name for reed or cane that is cognate with Greek *kanna* and was borrowed into Latin as *canna*, both ultimately from a Semitic root, *kanu*. In both Classical languages *canna* was applied both to reeds and to objects made from them: reed-mats and reed-fences in Greek, reed-pipes and small boats or poled gondolas in Latin (see *LSG, LSL*). *Arundo donax*, the pole-reed, denoted by *kanna* and *canna*, only thrives in hot countries: *Phragmites communis* is its economically important counterpart futher north. The word is thought to have taken a route of its own into northern European vocabularies. In Britain *Cano*- appears in two early place-names, both of which could be of Roman origin:

Canonium, the Roman settlement at Kelvedon, Essex, and *Canovium*, the Roman fort at Caerhun in Wales. Rivet and Smith (1979, 296–7), citing Jackson (*Britannia* 1970, 70), and Delamarre (2003, 102) derive *Canonium* and *Canovium* from a possibly Celtic **câno-*, 'reed' (cf. Welsh *cawn*) plus an **-on(o)* suffix. If CANI really is built on the same root, the segmented rod sometimes seen above this element of the inscription (Figure11) might be a pictogram for 'cane-', and/or symbolise a staff of office or a divine attribute, and **Cani-* can be taken as a Brittonic item of vocabulary, cf discussion of ANTEÐIO (above). This would be unsurprising in the eastern Icenian canton.

2. *Cani-* (with an -/i/-) is unattested in bona fide place-names in Britain and is absent from Sims-Williams' listings of ancient Celtic place-names in Europe and Asia Minor (2006) and of Celtic personal names in Roman inscriptions (Raybould and Sims-Williams 2007). *Cani-* is indeed unusual as a component even in Gaulish personal names, though Delamarre (2003, 102) cites two, *Canio* and *Canius*, that might be relevant here. these might derive from a different Indo-European root, *gan(dh)-* (*IEW*, 351), which is similar to Semitic *kanu* and has a parallel history of extended use, but has known derivatives only in Germanic (*HGE*, 210 sv *kanôn) and, doubtfully, in Celtic. It denotes a bowl or dish – both attested from countless prehistoric contexts as items of ritual as well as convivial significance – and reflections of *kanôn occur in early and modern Scandinavian languages and dialects as *kani, kana, kane,* and *kœne*, whilst in middle Low German *kane* also means 'boat', incidentally convergent with the secondary meanings of Latin *canna* (above) but for different reasons.

DVRO

DVRO can be read either as an entire word in its own right or as an abbreviation, **Duro-*, in either sense derived from IE **dhuor-, *dhur-*. This has long been recognised as the root for Italic, Celtic and Germanic words for door or town gate (*IEW*, 278; Delamarre 2003, 155–6; Rivet and Smith 1979, 346–7; Sims-Williams 2006, 75). Of relevance to the British Isles are Welsh and Cornish *dor* and OE *dur* (plural *duru*); *duru-* is also common in OE compounds. Originally the word designated the gap in a boundary ditch, fence or wall controlling the passage of people, goods and animals into and out of an enclosed space: Dutch *door*, German *durch*, and English *through* are philologically cognate words. Barriers of wood or other suitable materials installed to close and protect such portals – gates and doors – give the commonest secondary meanings built on the primitive root in several different languages.

In this inscription DVRO might, like similarly placed inscriptions on other Icenian silver coins, represent the first part of a personal name or, more likely, title of office meaning 'Gate-(?keeper)', cf Gothic *daurawards*, ON *duravördr*, OHG *turivart*, OLG *duruwarderi*, OE *dureweard*, 'janitor' (Carr 1939, 69). Janus, the ancient Roman god of doors and gates, faced both ways and presided over the opening and close of the year and of military campaigns; his priest, the *rex sacrorum,* had vestigial archaic functions that resembled those of a *sacerdos civitatis* or *Esuprastus* (see discussion below). *Duro-* is uncommon as a component in Celtic personal names and is not listed as such in Evans (1967), who relates the Gaulish name *Duratius* ('Unlucky') and a few others like it to compounds with the prefix *Du-*, meaning 'bad'. Delamarre, however (2003, 156), noted a cluster of possibly relevant Galatian names: *Durius, Duronius, Duronia, Durissa* and *Durialos*, which he cautiously likened to French 'Dubourg'. If this is relevant here, DVRO- might after all represent a personal name rather than a title. Either way, the format CANI- / DVRO- could resemble AL FE / SCAVO and SVB ESVPRASTO / ESICO FECIT and record two separate levels of authority to strike the coinage, with DVRO- 'under' CANI-.

DVRO can alternatively be taken as all or part of a place-name. Theoretically it could stand alone and represent the Latinised form *durum* of a similar vernacular word, *duron, with the Latin locative case-ending -*o*, meaning 'at (the) *Durum*', as in Cunobelinus' CAMVLODVNO, 'at Camulodunum' (VA 1977–1). *Durum* is a common element in Continental place-names, almost always coming second in position in the word (Delamarre 2003, 156), whereas in Britain, where its use is confined to the South, it only occurs in second position in *Lactodurum*, the Roman town at Towcester, Northants (Rivet and Smith 1979, 382–3). Instead, in British place-names, which might include this coin, it normally comes first. Rivet and Smith (1979, 346–54) list *Durobrivae* (Kent and Huntingdonshire), *Durocobrivis* (Bedfordshire), *Durocornovium* (Wiltshire), *Durolevum* (probably Kent), *Duroliponte* (Cambridge), *Durovernum Cantiacorum* (Canterbury) and *Durovigutum* (Huntingdonshire), and with the sole exception of the ethnonym *Durotrages* (Dorset, see Breeze 2002b; cf Gaulish *Durocasses*), these names were assigned to Roman forts and Romano-British towns, some of which almost certainly had Iron-Age antecedents. Of particular relevance to Norfolk, Delamarre (2003, 156) observed in his very thorough analysis of the word that a *duron* must be a settlement on a plain whilst a *dunon* was on a hill.

There were several large earthwork enclosures in north-western Norfolk in the late Iron Age, some ancient, including the hill-fort at Thetford Castle, and some probably more recently built (Davies 1999, 30; 2009, 95–100). None of these supported obvious domestic settlement in the late Iron Age but all had likely functions as places for intermittent assembly. More relevant to this particular coinage are a few much more recent agglomerations of denser but sprawling settlement clusters and monuments in the south and east of the county (Davies 2000, 119–25), and it is tempting to connect the latter with a recent history of internal political change and protracted engagement with the Catuvellauni in particular (see Section 3). *Duron would have been an apt and accurate name for any such place in Norfolk including Thetford and the Iron-Age predecessor of the Roman *Venta Icenorum*, Market of the Iceni, at Caistor St Edmund. In this role **Duron* would resemble Latin *Forum*, with which it is in fact linguistically cognate (*IEW*, 278), and in compound British place-names it is semantically identical with such Continental formations as *Forum Domitii*, *Forum Iulii*, *Forum Segusiavorum*, or *Forum Ligneum* ('Wood Market') high in the French Pyrenees. Places so designated typically hosted periodic assizes, the military levy, markets or fairs, and other large public gatherings in areas which – like late prehistoric Norfolk – had a large pastoral component in their economies and a population that mostly lived on private estates, isolated farms or in scattered hamlets. In rural Italy and in Cisalpine Gaul under the Roman Republic – still a Gaulish environment en route to Romanisation and not unlike parts of southern Britain in the 1st century AD – rural assembly-places and small market towns with local administrative functions were known generically as *fora et conciliabula* (Livy *ab urbe condita libri* 25.5.6; 39.14.7). If this is what DVRO- signifies on the Icenian silver coinage it could equally be a complete name in itself or the prefix to another compound place-name which did not need to be spelt out: such places were rare in Norfolk, and everyone whom CANI's coinage concerned would have known which *Duron* was intended.

Result: Inconclusive. Either two names or titles, both built on roots intelligible in Celtic and in Germanic; one such name plus (part of) the name for an assembly-place somewhere in Norfolk; or, perhaps least likely, a single compound place-name expressed in grammatical Latin.

7–8 ALE and ALI / R[.?.] SCAV and AL FE / SCAVO PF[?] (figs 12–14)

This set of rather Romanised coinages, mostly found in northern Norfolk, was struck at some point between *c* AD 30 and 43 (AC 235; de Jersey 2003; de Jersey 2007), at latest during upheavals around the time of Cunobelinus' death *c* AD 40/42 (Rudd 2008). By close analogy with SVB ESVPRASTO / ESICO FECIT (below) the AL FE / SCAVO inscriptions can best be understood as written in (abbreviated) Latin.

The obverse depicts a wild boar either standing still and alert (Figure 12) or charging forward (Figures 13–14). As the standard of engraving deteriorated on later dies in the series, evidently struck to meet pressing expenses or a military emergency, the animal begins to lose its original identity and comes to look rather canine, although its curly tail remained that of a boar. There are torc and ring-and-pellet symbols above it and the inscription AL FE, ALE or ALI. All reverses have the same horse leaping to the right with a solar ring-and-pellet symbol above. The main inscription appears below the horse, and on one early die in the charging-boar series the letter R also appears to the left of the solar emblem (Figure 13). It is not clear from the single coin so far known from these dies whether a second letter was engraved to the right of this motif, so at present expansion into R[EX] is not warranted, though it needs to be registered as an unconfirmed possibility.

All reverses show a horse with an inscription SCA, SCAV or SCAVO underneath in bold lettering identical with the obverse inscription. On what is probably a head of series die (Figure 12) the C was evidently omitted by mistake and inserted as a correction between the tops of the S and the A. In the space below the A, PF (perhaps PE) was separately engraved in a spidery but competent hand: once again, a clear reading will only be secured when a coin comes to light that was struck sufficiently off-centre on the anvil to show more of the outer area of the die design.

7a ALE and ALI

Probably an abbreviation, which limits understanding. It is spelt both ways, which suggests that the second vowel was unstressed and had a sound ambiguous between /i/ and /e/, rather like the vowel in South African English 'yes'. It might represent a prefix *ale-* or *al-* + *e*[...] or *i*[...] from the root *al-*, *ol-*, 'further, in addition' (*IEW*, 24–5) which has abundant derivatives in Italic, Celtic, Germanic, Slavic and other Indo-European language families. As *all-* it is represented in Gaulish, meaning 'other', and as *all-* and *al-* in Germanic, meaning 'all'. OE has a common prefix *al-* or *eal-* meaning All-, as in All-Wise or All-Seeing. The non-Celtic and non-Classical cognomina Aledus and Alio are attested amongst 2nd-century soldiers of the *I Tungrorum* at Vindolanda (Cheryl Clay pers comm).

7b AL FE

The placement of the four letters AL FE either side of the boar's front legs seems to indicate that they represent two abbreviated words, AL..., shortened from *ALE..., identical with ALE or ALI (above), plus FE..., abbreviated from Latin *fe*[*cit*]: 'Al... made [me/it]'. The fourth letter, sometimes looking like an F because it runs into the edge of the coin, is now confirmed as an E (Rudd 2006). It is possible that the boar's front legs were intended to be read as the alternative II form of E (de Jersey 2003), filling out the first abbreviated word to match the other inscriptions of its type.

8 SCA, SCAV and SCAVO

In view of the near identicality in design of all the reverse dies in both versions of this series, SCA and SCAV can safely be regarded as abbreviations of the fully expressed SCAVO. If the coins' obverse legends are indeed in Latin and can be expanded as *Ale*[...] *fe*[*cit*], SCAVO will also be a Latinised version of a vernacular name with the Latin dative or ablative case-ending that means 'for Scavus' or '[under] Scavus'.

Here, Celtic offers scant help in understanding the inscription unless Welsh *ysgaw*, 'elder trees' provides a link (A. Breeze, pers comm). West Germanic offers a stronger lead, based on an important verb derived from IE *keu-s-* (*IEW*, 588). This has many meanings that include to see, scrutinize, inspect things like omens and troops, and to give or provide, as in our own expression 'to see to'. Relevant West Germanic parallels for SCAVO include OSax *skawôn* 'to see, observe' (*HGE*, 337), OE *sceâwian* 'to see, scrutinise, inspect; to select, choose, provide; to show (favour, respect); to grant; OE *sceâwere* 'an observer, someone who looks into a matter; a mirror', and the later Germanic personal name *Scauwo* (*ADN*, 1306). On this interpretation, the inscription SCAVO could specify an official function meaning 'provider', 'seer' or 'overseer'. An apt semantic parallel occurs in western Britain in the inscription on a (lost) mosaic floor at the Romano-Celtic temple of Nodens at Lydney Park in Gloucestershire (Henig 1984, 136; de la Bédoyère 2007, 199). Here, the superintendent of the cult had the mosaic laid out of offerings with the assistance of the *interpres* or interpreter [of the will of the god from signs, portents and dreams].

Any tribe's patron deity could reasonably be described as all-seeing and all-providing (West 2007, 171–3), and the services of a tribal leader or community priest entrusted with his cult and interpreting his will for his people must also have played a role in composing die designs (Creighton 2000) and sanctioning the release of consecrated revenues for conversion into coinage. Such an official could aptly have borne the title **Scavus*. This might indeed shed light on the design of an earlier Icenian uninscribed Face–Horse silver unit (Figure 18; AC 145; *c* 30–10 BC; C. Rudd *List* 23 (1996) no. 30). This shows a male head with a blinded, sewn-up eye socket but with an open seeing eye issuing forth from his mouth. In later Norse mythology, which drew on a repertoire of very ancient stories, Odin, the most important of the Æsir, sacrificed an eye at Mimir's well to obtain the (divine) gift of foresight. Fore-sight is exactly what this uninscribed coin portrays, and divination exercised in the name of an all-seeing Icenian deity could have been one function of a **Scavus* or an **Esuprastus* (see below).

An alternative theoretical possibility is that SCAVO might be a vernacular version of the Latin name *Scaevus*, meaning 'left-handed', having undergone exactly the same sound-shift as *Prastus* from Latin *praestes* or *praestus* (below), in which case the legend would simply mean 'for (or under) Leftie'. Latin translations and Latinised renderings of Celtic and Germanic personal names are well known to exist in situations where the individuals concerned were involved with Romans, inhabited Roman provinces, or were named in Latin histories (eg the heavily Latinised Germanic names Arminius or Ariovistus or Latin Ursus and Ursula, 'bear' and 'little she-bear', from Gaulish Artos). It would, however, be difficult to account for the occurrence of this phenomenon on a British coinage struck in an area so remote from the Roman world as Norfolk before the Claudian conquest without a great deal of fanciful conjecture.

PF (?PE)

This item beneath the A of Scavo on one beautifully crafted die (Figure 12) is puzzling. It was engraved in spidery lettering that seems to differ from the bold hand of AL FE and SCAVO, and its position suspended below the inserted C of the main legend makes it look like a countersignature, perhaps to validate the correction and differentiate the inserted letter from confusion with an otherwise symbolically significant waning moon. On well centred strikings the extra letters are not seen at all. It may well have been important to formally correct a major compositional mistake in the design of a ritually charged object that was too complicated and expensive to simply discard and re-do, just as Roman priests were obliged to repeat sacrificial ceremonies if something inauspicious occurred during the performance. It may be for similar reasons that inaccurate attempts to reproduce misunderstood letters on dies in the later ECEN series were abandoned in favour of a graphic symbol that it was impossible to botch. On the SCAVO PF die it is by no means certain that the second visible letter is an F and not an E – that uncertainty will only be resolved when another coin is found that has been struck sufficiently off centre to clarify the reading. Until that happens it is pointless to try to interpret its significance.

Result: *Ali-* and *Ale-* are equally valid prefixes in Celtic and in Germanic. *Scavo* (Latinised dative or ablative of **Scavus*) is difficult to make sense of in Celtic but is intelligible as a title of priestly office in West Germanic meaning 'seer', 'overseer', 'interpreter' or 'provider'. A Latin reading of both inscriptions taken together makes most sense: '*Ale-* made [me/the coinage] for or under *Scavu*[*s*]' – an abbreviated version of the same formula seen in *sub Esuprasto / Esico fecit* (next below).

Face–Horse format silver units c AD 37–40 (Figure 15)

9–10 SVB ESVPRASTO / ESICO FECIT

This was probably the last Icenian coinage, struck on one or, more probably, several occasions between at earliest *c* AD 37–40, shortly before the Claudian invasion, and at latest the late 40s–early 50s AD under Claudius' dispensation (AD 41–54), when blanks for silver coins of some sort seem to have been made on the site of the 2nd-phase ritual monument at Thetford (Gregory 1991, 193–6). It is difficult on stylistic grounds to date the Esuprastus/Esico coinage with absolute confidence. Obverse dies (Figure 15) often resemble Julio-Claudian coin images and official portrait bronzes both of Gaius Caesar and of Claudius have been found in East Anglia. Chadburn (2006, 362) has made a strong case for ascribing the Esuprastus/Esico coinage to the time of Gaius, an accurately modelled official bronze bust of whom, atop a globe, has indeed been found near Colchester (Salway 1993, 45). The Catuvellauni–Trinovantes would have had to renew their alliance with Rome around the time of Gaius' accession in AD 37. Gaius famously spent the winter in Gaul in AD 39–

Boar–Horse silver units: AL FE / SCAVO PF; ALI / R SCAV; ALE / SCA

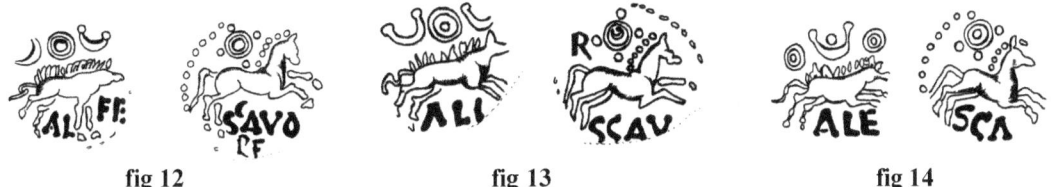

fig 12   fig 13   fig 14

Face–Horse silver unit: SVB ESVPRASTO / ESICO FECIT

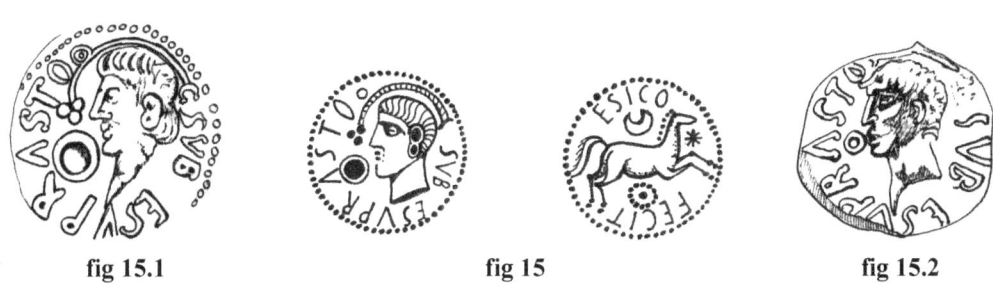

fig 15.1   fig 15   fig 15.2

Uninscribed gold staters   Uninscribed silver unit

fig 16   fig 17   fig 18

Images not to scale. Source of illustrations: figs 1–7; 9–11; 15 Amanda Chadburn, AC 275; 310; 360; 290; 315; 365; 400; 410; 230; 200; fig 8 Amanda Chadburn, AC 405, ed D Nash Briggs after C Rudd *List* 50 no. 80; figs 7a; 12–14; 15.1–2 D Nash Briggs after Chris Rudd *List* 70 no. 44; *Britannia* 1979 pl XII.8 (Joist Fen hd, Lakenheath, Suffolk) and CCI 98.2390 (fd 'Burnham Market' hd, SW Norfolk); CCI 00.0261 (fd 'Burnham Market' hd, SW Norfolk); 16–18 Chris Rudd *List* 23 no. 24; 58 no. 33; 23 no. 30.

40 and considered invading Britain, being much in need of a military triumph, and he did send a nominal detachment across, but otherwise confined himself to ostentatious diplomatic intervention (Braund 1996, 91–6). There was ample opportunity during this time for the Iceni, too, to make a treaty of official friendship with him, in which case they would have had to renew their credentials soon after Claudius' accession in AD 41 as well. If they did this, it may account for the reflection of various imperial portraits in this coin imagery. Any such event would have been accompanied by a handsome Roman cash subsidy, which may even have helped to fund a coinage and perhaps the impressive building works on the 2nd-phase ceremonial monument at Fison Way, Thetford (Davies 2009, 130–2).

There are two design formats (Figures 15.1, 15.2), but the inscription on both is identical and in perfect Latin, plainly stating that Esico made [this, *sc* the coinage? the dies? the payment?] under [the authority of] Esuprastus. Esuprastus' portrait in the most informative design (15.1) is crowned by a semicircular arching device, perhaps insignia of office, that is embellished with three symbols: three pellets ahead of him, a pellet in ring over his brow, and a crescent moon or torc behind his head. All three elements are also found on other Icenian coinages and may perhaps represent component parts of the federal territory. Sun disk and crescent moon are also known emblems on items like anthropoid short swords, calendars (Fitzpatrick 1996) and ritual headgear, all of which were of religious significance. Plausibly this device, together with the sun-disk or ceremonial shield that he also faces, identifies the portrait as that of a priest, which the accompanying inscription confirms. It is a beautifully composed design in every detail.

This coin's inscription contains two Latinised vernacular names or titles of office: ESVPRASTO and ESICO. The correct reading of the obverse legend is now absolutely clear from several well preserved coins that have come to light since Derek Allen and Henry Mossop first published the coin type in the 1970s and interpreted the incomplete and damaged lettering on all the specimens then available for study as the possible legend SVB RI PRASTO. In a scrupulously accurate drawing from a photograph of one of these coins that is often reproduced (e g Robinson and Gregory 1987, 27; Davies 2009, 135), stumps of what we now know to be the E and S of ESV can clearly be seen attached to the underside of the bust: the R and I of the old reading were understandable misinterpretations of a fragmentary inscription and can now be discarded.

9 ESVPRASTO

This is a compound word with two components, ESV- and -PRASTO.

ESV-

See AESV (above) and Chadburn (2006, 325). This was an honorific divine and human title known in this period both to stand alone as the euphemistic name of a deity and as the first element in numerous compound theophoric names (*Esuateros, Esugenus, Esumagius, Esunertus* etc: Evans 1967, 200). The Gaulish version *Esus* or *Esu-* was the form most compatible with Latin usage (eg Lucan, *Pharsalia* 1.445; cf Meid 1994, 36; M Green 1986, 110), which may account for its use here in a Latinised inscription in place of the earlier Icenian AESV-.

-PRASTO

This is Latinised and represents *PRASTVS with the ablative case ending -O that is demanded by the Latin preposition SVB, meaning 'under'. *Prastus* does not belong to any ancient Celtic or Germanic vocabulary set. Glen Prosen and the Prosen Water, to the north of Forfar in Scotland, contain what may be a related element (Prosen was *Glen-prostyn* in 1463), and has been compared with the Breton personal names *Prost-lon, -voret, Iud-prost*, and the Old Welsh *Onbraust*, but the etymology and meaning of *praust* or *prost* remain unknown (Paul Kavanagh pers comm, citing Watson 1922, 430). In the compound Icenian word ESVPRASTO, -PRASTO can however be understood as a useful and interesting loan-word representing Latin *praestes*: a presiding deity, official, or priest. See Sills (2003a) for a similar line of reasoning. Related vocabulary, with which any competent Latin speaker would have been familiar, included *praesto, praestu*: 'ready, near at hand; alert, keen'; *praestus* [colloquial and post-classical], 'out in front'; *praestare*: 'to stand in front, be excellent, superior'; *praestatio*: 'a guarantee, pledge'. Where the form of the naturalised loan-word is concerned, only the /a/ of Latin /ae/ was sounded perhaps partly because in Germanic the front of the diphthong in this position would have carried the accent. Latin *praestes* or *praestus* became Icenian *[*Esu*]prastus* whilst Latin *praeses* ('governor') became *prasu-* in Icenian Prasutagus (Tacitus *Ann.* 14.31.1) and Corieltavian ESVPRASV (VA 920, 924; see section 3). This resembles a sound-shift attested elsewhere in West Germanic in words where an original /ae/ preceded a following back vowel and moved to /a/, as for instance when Latin Caesar became Old English Casere (Campbell 1959, 203; Nielsen 1989, 149; Nielsen 1998, 100; 159). In contrast, in an Insular Celtic language Latin (or Germanic) /ae/ could be expected to move to /ei/ or /e/ – as in EISV not AESV on Dobunnic coins, not to /a/ (Jackson 1953, 335; see ibid 324–5 for discussion of the way in which IE /ai/ passed through /ei/ or /e/ in the insular Celtic of this period).

Latin *praestes* and *praestus* were rich in overtones of readiness (*praesto*), of standing out or being distinguished (*praestare*), and of giving or lending (*praestatio*). Above all, in the Latin of the 1st century AD, *praestes* was used to denote both a presiding *deity* and a human *priest*, a convenient ambiguity for a tribal ruler with priestly functions. For further discussion of innovative titles for community rulers in Norfolk and Lincolnshire in this last pre-conquest generation see section 3.

The inscription ESVPRASTVS probably means '(chief) priest of Esu(s)', denoting the sacral head of state, and as such resembles the parade of military, priestly and honorific titles on the Julio-Claudian coinage of the day: *Imp*(*erator*), *Augustus*, *Divi F*(*ilius*), *Pont*(*ifex*) *Max*(*imus*) etc.

10 ESICO

A name or title of uncertain etymology, probably built on the Latin-friendly ESV- version of AESV-. Place-names of similar form are recorded at *Aesica* or *Esica* (Great Chesters fort on Hadrian's Wall) and in Italy and Bithynia (Evans 1964, 200-1; Rivet and Smith 1979, 242), but are are not included amongst the Celtic toponyms listed in Sims-Williams (2006). The version *Aesica* is phonologically similar to Icenian *Aesu* and *Aesuminus* and might be based on another West Germanic version of Brittonic/Latin *Esu-*. This could readily have occurred in Northumberland: for some plainly Germanic names on Hadrian's wall see Clay (2007). The coin's inscription makes it clear that ESICO is a personal masculine name or title with an -o ending that puts it in a different grammatical declension from Aesica. Personal names in Gaul are occasionally known to have ended in *-ico*, including Vertico, a Nervian from the Germanic–Celtic language contact zone (Caesar *BG* 5.45.2; 5.49.2; cf Evans 1967, 385). Gaulish and Brittonic also had an *-icos* ending, Latinised as *-icus*, which occurs in personal names. It is clear, however, that the Icenian name is not *Esicos but *Esico*: there was plenty of room on the die for a final S in this carefully composed inscription had it in fact been sounded.

Esico is otherwise unrecorded in any linguistically Celtic context, but it and several other very similar names are liberally attested in early Germanic literary and inscriptional contexts, including some built on **Ansi-*: *Asico, Etsico* and *Asicho* (*ADN*: 121) and others built on **Aza-*, minus the -n- of **Ansi,*: *Esico, Ezico, Ezzico, Aesica, Esic, Esik* and *Esich* (*ADN*, 219–220). The Romanised name, *Esicus*, of a bishop of Poitiers *c* AD 500 is in the same continuum and is analysed by Kaufmann (1968, 219) as **Aid-s-ic-*. Icenian ESICO would be the earliest known example of this name-form. As a personal name built on **(A)Esu-* it would mean 'belonging or dedicated to Esus', in a continuum with *Aesuminus, Aessicunia* and *Aesibuas* (above). As a title of office it might indicate another priesthood of Esus, cognate with the Roman (*Flamen*) *Dialis* (of Jupiter) or (*Flamen*) *Martialis* (of Mars).

Result: Probably one title of senior political and sacral office (ESVPRASTO) and one theophoric personal name or title of office (ESICO). Some promising parallels in early West Germanic for both names.

3 Discussion

The findings above can be summarised thus:

NAME	Celtic?	Either Celtic or Germanic	Germanic?	Latin loan-word?
ANTEÐI[O]	YES			
ECEN			YES	
ECE			YES	
SAENV			YES	
AESV			YES	
CANI		YES		
DVRO		YES		
ALI or ALE		YES		
SCAVO			YES	
ESV-		YES		
-PRASTO				YES
ESICO		?	YES	

This gives what may be two to four titles of office (SCAVO, ESVPRASTO and possibly ANTEÐI[O] and ESICO), four to seven that probably represent epithets of tribal deities upon which district, clan or personal names and titles of office could be based (ECEN, ECE, SAENV, AESV and possibly ANTEÐI[O], CANI and DVRO), two to four that might simply be personal names (ANTEÐI[O], ESICO and possibly CANI and DVRO), and one that may represent a place-name (DVRO).

So where does this leave us? Here there is only space to draw together a few pointers for further research.

Traces of an ancient Germanic language in pre-Roman Britain?

Where the linguistic status of the names from early British inscriptions is concerned the phonology of AESV, AESVMINVS, SAENV, -PRASTO and Corieltavian -PRASV is self-consistent and compatible with reconstructions of some early West Germanic speech forms. Apart, probably, from ANTEÐI[O] and possibly *duron as a place-name, all the names on Icenian coinage might have been drawn from an early Germanic language. Even if this cannot be definitively proven, it cannot be ruled out. Some of this vocabulary does seem to make deliberately Germanic choices: Germanic *ece-* not Celtic *dru-* for 'oak', *sae-* not *mor-* for dangerous waters, and *Aesu-* not *Esu-* or *Eisu-* when not embedded in Latin.

The presence in pre-Roman Britain of scraps of a philologically Germanic onomastic vocabulary does not of course mean that its users would necessarily have spoken the language from which they were conscripted – they might for instance reflect an archaic language of sacred song – only that they might have done. Neither does it mean that any such vernacular, if indeed in current use in Norfolk, was identical with contemporary vernaculars in Flanders or Frisia (which it probably was not), nor that it would necessarily have been the only language of

Iron-Age Norfolk, which it was manifestly not, since a standard form of Gaulish or Brittonic is recorded on some Icenian and almost all other inscribed ancient British coins and a majority of recorded ancient place-names, so was obviously familiar at least to all of ancient Britain's political elites.

Even if some of the Iceni did speak a non-Celtic language amongst themselves, emblematic perhaps of a North-Sea regional identity, we could expect to find some Brittonic names amongst them, just as British names later occurred in Anglo-Saxon dynasties. If, however, *Ecen, Ece, Saenu/Saeviu, Aesu, Scavo* and *Esico* are indeed as Germanic as they look, the stock from which they were drawn must at some point have been current in a living community; and if these names are juxtaposed with what may be a West-Germanic phonetic treatment of two Latin loan-words, we would have to wonder why the Iceni were doing that if at least some of their most influential families did not actually speak that kind of language.

It is pointless to deny the significance at least in north-western Norfolk of seaborne contact with Continental northern Europe. Norfolk's post-glacial founder population was from northern Europe and took permanent root on the British seaboard when the North Sea flooded the Dogger lowlands. There is no subsequent break in the cultural continuity of rural life in pre-Roman Norfolk, though the Iceni and their ancestors did engage culturally and intermarry with inland Britons of ultimately Atlantic extraction (Davies 2009; Oppenheimer 2007, 138; 159; 223 and *passim*). The Iceni must surely count amongst what Julius Caesar described as Britain's aboriginal peoples (*BG* 5.12.1). What is more, the Iceni and their forebears were immensely rich and influential: cultural activity and craftsmanship were concentrated in the fen edge during the late Bronze Age and in western Norfolk in the later first millennium BC (Robinson and Gregory 1987; Davies 1999; Davies 2009), facing the Wash and the open sea. Their principal Iron-Age port(s), long lost from view by a changing shoreline, cannot have been far from where the Icknield way met the coast, somewhere near Snettisham, Hunstanton, or Brancaster, and we can safely infer the presence of some actual German visitors further down the Icknield Way during the brief 2nd phase (40s–early 50s AD) of the monument at Fison Way, Thetford, complete with household belongings and genetically German house-mice (Searle et al 2008; Gregory 1991, 175). Even in the Roman period the old aristocratic environment of western Norfolk retained a highly distinctive social profile with numerous large country estates but minimal town development, and it may be relevant in this connection that it was precisely to this part of the federal territory that, on purely internal numismatic grounds, Amanda Chadburn (2006, 479) tentatively ascribed the majority of the Icenian coins that bear the non-Celtic inscriptions.

On both sides of this part of the North Sea wetland communities with their self-sufficiently prosperous and rather specialised ways of life seem to have been conspicuously stable within their territories over immensely long periods: this might reasonably be expected to have gone hand in hand with a comparable stability in whatever vernacular languages they spoke. Nielsen (1989, 109–143) has provided apt examples from several other historical situations to illustrate the disproportionately strong and long-enduring influence that the language or dialect of a founder population, however small compared with whatever succeeded it, can have upon the linguistic history of the area concerned. Given its history and its geographical status as a near-peninsula in the North Sea, it is by no means unthinkable that the Iron-Age vernacular language at least of north-western Norfolk might have developed there *in situ* over several centuries as an insular instance in its own right of the West Germanic (Ingvaeonic) languages concurrently emergent in the coastlands of what are now Belgium, the Netherlands and Denmark.

It is unreasonable to suppose that tribal vernaculars can ever have been uniform thoughout mainland Britain or that specific dialects and ways of saying things were not fiercely defended aspects of individual, social and political identity. Members of social and military elites, however, and religious specialists, all of whom spent a lot of their lives interacting with outsiders to their communities of origin, must always have had fluent use of languages that were mutually understood and were not unduly inflammatory to speak with rival regional groups and with strangers. In the late pre-Roman Iron Age, Brittonic, as spoken for instance by the Catuvellaunian elite and employed for most non-Latin British coin inscriptions, must have been the most important medium for inter-tribal communication precisely because it was not a home vernacular peculiar to any one regional group or faction. It was also formally almost identical to Gaulish, which had for centuries served exactly the same purpose on the Continent south of the Rhine, bridging several markedly different sets of regional vernaculars (Caesar BG 1.1.2). Claudius' administrators will constantly have had to use interpreters when dealing with people who didn't speak Latin, and Brittonic, the public language of the southern British elites on whose cooperation the Romans depended, must have been the routine filter through which all kinds of information, including non-Brittonic names and place-names, were transmitted into Latin. By way of comparison, Swahili functioned in much this way in early 20th-century British East Africa. Soon after Claudius' invasion, probably in AD 45/6, a census will have had to be held as a first step in the routine of setting Britain up as a province (Isserlin 2007). Tribal and place-names were then inventoried and officially recorded, and from this point onwards Brittonic and Romanised versions of such names dominate the written record.

Whatever tribal vernaculars were also still spoken – and *Aesuminus, Aessicunia* and *Aesibuas* hint that at least some lightly modified Germanic names were to be found in Roman Britain in the 2nd to 4th centuries AD – Brittonic must have served as a ready means of communication wherever Latin was unfamiliar or known only to townsmen or educated elites. Nielsen (1998, 62; 153) noted that British languages must always have been spoken in the countryside, that Romano-British place-names taken over into Anglo-Saxon reflect vernacular, not Latin, pronunciation, and that Latin vocabulary borrowed into Old English has sound features typical of vulgar, not educated, Latin.

It is a fair presumption in the absence of any conflicting linguistic evidence and in the light of all that is known of its archaeology and history, that in western and some of central and southern Britain most tribal vernaculars in the first century AD were in fact philologically Celtic. It is at least open to question whether this was equally true of coastal eastern Britain, above all in northern and western Norfolk, where Continental Germanic must always have been understood and there may long have existed a localized insular form of an early West Germanic language.

Titles of office

Icenian inscribed coinage does not appear, on the evidence here presented, to name individual rulers or officials by ordinary personal names. *Esuprastus* has understandably been identified with *Rex Icenorum Prasutagus* '[the] king of the Iceni, Prasutagus' (Tacitus *Ann*. 14.31.1) whose death in AD 60 was the first in a chain of events leading to Boudica's uprising. Tacitus was a dramatic writer introducing a dangerous episode in recent Roman history. He wasn't writing historical anthropology, and he gave the Icenian head of state the title with which any tribal leader who was also an official friend of Rome would have been dignified to his readers. *Rex* tells us nothing about Prasutagus' title of office amongst his own people. In fact, *Prasutagus* is itself almost certainly the title of highest office in the Icenian confederacy, held by a man whose personal name is unknown. The word can be analysed as a compound of two loan-words, *Prasu-* and *-tagus*, the first straight from Latin and the second from Gaulish via Latin, with a good parallel in Northern Italy.

Prasu- is from Latin *praeses*, meaning guardian, protector, or the governor of a Roman province. It will have entered Icenian vocabulary by exactly the same route and with the same sound modification as -PRASTO, discussed above. It also occurs in Lincolnshire on coins of the Corieltavi inscribed ESVPRASV (Williams 2001, 13; Sills 2003a), where *prasu*, 'guardian, governor', was compounded with the honorific sacral name *Esu-* to give what is probably a third power-title in the same regional continuum. A Roman provincial governor was in charge of military affairs in his province – in this period the model would have been Gaul – and *prasu* may have been adopted specifically to denote a ruler's responsibility for the military levy in a tribal confederacy run by an assembly. Its currency already in first-century Britain could incidentally have relevance to the survival of a semantically related *prass* word in Welsh and Old English long after the Romans had departed (Breeze 1992).

-tagus seems to be exactly the same word as Gaulish *tagos*, meaning 'magistrate', as in the *tagos toutas* attested in Cisalpine Gaul, where it meant community magistrate (Meid 1994, 13–16). *Prasutagus* would then translate as '(military) governor and head of state'. If the title *Esuprastus* denoted the chief priest or *sacerdos civitatis* (Tacitus *Ger*. 10), entrusted with divination and sacrifice on behalf of the entire confederated tribe, *Prasutagus* would have been its *summus magistratus* responsible, amongst other things, for supervising the military levy and for representing the tribe in its dealings with outsiders. *Prasutagus* and *Esuprastus* would therefore have been the secular and sacral titles respectively for the office of supreme confederate ruler, qualification for which could well have run in an old royal lineage. There is no reason why the same official should not have held several offices at the same time and be known by different titles in different functional contexts. *Esu-, -Prastu(s), Prasu-, -tagus* and possibly *Anteði*, all borrowings from Catuvellaunian, Gaulish and Roman usage, seem to have supplied versatile elements from which a new terminology of state office could be built in these socially conservative and probably linguistically mixed British tribal areas, and the use of Latin loan-words suggests a context for this development in the early 1st century AD.

What we do not seem to find on Icenian coinage is a parade of the compound personal power-names of rulers like Tincomaros, Aððedomarus, Tasciovanus, or Cunobelinus, all of whom must have been sovereign overlords or high kings in the strictest sense, the specific title for which was Gaulish and Brittonic *Rix* and Roman *Rex*. This was a foreign role without a name in primitive Germanic, but Celtic *Rix* was adopted relatively early into the Continental Germanic languages to denote a style of personal dominance that was starting to emerge during the period of Roman occupation of Gaul and Britain (Thompson 1965). Germans had other vocabulary for their own styles of kingship and magistracy in societies run by citizen assemblies (D.H. Green 1998, 7–140; 151–2; Nielsen 1989, 27; Thompson 1965). Amongst the Iceni, too, there is as yet no confirmed example of the title *Rix* or *Rex* on their coinage.

Nothing currently known about them suggests that they ever had, or would have accepted, the sovereign overlordship of a High King or *Rix* on the Belgic or Catuvellaunian model. The polyfocal federated state which they seem to have succeeded in creating must have been governed otherwise. Thus, as late as AD 47, when Aulus Plautius must have attempted to impose the *lex Iulia de armis* upon all the Iceni, some of them rose in arms and with associates of their own were defeated at a wetland stronghold: they might as well have been asked to surrender their manhood as to renounce carrying weapons with which they had probably been presented when they qualified as adults to attend the tribal assembly (cf Tacitus *Germania* 13). Despite the military cost of defeating these insurgents, the Romans seem not to have held a named Icenian king responsible for the uprising, and afterwards the Iceni were left to continue self-governance until AD 61. Their titular head of state, presumably Tacitus' Prasutagus, might in fact sincerely have made exactly the same excuses for not having prevented the AD 47 uprising as Ambiorix, joint head of state with Catuvolcus of the Eburones (Belgic Gaul), made to Julius Caesar in 54 BC (*BG* 5.27.3). He said it was in the nature of his powers to command (*imperia*) that the armed assembly (*multitudo*) had no less binding authority (*iuris*) over him than he had over the assembly.

The civitas Icenorum in the 1st century AD

Can a dozen coin inscriptions really add much to an understanding of Norfolk in the Late Iron Age? I think they can. At very least they confirm an impression apparent also from aspects of their archaeology that the Iceni had a strong sense of a distinctive cultural identity and that they preferred to conduct their affairs in their own way. For instance they wanted, and obtained, a lot of gold, silver, copper and tin and supported incomparably fine metalsmiths, but must at the same time have actively maintained a self-imposed ban upon the importation of wine and associated drinking wares in the 1st century AD: no outside authority could have have stopped them trading by sea for the luxuries of city civilisation, had they wanted them. In this they concurred with the Continental northern Belgae and Germans who refused to import such things on the grounds that they would soften the spirits of war-hardened men (Caesar *BG* 1.1.3; 2.15.4; 4.2.1, 6). Worse still, they were known to promote the fortunes of would-be overlords.

The oldest Icenian heartlands faced the North Sea and their inscribed coinage seems to display some of the more Germanic aspects of their vocabulary and pronunciation. This in fact was nothing new: two earlier Icenian coin types evoked north European mythological themes that are otherwise well attested only in the Scandinavian narrative tradition. One is the tale of how Odin lost his eye, seemingly illustrated on an Icenian silver unit (fig 18, see under SCAVO above). The other concerns wolves (Nash Briggs 2009c; 2010). In one version, cosmic wolves continually chase and eventually catch both sun and moon, whilst in the other a monstrous primordial beast, sometimes pictured as a wolf, bursts free from magical restraint at the crack of Doom to splatter the heavens with blood and swallow the sun, moon and heavenly bodies (and in Norse mythology, Odin himself) before a fresh cosmic cycle begins (Simek 1993, 80–1; Debord 1991). Both themes are implicit in the design of the first extensive gold coinage of East Anglia (figs 16–17, AC 20–30): this famously stands apart from all other British stater coinages of its time, which bore stock versions of a formulaic solar horse on their reverses (Sills 1998). It is of some relevance in this connection that the name by which this particular cosmic monster was later known in Scandinavia – Fenrir or the Fenriswolf – can be understood as 'fen-dweller' (Simek 1993, 81), having been fettered and bound on a sacred island in a lake. We do not know what the Iceni called their own mythic wolf or their fens, but images of three wetland birds – avocet, bittern, and lapwing – were worked into the upper background design of Norfolk Wolf B gold staters (fig 17; Kretz 1999), making him a wolf in a fen – something an Icenian champion warrior or charioteer might also have felt himself to be. Wolves were emblematic of the most dangerous kind of early Germanic warband, wolf-warriors, akin to the berserks (Simek 1993, 35; 338). Curiously, totem wolves recur in East Anglia in the post-Roman period in the name of the Wuffing royal dynasty.

Norfolk Wolf gold staters were first struck between 56 and 54 BC to finance opposition to Julius Caesar's invasions, with a second series soon after 54 BC, when Caesar left the defeated Cassivellaunus and his allies with a punitive tribute to pay in three annual installments (Sills 1998; Sills 2000). Cassivellaunus must have taken energetic measures to assemble all that gold, and the wealthy Iceni must have been tempting neighbours to lean upon for contributions (Kretz 1999; Sills 2000; Rudd 2008). Norfolk Wolf staters are distributed towards the north and west of the county and were struck in such large quantities that towards the end of the series the quality both of die engraving and gold alloy deteriorated, suggestive of a period of extremely high and eventually unsustainable mint activity.

Under Cassivellaunus' successors the Catuvellauni thrived and expanded, eventually gaining control of Camulodunum and presumably also of the Trinovantes. The Iceni must have found this a threatening development, but were well protected from a similar fate by their independent wealth, daunting geography, free access to the sea, and their polyfocal tribal structure. They could, and did, maintain a social distance. Very little of Cunobelinus' coinage is found in Icenian lands: nowhere did Catuvellaunian coinage replace that of a pre-existing Icenian authority and even the Romans left them to manage their own affairs until AD 61. The Catuvellauni could, nonetheless, have caused the Iceni great trouble and expense in other ways, and the distribution of later Icenian coinages is biased towards their landward frontiers, in areas where there are other reasons to think that political activity was becoming focussed (Davies 2009, 119–25; Nash Briggs 2009c).

Chris Rudd (2008) has given a persuasive account of relations between the later Catuvellaunian kings and the Iceni, with which I largely concur. They probably struck a series of increasingly unequal treaties whose main purpose for the Iceni was to secure freedom from destructive interference and for the Catuvellauni to secure access on favourable terms to slaves, raw materials, livestock, metalwork, and a range of specialised services. Such treaties were devices that tended to promote social change in both partners and were something that the Romans, in particular, excelled in exploiting (Nash 1987; Braund 1984; Braund 1996): theirs was an example open to emulation by any ambitious regime. Such relations with their most powerful neighbour could account for the deferential display of Catuvellaunian design motifs on many of the later Icenian coinages and provide a context for the adoption of Brittonic and Latin vocabulary into the language of Icenian governance. The latest treaty with the Catuvellauni will have lapsed on Cunobelinus' death, and would have had to be renegotiated with his successors. The Esico/Esuprasto coinage suggests that the Iceni also had an independent treaty of friendship with Rome under Gaius and Claudius that would have safeguarded their domestic interests in the event of political instability on their borders at the end of Cunobelinus' long reign.

I think Icenian coinage and archaeology together suggest that during the 1st century AD at least some sections of the Icenian people must have begun to forge the more cohesive political institutions that long-term peaceful engagement with powerful outsiders now demanded, and were attempting to do so without abandoning collective social norms. I envisage a process that was broadly similar to developments in parts of central Gaul in the 2nd and 1st centuries BC (Nash 1978), though with a different outcome that may have leaned heavily upon religion to hold a polyfocal and perhaps ethnically diverse society together (Nash Briggs 2009c).

State formation seldom proceeds without bloodshed and we cannot exclude the possibility of episodic conflict, always expensive, amongst factions with opposing interests in Norfolk in the first half of the 1st century AD. Some of them certainly did strike a lot of silver coinage, probably in the 30s AD, which is seldom found far from home territory and never replaced the coinage of any neighbouring people. Instead, this outpouring reflects intermittently very high levels of internal expenditure, whilst the consignment of exceptionally large quantities of it to the ground probably testifies to the intensive ritual activity characteristic of Icenian public life (Nash Briggs 2009c; cf Haselgrove and Wigg-Wolf 2005). In this process they seem not to have instituted a tributary kingdom under personal control on the Catuvellaunian model. Instead, the political model that may provide the best fit for their coinage and pre-conquest archaeology is one in which sovereign authority remained vested in tribal and district assemblies of all free adult males, resembling what Caesar (*BG* 6.23.5) described in German societies across the Rhine: 'In peace-time they had no community magistrates, but the leading figures of districts and *pagi* dispensed justice and arbitrated disputes'. They would come together in larger groupings under appointed or elected war leaders only when specific circumstances demanded, and were otherwise held together by the organized religious activity for which there is ample evidence in late prehistoric Norfolk. The absence throughout most of Norfolk's earlier prehistory of permanently settled central places with potential administrative and redistributive functions comparable with *oppida* elsewhere in lowland Britain is congruent with this picture, as is the presence, concentrated in the north-western Norfolk landscape, of a number of boundaried features (Davies 1999, 30) that could well have served, amongst other functions, as assembly-points for district meetings or the tribal levy – times when it was important to be able the shut the gates on the proceedings (cf Caesar *BG* 5.56.2). In such a society the *Esuprastus* or *Prasutagus* would probably have spent most of his year moving around the territory from estate to estate of the senior nobility and cantonal 'kings', consuming their surpluses, resolving disputes, dispensing justice and conducting sacrifice.

Long-term involvement with rich foreign states always made it difficult for nominally egalitarian agro-pastoralist elites to control the activities of ambitious individuals and avoid forming more permanently centralised political institutions (Thompson 1965). There may indeed be hints in Icenian archaeology of a coming-together at the end of the pre-Roman Iron Age of some larger clusters of landholders in sprawling settlements to the south and east of the old north-western focus: Thetford, Saham Toney, Ashill, and Caistor St Edmund (with its own distinguished local prehistory) were certainly amongst them (Davies 1996, 80; Davies 1999; Davies 2009, 119–25). If formal confederation did indeed occur in the 1st century AD it may be reflected in successive and extremely expensive changes to the impressive ceremonial site at Fison Way, Thetford (Robinson and Gregory 1987, 44–7; Gregory 1991; Bradley 2005, 184–8; Davies 2009, 130–2): in its final configuration in the 50s AD, perhaps partially financed with a hefty loan from Nero and his rapacious mentor Seneca (Cassius Dio *Roman History* 62.2.1), a single very large roundhouse built in the 40s or early 50s AD was flanked by two others, each fronted by a further circular feature as though to reflect a formalized union amongst a politico–religious threesome. At the same time the boundary features of the site were dramatically enlarged and embellished for the second time in under twenty years. By way of possible analogy for this ostentatious public performance, the city of Rome had an ancient (though, in their case, inconspicuous) ritual boundary, the *pomerium*, that defined the space within which the urban auspices were taken. It went unchanged for centuries until in the course of constitutional reforms and to mark the addition of new territories to the Roman state, it was enlarged in turn by Sulla (81 BC), Julius Caesar (40s BC) and Claudius (40s AD: Braund 1996, 107).

Material legacies of this period include visible changes in settlement pattern, the outpouring of silver coinage, and the creation of public monuments. Cultural legacies include the influence of Brittonic and Latin upon the traces that remain of a tribal vernacular language within the *civitas Icenorum*, biassed as ancient inscriptions and documentary sources inevitably are towards the official languages of political elites. Unless and until a scrap of connected text is discovered to confirm its linguistic identity, evidence for use of a non-Latin, non-Brittonic, but possibly coastal West Germanic language in late prehistoric and Roman Norfolk must depend upon analysis of personal names, theonyms, and political titles, beginning with Late Iron-Age coin inscriptions.

Acknowledgements

This paper is a revision of a short pilot study (Nash Briggs 2008) and I am grateful to the many colleagues who have read, commented upon and constructively criticised intermediate drafts along the way. Most especially I would like to thank Amanda Chadburn (Figures 1–7; 9–11; 15) and Chris Rudd (Figures 16–18) for permission to reproduce drawings and photographs of coins, Andrew Breeze and Frances White for advice and critical attention in matters concerning linguistic research, Thomas Charles-Edwards, Richard Dance, Martin Henig, Nicolas Jacobs, Paul Kavanagh, Heather O'Donoghue and Patrick Sims-Williams for helpful guidance on particular points, and Stephen Oppenheimer for raising questions that piqued my curiosity and led me into this enquiry in the first place (Oppenheimer 2007, 323–39). I am of course solely responsible for the views I have expressed in this paper.

Coda 1: The letter Đ

Đ first occurs in Gaul and Belgica in the late 1st century BC, where it can alternate in the same word with Θ, D, S and a barred S. On British coins it alternates with D and Θ. It was an innovative addition to the Roman alphabet and we cannot exclude the possibility that one of the seats of alphabetic experimentation was in Britain itself, which had an influential centre of druidic learning (Caesar *BG* 6.13.11). Both Gaulish and German priests and officials are known to have used writing for ritual and administrative purposes that included divination or sortilege (Caesar *BG* 6.14.3; Tacitus *Ger*.10). Several scripts were in concurrent use in different areas in the 1st centuries BC and AD, including ones based on Greek, North Italic, Celtiberian and Roman alphabets (Williams 2001; Clay 2007, 53; Russell 1995, 198–207). There were also alphabetic or syllabic symbols of peoples' own devising (e.g. Sills 2004), including early forms of Germanic runes (Elliott 1959; see Scheers 1977, 237 for an example). British coinage largely sticks to the Roman alphabet then current in Gaul, with the additional letters Θ and Đ.

Both Gaulish and Germanic had consonantal sounds that were alien to Latin and impossible to represent accurately in the standard Roman alphabet. In Gaulish and Brittonic Đ replaced the approximations -s-, -ss- or Greek single or double *theta* (Θ) to represent a distinctive, faintly sibilant, dental fricative that the Romans called *tau gallicum*. It is alien to modern English also, but seems to have hissed at the end of the tongue behind the teeth, sounding something like /-ts/ or /-ds/ (Russell 1995, 207). In Celtic-language inscriptions of this period Đ is commonly doubled up, suggesting an emphatic double consonant, as on British coins naming the Trinovantian ruler AĐĐEDOMAROS (VA 1605–1635; de Jersey 2005). This is thought to have been pronounced something like /Ads-sedomaros/, meaning 'great charioteer'. In contast all three versions of Dobunnic and Icenian ANTEĐI are spelt with a single Đ, suggesting a less emphatic single sound.

Whether in the period of active alphabetic experimentation before the Roman conquest Đ was ever used in southern Britain to represent a Germanic sound is doubtful. Germanic did not have the Brittonic hissing /ts/ or /ds/, but had instead a version of the unvoiced /th/ of English 'thing'. This was not yet a feature of educated Latin speech, where written TH was still a strongly emphatic /t/ (Allen 1978, 26–7), but unvoiced /th/ had begun to be heard in some regional Greek and Latin accents (Allen 1987, 23) allowing TH to serve well enough for Germanic /th/, as reflected in a dedication to *Mars Thingsus* on Hadrian's Wall (Clay 2007, 51; 56). Đ seems not to have been used in post-Roman British inscriptions and was not conscripted into the earliest Germanic alphabets: the old Runic futhark, which improvised on north Italic scripts, created Þ to represent unvoiced /th/ (Elliott 1959). The old grapheme Đ did, nonetheless, survive somehow to be resurrected after the end of Antiquity, perhaps by Irish monks, and was adopted into Old English as the letter *eth* for the voiced /th/ of 'the' (Campbell 1959, 25; 29; Nielsen 1998, 108 n 23).

Coda 2: Eceni or Iceni?

The inscription ECEN (never ICEN) on Pattern–Horse coins can be read on silver issues as ECENI if the horse's nearest front leg is taken as an I (Figure 5). **Eceni* is often regarded as probably synonymous with the name of the Romano-British *civitas Icenorum* (eg Rivet and Smith 1979, 373), but it seems prudent to continue treating the two as potentially separate lexical items (Chadburn 2006, 68–9). Aulus Plautius' administration would have been able to verify from the still abundant Icenian silver coinage how the tribal name was spelt if it had indeed been ECENI, whilst five lead ingots retrieved from a shipwreck off Sept-Îles in 1983 were stamped CIVITI ICENOR PCCC and CIVITICIINP, confirming the Gallo-Roman spelling of *Iceni* (Chadburn 2006, 68). Attempts have been made to relate the Gallo-Roman ethnonym to an obsolete or substrate word for water, **ico-*, of unknown etymology, and whilst this suggestion might still be defended, it has met with detemined opposition (summarised in Rivet and Smith 1979, 374). *Iceni* is not listed as a potentially Celtic ethnonym by Sims-Williams (2006). I myself attempted (Nash Briggs 2008) to relate it to a Germanic root, **aukanan* (*HGE*, 29), invoking an OE verb *eacen* or *iecan*, 'to augment or increase', but this ran into what may be insuperable phonological objections. Understanding *Iceni* is further complicated by Julius Caesar's mention of *Cenimagni* or *Cenomanni* at the head of a list of five British tribal delegations who sought his friendship in 54 BC (*BG* 5.21.1), the other four of whom are never heard of again. *Cenimagni* could equally be a fifth group of otherwise unattested 1st-century British tribesmen. Nonetheless, Caesar's [*I*]*cenimagni* is commonly – and attractively – accepted as the earliest record of the Iceni, even though it requires all surviving versions of the text to be emended. For what it is worth, successive ancient and medieval manuscript copyists did not themselves connect Cenimagni with the Romano-British *civitas Icenorum*, familiar though the latter may have been because of Boudica's uprising. If anything, the name reminded them of the Cenomani of northern Italy and Gaul. Further investigation of Icenian names unreliably transmitted in ancient texts will have to be postponed.

Oxford, 3.11.09

Spelling conventions

Letters between a pair of double slashes, as in /ae/, indicate phonemes, or units of sound. A circumflex has been used to indicate a long vowel, as in *êk*. An asterisk indicates a word that is conjectural or reconstructed, as in **Scavus*. Words in capital letters represent the form in which they appear on coins or inscriptions.

Abbreviations

AC: Chadburn (2006). Numbers follow her classification.
ADN: Förstemann, E, 1900, *Altdeutsches Namenbuch*, Bonn
HGE: Orel, V, 2003, *A handbook of Germanic etymology*, Leiden
IE: Indo-European
IEW: Pokorny, J, 1959, *Indogermanisches etymologisches Wörterbuch*, Tübingen
LSG: Liddell, H G and Scott, R, 1940, *A Greek-English lexicon*, 8th edn, Oxford
LSL: Lewis, C T and Short, C, 1879, *A Latin dictionary*, Oxford
LT: de la Tour, H, 1968 (1892), *Atlas des monnaies Gauloises,* London (Paris)
OE: Old English
OFris: Old Frisian
OHG: Old High German
OLG: Old Low German
OIcel: Old Icelandic
ON: Old Norse
OSax: Old Saxon
VA: Van Arsdell, R D, 1989, *Celtic coinage of Britain*, London

Bibliography

Allen, W. S. 1978. *Vox Latina: the pronunciation of Classical Latin*, 2nd ed. Cambridge.
Allen, W. S. 1987. *Vox Graeca: the pronunciation of Classical Greek*, 3rd ed. Cambridge.
Bradley, R. 2005. *Ritual and domestic life in prehistoric Europe*. London.
Braund, D. 1984. *Rome and the friendly king: the character of the client kingship*. London.
Braund, D. 1996. *Ruling Roman Britain*. London.
Breeze, A. 1992. Maldon 68 *mid prasse bestodon*. *English Studies* 73.4, 289–91.
Breeze, A. 2002a. Does Corieltavi mean 'warband of many rivers'?. *Antiquaries Journal* 82, 307–9.
Breeze, A. 2002b. Not Durotriges but Durotrages. *Notes and Queries for Somerset and Dorset* 35/357 (2003), 213–15.
Campbell, A. 1959. *Old English grammar*. Oxford.
Carr, C. T. 1939. *Nominal compounds in Germanic*. London.
Chadburn, A. 2006. *Aspects of the Iron-Age coinages of northern East Anglia with especial reference to hoards*. Unpub PhD thesis, University of Nottingham.
Clay, C. 2007. Before there were Angles, Saxons and Jutes: an epigraphic study of the Germanic social, religious and linguistic relations on Hadrian's Wall. In Gilmour (2007), 47–63.
Creighton, J. 2000. *Coins and power in late Iron Age Britain*. Cambridge.
Davies, J. A. 1996. Where eagles dare: the Iron Age of Norfolk. *Proc Prehist Soc* 62, 63–92.
Davies, J. A. 1999. Patterns, power and political progress in Iron Age Norfolk. In Davies, J A and Williamson, T (eds), *Land of the Iceni: the Iron Age in northern East Anglia*, Norwich, 14–43.
Davies, J. A. 2009. *The land of Boudica: prehistoric and Roman Norfolk*. Oxford.
Debord, J. 1991. Figuration d'une légende de la mythologie germanique sure une monnaie gauloise tardive en potin. *Proceedings of the XIth International Numismatic Congress, Brussels, 1991*: Vol 2, 37–42.
de Jersey, P. 2003. ALIIF SCAVO and ALE SCA. *Chris Rudd* List 70, 4–6.
de Jersey, P. 2005. Ancient British kings: Addedomaros. *Chris Rudd* List 80, 2–4.
de Jersey, P. 2007. Ancient British kings, and a queen: East Anglia – and some loose ends. *Chris Rudd* List 96, 2–4.
de la Bédoyère, G. 2007. *Gods with thunderbolts: religion in Roman Britain*. Stroud.
Delamarre, X. 2003. *Dictionnaire de la langue gauloise: une approche linguistique du vieux-celtique continental*. Paris.
Elliott, R. W. V. 1959. *Runes: an introduction*. Manchester.
Evans, D. Ellis 1967. *Gaulish personal names: a study of some Continental Celtic formations*. Oxford.
Fitzpatrick, A. 1996. Night and day: the symbolism of astral signs on later Iron Age anthropomorphic short swords. *Proceedings of the Prehistoric Society* 62, 373–398.
Gilmour, L. (ed.) 2007. *Pagans and Christians – from Antiquity to the Middle Ages: papers in honour of Martin Henig, presented on the occasion of his 65th birthday*. British Archaeological Report International Series 1610, Oxford.
Green, D. H. 1998. *Language and history in the early Germanic world*. Cambridge.
Green, M. J. 1986. *The gods of the Celts*. Stroud.
Green, M. J. 1997. *Exploring the world of the druids*. London.
Gregory. T. 1991. *Excavations in Thetford, 1980–1982, Fison Way*. East Anglian Archaeology 53.
Haselgrove, C. and Wigg-Wolf, D. 2005. Introduction: Iron Age coinage and ritual practices, in Haselgrove,

C. and Wigg-Wolf, D. (eds), *Iron Age coinage and ritual practices*. Mainz am Rhein, 9–22.

Henig, M. 1984. *Religion in Roman Britain*. London.

Hutcheson, N. C. G. 2004. *Later Iron Age Norfolk: metalwork, landscape and society*. British Archaeological Report British Series 361.

Isserlin, R. M. J. 2007. Some leaves from the invisible archive. In Gilmour (2007), 163–70.

Jackson, K, 1953. *Language and history in early Britain*. Dublin.

Kaufmann, H. 1968. *Altdeutsche Personennamen Ergänzungsband: Ergänzungsband zu Ernst Förstemann Personennamen*. Munich.

Kretz, R. 1999. On the track of the Norfolk Wolf. *Chris Rudd,* List 48, 3–9.

Lambert, P.-Y. 1994. *La Langue gauloise*. Paris.

Meid, W. 1994. *Gaulish inscriptions: their interpretation in the light of archaeological evidence and their value as a source of linguistic and sociological information*. Budapest.

Nash, D. 1978. Territory and state formation in central Gaul, in Green, D., Haselgrove, C., Spriggs, M. (eds.), *Social organisation and settlement. BAR* IS 47(ii), 455–72.

Nash, D. 1987. Imperial expansion under the Roman Republic, in Rowlands, M., Larsen, M, Kristiansen, K. (eds.), *Centre and periphery in the ancient world*. Cambridge.

Nash Briggs, D. 2008. Identifying the Iceni. Unpub conference paper at *Land of the Iceni: current work on the Iron Age in northern East Anglia*. Convenor J. Davies, Norwich.

Nash Briggs, D. 2009a. Reading the images on Iron-Age coins: 1. the sun-boat and its passengers. *Chris Rudd,* List 104, 2–4.

Nash Briggs, D. 2009b. Reading the images on Iron-Age coins: 2. horses of the day and night. *Chris Rudd,* List 106, 2–4.

Nash Briggs, D. 2009c. Religion, ritual and cosmology in late prehistoric Norfolk. Conference paper at *Icon? Art of faith in Norfolk*, UEL/Norwich Castle, Norwich, 9.10.2009, in prep as Sacred image and regional identity in late prehistoric Norfolk, for M Thøfner and S Heslop (eds) *Icon? Art and Belief in Norfolk*.

Nash Briggs, D. 2010. Reading the images on Iron-Age coins: 3. some cosmic wolves. *Chris Rudd,* List 110, 2–4.

Nielsen, H. F. 1989. *The Germanic languages: origins and early dialectal interrelations*. London.

Nielsen, H. F. 1998. *The Continental backgrounds of English and its insular development until 1154*. Odense.

Oppenheimer, S. 2007. *The origins of the British: a genetic detective story*. Revised edn, London.

Pryor, F. 2001. *Seahenge: a quest for life and death in Bronze Age Britain*. London.

Puhvel, J. 1987. *Comparative mythology*. London.

Raybould, M. E. and Sims-Williams, P. 2007. *The geography of Celtic personal names in the Latin inscriptions of the Roman empire*. Aberystwyth.

Reichert, H. 1987. *Lexikon der Altgermanischen Namen*. Vienna.

Rivet, A. L. F. and Smith, C. 1979. *The place-names of Roman Britain*. London.

Robinson, B. and Gregory, T. 1987. *Norfolk origins 3: Celtic fire and Roman rule*. North Walsham.

Rudd, C. 2004. Aedic is Anted. *Chris Rudd* List 76, 6–7.

Rudd, C,. 2006. Inamn(uetoutos?) and Al fe(cit) Scavo. *Chris Rudd* List 88, 2–5.

Rudd, C. 2007. Where was Caniduro? *Chris Rudd* List 93, 2-7.

Rudd, C. 2008. Did Cunobelin control the Iceni? *Chris Rudd* List 102, 2–6.

Russell, P. 1995. *An introduction to the Celtic languages*. London.

Salway, P. 1993. *The Oxford illustrated history of Roman Britain*. Oxford.

Scheers, S. 1977. *Traité de numismatique celtique. II la Gaule belgique*. Paris.

Searle, J. B.; Jones, C. S.; Gündüz, I.; Scascitelli, M.; Jones, E. P.; Herman, J. S.; Rambau, R. V.; Noble, L. R.; Berry, R. J.; Giménez, M. D.; Jóhannesdóttir, F. 2008, Of mice and (Viking?) men: phylogeography of British and Irish house mice, online pub *Proc. R. Soc. B*; doi: 10.1098/rspb.2008.0958.

Sills, J. 1998. The ABC of Westerham gold. *Chris Rudd* List 33, 2–4.

Sills, J. 2000. The Ingoldisthorpe stater and the study of Iron Age coins. *Chris Rudd* List 49, 2–3.

Sills, J. 2003a. Celtic or Roman? AGR and ESVPRASTO. *Chris Rudd* List 70, 2–4.

Sills, J. 2003b. Dobunnic staters: a new sequence. *Chris Rudd* List 72, 4–7.

Sills, J. 2003c. *Gaulish and early British gold coinage*. London.

Sills, J, 2004. The Italian connection – personal names on Philippus and Alexander copies. *Chris Rudd* List 76, 2–6.

Sills, J. 2005. Identifying Gallic War uniface staters. *Chris Rudd* List, 2–6.

Simek, R. 1993 *Dictionary of northern mythology*. Cambridge.

Sims-Williams, P. 2006. *Ancient Celtic place-names in Europe and Asia Minor*. Oxford.

Thompson, E. A. 1965. *The early Germans*. Oxford.

Tomlin, R. S. O. 1988. *Tabellae Sulis: Roman inscribed tablets of tin and lead from the sacred spring at Bath*. Oxford.

Watson, W. J. 1922. *The Celtic place-names of Scotland*, repr Shannon 1973.

West, M. 2007. *Indo-European poetry and myth*. Oxford.

Whatmough, J. 1970. *The dialects of ancient Gaul*. Cambridge Mass.

Williams, J. 2001. Coin inscriptions and the origins of writing in pre-Roman Britain. *British Numismatic Journal* 71, 1–17.

Closing thoughts

John Davies

The 2008 conference brought together a number of scholars who have been working on different aspects of the Iron Age in northern East Anglia. Some of the main studies have been presented in this volume as separate papers. The conference also served to stimulate lively discussion, which further developed some of the ideas presented on the day. Here, I will pull together some of the strands of the debate, which together may serve to suggest a direction for future research.

Until relatively recently a common approach to Iron Age studies was to compare local archaeology, across different parts of the country, with what was considered to be 'the norm' for Britain. The 'norm' was generally taken to be a picture established for Iron Age life in Wessex and the Thames Valley, often expressed through the presence of a series of common characteristics such as hillforts, rich furnished burials, imported Mediterranean goods and *oppida*. The perception of East Anglia being different to the rest of Britain in later prehistory, lacking the common characteristics associated with that picture, is rooted in earlier studies (Clarke 1939; contributions in Gardiner (ed.) 1993). By the mid-1990s it was being appreciated across the country that we could no longer generalise about a homogenous British Iron Age. 'Different Iron Ages' were being identified and characterised right across Britain and temperate Europe (for example Hill and Cumberpatch 1995). It was at this time that the Iron Age of Norfolk became the focus of a regional study. We began to construct a picture of life in the *Land of the Iceni* that was distinctive and could stand alone.

A number of characteristics were identified about the society that inhabited this area during the Iron Age. It will be helpful to briefly summarise some of these features here (see in particular Clarke 1939; Davies 1996; Davies 2009; Davies and Williamson 1999; Hill 1999):

- They possessed great wealth, as evidenced by sites in the west of Norfolk, including Snettisham, Sedgeford and Bawsey.
- They produced fine decorated and enamelled metalwork (Hutcheson 2004).
- They made deposits of fine metalwork. Examples have been recovered from the sites of Snettisham (Stead 1991), Ringstead (Clarke 1951), Saham Toney (Clarke 1939; Bates 2000) and Carleton Rode (unpublished deposit of horse equipment, held at Norwich Castle Museum).
- There is an emphasis on horse-related equipment amongst their material culture.
- There was a continued use of flint tools in the region (Gardiner 1993).
- The use of silver was rapidly adopted after its introduction early in the first century BC. Imported silver items were subsequently adapted, through re-working into new forms, including torcs and coinage (Dennis 2003).
- There was a lack of decorated pottery in the area (contrasting with other adjacent parts of eastern Britain) (Percival 1999).
- There was an absence of Roman influences and imports in the region.
- There is an absence of chieftain type burials, as seen in the south and east of Britain.
- There is generally very little evidence for burials and how they disposed of their dead (Davies 1996).
- Distinctive and recurring symbols were used on their coins and in other aspects of their material culture and the symbols appear to have had meaning to these people.
- They lived in unenclosed farmsteads.
- They constructed few large monuments.
- Their settlements could sprawl over large areas, in a 'splurgy' pattern (Hill 1999).
- They had a polyfocal tribal structure.
- Some major concentrations of population have been recognised in central and south Norfolk, at Thetford, Saham Toney and Caistor St Edmund (Davies 1996).
- Some significant linear earthworks in central-west Norfolk appear to have an origin in the Iron Age (Davies 1996).

Recent and current studies

In addition to the features identified and listed above, which have been drawn from earlier work, both formal presentations and informal discussion at the 2008 conference led us further towards a fuller understanding of the characteristics of the society living in this region. Additional features can be expressed, both in terms of what was *absent* and what was *present* in the land of the Iceni. These will be listed in turn.

What the Iceni didn't have (which are present elsewhere in Britain)

- There is an absence of the large Wessex type storage pits in northern East Anglia, except at major sites like Fison Way, Thetford (Gregory 1992). This may possibly be due to local soil conditions.
- Corn driers are not commonly encountered.
- In general, we don't have evidence for a significant production of cereals, for storage and possibly redistribution, as been assumed. 'Chaff' (the husks separated during the threshing process) tends to be absent from many sites in the region (Val Fryer, *pers comm*). This indicates that agriculture was not as biased towards growing corn at this time, as had been assumed. It may have been more pastoral, based on sheep and cattle herding.
- There is an absence of high status 'furnished' burials.
- Despite the many finds of different object types, Iron Age mirrors are absent from this area.
- There is an absence of evidence for exotic items imported from the Mediterranean world into other parts of southern Britain during the Late Iron Age.
- There is an absence of pottery types that were being imported into other parts of southern Britain including:

  amphorae
  mortaria
  Black Burnished Ware - BB1
  fine foreign pottery, such as:
      Lyon Ware
      Arretine (Tyers 1996, p111)
      Terra rubra (Tyers 1996, p165)
      Terra Nigra (Tyers 1996, p165)

Amanda Chadburn argued that the Iceni were *deliberately* excluding items from the Roman world that were entering other parts of Britain, together with Roman ways of doing things, such as wine consumption. (We are told by Caesar that the Germans and Continental Belgae similarly barred such imports (*Gallic War*).

What the Iceni did have that are less predominant in other parts of Britain

- Torcs are a feature of their culture.
- Horses were highly important in their society.
- They used the wolf as a symbol on their coinage (which was not used by any other tribe).
- They liked beer (while not accepting wine).
- There was a strong maritime influence within their culture. Their landscape and territory was dominated by water. It was surrounded on three sides by a long coastline to the north and east, with the fenland and Wash to the west. A great estuary stretched inland from the area now covered by Great Yarmouth (Davies 2009) and major rivers radiated inland from this point. The River Waveney, which today separates Norfolk from Suffolk, also provided a watery barrier running from west to east and may have been a southern tribal boundary for periods of time.

An identity established

In conclusion, it is becoming possible to begin to recognise a series of *cultural indicators*, through which we can start to construct a picture showing the unique identity of the people of northern East Anglia, in relation to other tribal groupings of Iron Age Britain. Alongside these indicators, we may also be seeing the possible deliberate exclusion of Mediterranean style goods and ways of doing things adopted by their neighbours to the south, such as chieftain burials.

Most interestingly, through the work of Daphne Nash Briggs, we are beginning to see specific external cultural links with Germany. Elsewhere, a genetic component of Norfolk's rural population has also been shown to have originally been of north European origin (Oppenheimer 2006).

The work of John Talbot has shown that the Iceni operated a more sophisticated system of coinage than has previously been recognised. They were using a bi-metallic, multi-denominational coin system. Talbot has called them 'a very sophisticated people, using and making money in a sophisticated way'. In relation to the symbols used on the coinage by the Iceni, Talbot considers that they had a meaning to these people and that there was 'a symbolic logic' going on.

A people apart

The evidence presented through this volume and previous work cited above suggests that the Iceni appear to have protected their own society and way of life and rejected the ways of other British and most foreign peoples. Additional evidence for this interpretation may come in the form of a site excavated some thirty years ago. The purpose and function of the remarkable enclosure at Fison Way Thetford (Gregory 1992) has long remained a problem. More recently, Richard Bradley has suggested that this sanctuary may have represented a symbol of native resistance to foreign rule (Bradley 2005). Now, in the light of current work on the Iceni, its unique construction and apparent ceremonial association might readily be interpreted as an ostentatious expression of independence, situated at a key location that people would have needed to pass by as they entered Icenian territory.

In the first century AD and following the initial Roman conquest in the south of Britain, the Iceni entered into a client alliance with Rome. It may have been a perception over the years that the Iceni had become closely affiliated with the new rulers through this arrangement. However, evidence may now be suggesting that it actually provided an opportunity for them to achieve just the opposite. They were given a mechanism by which they were able to safeguard, reinforce and preserve their own cherished identity, as well as enabling them to promote some of the more Germanic aspects of their tribal culture.

I shall end by referring to the more recent Norfolk saying, '*In Norfolk We Do Different*'. We are now seeing that the people of this part of East Anglia always did *do different*. And we are now beginning to be able to define just how far they did *do different* at that time. The Iceni were indeed a people apart.

Acknowledgements

This paper has been developed from some of the conclusions and discussion on the day of the conference. Thanks to all of those who were involved in, and contributed to, the conference and also those who attended. May we all re-assemble once again, 20 years on.

Bibliography

Bates, S. 2000. Excavations at Quidney Farm, Saham Toney, Norfolk 1995. *Britannia* 31, 201-237.

Bradley, R. 2005. Ritual and Domestic Life in Prehistoric Europe. London, Routledge.

Clarke, R. 1939. The Iron Age in Norfolk and Suffolk. *Archaeological Journal* 96, 1-113.

Clarke, R. 1951. A hoard of the Early Iron Age from Ringstead, Norfolk. *Proeedings of the. Prehistoric Society* 17, 214-225.

Davies, J. A. 1996. Where eagles dare: the Iron Age of Norfolk. *Proeedings of the. Prehistoric Society.* 62, 63-92.

Davies, J. A. 2009. *The Land of Boudica: Prehistoric and Roman Norfolk*. Oxford, Oxbow Books.

Davies J. and Williamson T. (eds) 1999. *Land of the Iceni: the Iron Age in Northern East Anglia.* Norwich, Centre of East Anglian Studies.

Dennis M. 2003. *Silver in Late Iron Age and Early Roman East Anglia: A Study of Archaeological Contexts*. Unpublished MLitt thesis, School of Archaeology, Oxford University.

Gardiner, J. 1993. The flint assemblage. In J. A. Davies, Excavation of an Iron Age pit group at London Road, Thetford. *Norfolk Archaeology* 41, 456-58.

Gardiner, J. (ed) 1993. Flatlands and Wetlands: current themes in East Anglian archaeology. East Anglian Archaeology 50. Norwich.

Gregory, T. 1992. Excavations in Thetford, 1980-1982, Fison Way. East Anglian Archaeology 53.

Hill, J. D. 1999. Settlement. landscape and regionality: Norfolk and Suffolk in the pre-Roman Iron Age of Britain and beyond. In J. Davies and T. Williamson (eds), *Land of the Iceni: the Iron Age in Northern East Anglia,* 185-207. Norwich, Centre of East Anglian Studies.

Hill, J. D. and Cumberpatch, C. G. 1995. *Different Iron Ages: studies on the Iron Age in Temperate Europe.* British Archaeological Report, International Series 602.

Hutcheson, N. C. G. 2004. *Later Iron Age Norfolk: metalwork, landscape and society.* British Archaeological Report, British Series 361.

Oppenheimer, S. 2006. *The origins of the British: a genetic detective story*. London, Constable.

Percival, S. 1999. Iron Age pottery in Norfolk. In J. Davies and T. Williamson (eds), *Land of the Iceni: the Iron Age in Northern East Anglia,* 173-184. Norwich, Centre of East Anglian Studies.

Stead, I. M. 1991. The Snettisham treasure: excavations in 1990. *Antiquity* 65, 447-465.

Tyers, P. 1996. Roman pottery in Britain. London, Routledge.

www.ingramcontent.com/pod-product-compliance
Lightning Source LLC
Chambersburg PA
CBHW041708290426
44108CB00027B/2895